Tapwe: Selected Columns of Doug Cuthand

Library and Archives Canada Cataloguing in Publication

Cuthand, Doug
   Tapwe : selected columns of Doug Cuthand.

ISBN 1-894778-21-9

   1. Native peoples--Saskatchewan. 2. Native peoples--
Saskatchewan--Social conditions. I. Title.

E78.C2C98 2005   971.24004'97   C2005-902954-4

Editor: Liv Marken
Design: Suzanne Bates
Cover Design: Kevin Hogarth
Copyedit: Chick Gabriel
Proofing: Anita Large

Theytus Books Ltd
Green Mountain Rd., Lot 45
RR#2, Site 50, Comp. 8
Penticton, BC, V2A 6J7

Printed in Canada by Gauvin Press

We acknowledge the financial support of the Government of Canada through the Book Pubishing Industry
Development program (BPIDP) for our publishing activites.

We acknowledge the support of the Canada Council for the Arts which last year invested $20.3 million in writ-
ing and publishing throughout Canada.
Nous remercions de son soutien le Conseil des Arts du Canada, qui a investi 20,3 millions de dollars l'an
demier dans les lettres et l'édition à travers le Canada.

We acknowledge the support of the Province of the British Columbia through the British Columbia through
the British Columbia Arts Council.

Tapwe
Acknowledgements

I would like to thank the various editors I have worked with over the years. Trevor Sutter, with the *Regina Leader Post* was the first to ask me to write a weekly column and he was later replaced by Dave Ramsey. Sadly, Trevor left a promising career in journalism to work for the colonial office.

Lawrence Thoner handled my column at *The Star Phoenix* until his retirement and he was replaced by Gerry Klien. Lately, I have written a companion column for the *Winnipeg Free Press* with John Sullivan editing my work.

I would also like to thank Murry Mandryck for writing the Foreward and sharing his thoughts with me over the years as we both try to address the issues and craziness in our respective constituencies.

I would like to thank Christine Fiddler who worked with me following her graduation from the University of Saskatchewan. She sorted out all 600 columns according to topic. The original draft was edited and completed by Liv Marken who juggled childcare and her family life to complete the job. I would also like to thank my friend Kevin Hogarth who created the cover and shot its photo.

I would also like to thank my wife and family who have put up with my preoccupation with each week's column. On more than one occasion my wife has been speaking to me only to discover that I wasn't even listening, but formulating the week's column in my mind.

And of course I would like to thank all my loyal readers who may or may not agree with my particular point of view. I appreciate the letters and comments, positive and otherwise. It keeps me aware that I am being read and drawing reaction.

Tapwe: Selected Columns of Doug Cuthand

Table of Contents

Tapwe: Selected Columns of Doug Cuthand

Theytus Books Ltd.

Penticton B.C.

Foreward

The brethren of journalism tend to be a small circle, especially when it comes to that subgroup known as the newspaper columnist. Because of this reality, we columnists tend to coalesce in our own little support group where we commiserate on the frustrations of our little world – frustrations ranging from the pressure of deadlines, to the idiocy of editors and newspaper owners, to the delicate balancing act of criticizing the very people who are our sources of information.

And while we like to view ourselves as a unique lot with our own unique problems, what's actually surprising is how similar we are, and, frankly, how mainstream we are. Sure, maybe journalism is less of the old boys' club it once was. The influx of women reporters in the past generation has given the "brethren" significantly more gender balance.

But journalism still has a long way to go before it accurately reflects society. The demographics of the profession tend to be overwhelmingly white, middle-class, and, especially in the aforementioned sub-group of the columnist, male. This doesn't exactly put us in good stead when it comes to providing insight into those growing segments of Canadian society that are no longer white, male, and middle-class. It also doesn't provide most of us with the authoritative background to be a voice of advocacy for the socially disadvantaged or the disenfranchised.

It is here where Doug Cuthand has become a welcome addition to the brethren these past 10 years. Doug's contribution to a better understanding of First Nations' issues in a decade of newspaper columns has gone well beyond his patient and clear explanations of Native culture and history. In themselves, the explanations have often been invaluable to putting into perspective social, economic, and political issues affecting the Aboriginal community.

But even more important has been Doug's relentless determination to remind us that First Nations communities are neither homogeneous nor even completely united in their issues, problems, and approaches to solving those problems.

Doug wrote in a column in the wake of the occupations at Ipperwash Provincial Park in Ontario and Gustafson Lake in B.C., "One constant source of amusement for First Nations people is the attempt to lump all of us together and make us fit into the same mould. . . . [but] both groups are very different, as well as the issues." That two First Nations communities separated by thousands of miles would somehow have very different interests, issues, and approaches to problems should not be a difficult concept to grasp. After all, non-Native communities separated by four provinces are generally seen to have very different issues.

Yet the media tends to suspend such common sense when it comes to First Nations issues, as Doug has often reminded us. Doug's column once gave an example:

"The other day, I received a call from an eastern reporter who told me that Ovide Mercredi was proposing a training centre for non-violent protest, and 'how was it going over in Saskatchewan?'"

"I said that was the first I had heard of it, and it was probably not a burning issue out here. He sounded genuinely confused and couldn't see why it wasn't the centre of our attention."

"He hung up and continued his search for someone who would give him the comment he wanted."

Doug concluded, "For all I know, he's still looking."

Doug has insisted on providing us with a complete and textured understanding of First Nation issues, but he's managed to do so while being an advocate for First Nations people, their problems, and their issues. This, too, has been an important contribution to the newspaper world where a growing number of columnists seem uncomfortable with taking any advocacy role, and, if they do take an advocacy role, they tend to advocate the male, conservative, and middle-class social values from which most of them spring.

After all, it's one thing to advocate programs to deal with fetal alcohol syndrome, residential school compensation, and diabetes and substance abuse, which Doug has often done. But it's quite another to take a strong, persuasive stance in favour of treaty rights and land claims, self-governance, and lowering rates of incarceration. Doug has ventured into places where other journalists have feared to tread. Such advocacy has made many, both inside and outside the world of journalism, uncomfortable. But both his ability to put forth compelling arguments that support his points, and his vantage that allows us to explore these issues from the point of view of a First Nations person, have made his columns important.

Moreover, anyone who has simply written Doug off as simply an apologist for First Nations people would be well served to read this book and review what he has said.

"We can't accept the old bromides that all the problems stem from white people, boarding schools, Indian agents, and any other convenient excuse that comes along," Doug once wrote. It's never been particularly easy to criticize a socially disadvantaged group, and it's far more difficult if you happen to come from that group. Those of us in the newspaper brethren, and particularly those of us who write columns, understand that. But here, too, Doug has been fearless. In providing us with honest commentary, he's not only taught us about First Nations issues, but he's also taught us a lot about many other issues. In doing so, he's certainly been a welcome addition to our brethren.

Murray Mandryk
The Regina Leader Post

Introduction

Tapwe, As I See It

In 1970, when I first began my career as a writer and journalist, I was hired by the Alberta Native Communications Society to develop and edit a province-wide Aboriginal newspaper.

The president of the organization, Jim Ducharme, was a Métis leader with years of experience. He became my mentor and a good friend. One day, he told me that our role as communicators was to provide Aboriginal people with the best information we could. We had to be fair and accurate because people who are well informed will make the best decisions. He told me that in the years to come, our people would be called upon to make decisions on self-government, economic development, and other issues that we hadn't even anticipated. As it turns out, he was exactly right.

Jim Ducharme's prediction resonated with me over the years, but I now believe that it extends to the general public. The people of western Canada have to make some crucial decisions about our place as partners and neighbours. I hope that through my columns I have shed some light on the issues and put a human face where there is fear and misunderstanding.

And do we have issues! Rapid population growth, urbanization, and sweeping change coming from the Charter of Rights and Freedoms and the Courts are huge issues that we will face long into the future. In 1972, when I began working for the Federation of Saskatchewan Indian Nations, there was a population of 36,000 predominantly rural Indian people in Saskatchewan. When I write this in 2004, there are close to 120,000 Indian people in Saskatchewan and over half are urban residents.

Because of the wide range of issues, sometimes I think people see me as a crisis manager. I regularly get calls to write something about what a certain individual has said, or about some particularly galling event, but I prefer to follow my own agenda. My agenda has been laid out in advance by my own investigations of the issues, and especially their historical contexts.

Once, at the same time as I was writing a column on the devastating effects of diabetes on our people, a federal politician made some stupid remark about

First Nations. I received calls to "do something about this guy." I could have been reactive or proactive, so I chose the latter and stuck to my column on diabetes; in the long run, it was a bigger story and more important.

I prefer to be in the forefront of exploring new areas rather than being reactionary and appearing like an opposition politician, too often opposing and rarely providing positive alternatives.

Simply reacting to situations as they surface places us in a position where we are not in control of our agenda. When people tell me that some politician or political party must be put down, I take the long view of history. We have been here for thousands of years, and we will be here for long into the future. Detractors and naysayers will go away, but we will remain. We've been around for centuries, and we'll be here for a long time to come.

While trying to avoid rhetoric and rants, every so often some sneak in. I remember my mother's words when she told me that "there is nothing wrong with righteous wrath." I find racism, violence against women, and exploitation of any people particularly galling.

On the lighter side, I invented the character of Abe Original. He is my alter-ego and allows me to play the straight man. Abe and his friend Luke Warm Water tilt at windmills and allow me to inject some humour into the issues of the day instead of always being so damn serious.

Between the times I was a newspaper editor and a freelance filmmaker, I was Vice Chief of the Executive of the Federation of Saskatchewan Indian Nations from 1977 to 1982. During this time, we organized politically, worked to establish the province's post-secondary institutions, and participated in the constitutional negotiations. It was an exciting time, an important part of my experience, and it is where I draw much of the information for my writing.

I have been a journalist and observer for close to 35 years now, and for the last 13 years, I have written a column for the *Regina Leader Post* and the *Saskatoon Star Phoenix*. In the past year, I started running an expanded column in the *Winnipeg Free Press*. I was surprised to discover that I had written over 600 columns on three different laptop computers and in three different programs. It was quite a job to sort them out, and, as the old saying goes, separate the wheat from the chaff.

After I completed my manuscript, my publisher told me that a title might be a good idea. It wasn't easy to come up with a title because I had such an eclectic mix of topics. In the 1970s, I ran a column in *The Saskatchewan Indian* called "Tapwe." The word "tapwe" means "the truth" in Cree. When someone is telling a story, a listener will add the word "Tapwe" every so often, indicating that he or she agrees, and that what is being told is the truth.

So what follows is *tapwe*, as seen from my point of view.

Chapter 1

Race Relations in a
Changing World

The Moose Metaphor Still Applies

Teaching in the Aboriginal world is done through metaphors and stories that either directly or indirectly teach a lesson. I recall asking my father one time what I thought was a simple question, and when he sat back and began, "In 1931, your grandfather ...," I knew I was in for a long but interesting answer.

The reason for this type of teaching is to avoid being preachy or didactic. The story must be timeless and make the listener think and remember, but a little bit of humour doesn't hurt either.

The following story about Wesakechak teaches us an important lesson, but it does it in our own unique way.

The stories of Wesakechak are shared with other cultures. For example, the Ojibway have Nanabush and the Blackfoot have Napi. Nanabush and Napi are the same individual as Wesakechak, but the stories are told in different languages. Wesakechak was the emissary from the Creator. He was sent down on earth to create the animals and the people intended to inherit the new land that the Almighty had created.

The First Nations' creation story is one of trial and error, and the individual features of each animal happen because Wesakechak made them either through accident or design. Stories are told of the different animals and how they interacted with each other or how they developed strange characteristics. This is a far cry from the serious creation story in the Bible, and in a way it reflects the worldview of the First Nations people compared to that of the uptight, Judeo-Christian world view. Wesakechak was a figure with human weaknesses and a sense of humour, and many of his creations reflected this.

When Wesakechak had finished creating all the animals of the earth, he looked around and found some spare parts that hadn't been used. He found a large, floppy coat of dark hair. There was a big nose, two floppy ears, some long legs, and a set of large, flat antlers.

1

He took these odds and ends and created the last animal. He wasn't sure what it was, but after he got it together, he gave it life, and it walked around admiring itself. The animal was a moose, and this moose was very proud about the way he looked. He had a beautiful black coat, two wonderful ears, tall legs, and a lovely rack of flat antlers.

He went down to the lake and admired his reflection. He was very pleased. But the other animals were not so kind. They laughed at him and called him "ugly" and "clumsy". They made fun of his flat antlers and large nose.

The moose was devastated. He thought that he looked just fine, and here were all the other animals laughing at him: Rabbit with his long ears and big feet, Beaver with his funny flat tail and large teeth, and Pelican with his large bill. Why should they laugh at him when they looked just as funny?

But the poor moose continued to be teased and laughed at by the other animals. So he told them, "I will go away and live in dark, swampy places by myself." And he went deep into the forest and lived by himself in dark, damp places.

Today if you want to find a moose, you have to go into the forest and find a secluded, swampy area. He lives alone and mostly moves about in the early morning hours when nobody is awake. He doesn't even associate with members of his own kind like other large animals that live in herds, such as the elk or caribou.

He was only a moose, but he had feelings and the ridicule changed his way of life forever. This story is told so the children can see the damage that teasing and prejudice can do to people.

This is also a story of tolerance toward people from other races and backgrounds. Racism hurts, and those who suffer its sting often want to withdraw from the world and go somewhere they can be themselves.

The reaction of the moose to prejudice was a universal reaction, and his story illustrates the pain and lasting effects that prejudice has on us all.

Racism Is the Old Battle Between Good and Evil

In the Cree tradition, the seasons are the result of an ongoing quarrel between Kewatin, the north wind, and Sawin, the south wind. They are fighting and quarrelling brothers. In the fall, Kewatin chases Sawin away to his home in the south. He brings the storms of winter and the cold that freezes the land. In the spring, Sawin returns refreshed and chases Kewatin back to his home in the north. Sawin is known as "the healing wind," healing the land by bringing back the warm air and the large, puffy clouds. He also brings back the green grass, the birds, and the flowers. He is the giver of life.

It's the classic story of the never-ending battle between good and evil.

Like the conflict between Sawin and Kewatin, racism is also the continuing struggle between good and evil.

The origins of the International Day for the Elimination of Racism are tragic and should never be forgotten because they continue to remind us of the evils of racism. On March 21, 1960, about 5,000 unarmed Black South Africans marched on a police station in the town of Sharpeville to protest the despised "pass law." All Black South Africans were obliged to carry a pass that showed their identification and address. By law, they were segregated from the minority white population. "Apartheid" or "living apart" was the official racial policy of South Africa.

The police reacted swiftly to the demonstration and opened fire, killing 69 and wounding another 180. This act of treachery and cowardice became the turning point for the long battle against racism that was to follow.

South Africa is now a multiracial country, but racial discrimination has not been eliminated. The economic disparities still exist, and services for the poor are still substandard.

Racial discrimination takes many forms. It can be overt, as seen in the former South Africa, or it can be more subtle, in the form of government policies and legislation.

It's easy for Canadians to point to the segregated society in South Africa or the United States and morally proclaim that "we never had that in Canada." But ask Black Canadians from Nova Scotia about segregation, and they will point out that their society was just as segregated as that of the southern United States.

In fact, Canada has a long history of racism against non-white immigrants and Aboriginal people. Chinese immigrants were largely male and employed in the construction of the Trans-Canada Railway. When they raised enough money to bring in their families, they were charged a head tax. Starting in 1885, to bring a Chinese person into the country, one had to pay an additional tax of $50.00. No other group of immigrants was penalized in the same manner.

In 1912, the Saskatchewan government made it illegal for a Chinese Canadian to employ white women. In Moose Jaw, Quong Wing was fined $5.00 for employing two white women in his restaurant. He refused to pay and took the case to the Supreme Court where he lost.

And war brings out the worst in governments; paranoia and hatred take over from common sense. For example, during the First World War, members of the Ukrainian community were placed in holding camps because they were felt to be a security risk.

And, of course, there was the shameful treatment of Japanese Canadians during the Second World War. The majority of the Japanese community lived on the West Coast, where they had fishing boats or worked in the fish canneries. They lost their property, including their homes and boats. They were sent to the interior and interned in camps until the end of the war. Today, Japanese Canadians are scattered throughout Canada. Their original thriving communities on the West Coast are no more.

Today, there is hatred for and paranoia about Muslim Canadians. It would seem that we have not learned from history.

Of course, our own stories as First Nations are a part of Canada's shameful past. The historical record includes boarding school abuse; repressive Indian Agents; and legislation that forbade freedom of movement, such as freedom of religion, freedom of assembly, and freedom to organize politically.

First Nations people are a rapidly growing group within Canadian society, particularly in the West. Our challenge for the future is going to be in finding a way to live together in harmony and mutual benefit. Racism hurts all parties. It retards community, creates depression, and it misplaces our energy. We need to understand and learn from each other rather than waste energy.

Racial discrimination in Saskatchewan is seen in the fear and misunderstandings that people have about the changing demographic. Today, First Nations are the fastest growing population in the country. We are also evolving rapidly as we react to the change from a rural to urban lifestyle, and to a wage economy.

Programs that offer affirmative action are seen as discriminatory because they have an impact on society's spoiled brats: white males who have had an easy ride in the past. White men automatically got the best jobs, the most lucrative careers, and the bulk of business opportunities. Even now, they statistically get lighter sentences when they get in trouble with the law.

White men no longer dominate as strongly, though. With more women and minorities in the workforce, it's only natural that the workplace will shift to reflect this fact. But it has been a steep, uphill path to obtain parity.

When I was growing up, my father told me that I can't be equal to white people and expect to succeed. I had to be better. Affirmative action is a way of addressing this situation, but we hear the tired old clichés of "reverse discrimination" and "not having a level playing field." I have to laugh at the latter because how do we know if the playing field was level if we were never allowed on it in the first place?

Racism is truly unnecessary if one examines it objectively. We are all the result of an accident of birth. To illustrate, I have in my mind this image of a bunch of baby souls lined up in a waiting room in heaven. There is this bureaucrat (I'm sure God needs a bureaucracy to keep track of things), and he is sporting a pair of reading glasses, a green eyeshade, and a clipboard. He is wearing a white shirt and a black vest. He runs around, preoccupied with his task, handing out wombs.

"You! You're going to Buckingham Palace."

"You are going to the Southern Sudan."

"You're off to India where you will be a low-caste Hindu." "You go to southern California for a life of spoiled privilege."

"You are headed for China, and you can go to Alphabet City in Saskatoon."

The little souls obediently fly off to their assigned wombs.

We all come from the same Creator, and we will return to the same Creator, so why do we pick on each other?

On March 21st, Sawin returns to heal the land and the people. It is fitting, therefore, that the south wind should return on that day to eliminate racial discrimination. Sawin brings hope, including a renewal of life and nourishment for the soul. It is nourishment that we need if we are to eliminate racism.

Population Growth: The Monster That Ate Saskatchewan

Every so often, a news story comes out that states the obvious. The Aboriginal population is growing at a phenomenal rate, and it's going to be problematic for the country and the provinces. Nobody ever seems to think that our population growth could be a good thing: instead, it appears to be some kind of problem.

But look at it from the Aboriginal point of view: eventually we will take over the province and run it politically and economically. With land claims and Treaty Land Entitlement, we will eat up most of the land base. Once again, Saskatchewan will truly be Indian country.

But alas, our dreams are also the fears of others.

The First Nations population explosion is the result of improved public health and living conditions following the Second World War. We experienced the same postwar population boom as the rest of the country, but we just didn't quit.

At the turn of the century, there were only about 11,000 Status Indian people in Saskatchewan. By the end of the century, our population exceeded 100,000, almost ten times that of a century earlier.

The First Nations population was so low at the turn of the century because we had come through several decades of famines and plagues. Our people had no resistance to European diseases, and so measles, small pox, and influenza killed off our people in appalling numbers.

Following the Second World War, though, public health became accessible on reserves. While the birth rate had always been high, now infant mortality dropped and the population began to grow.

I grew up on the reserve during this period. The nurse was a regular visitor in our school, and every fall we received our needles. Later, during high school, all the Indian kids would be called out to have our shots at different times throughout the year. At the time, it was a fearful experience, but the result was that our people were healthier and our population grew.

One should keep in mind that while our population grew, we continued to suffer from high mortality rates from poor housing and deteriorating social conditions.

By 1970, there were 35,000 Status Indians in Saskatchewan, and by 1985, our population had doubled to 70,000. By the year 2000, our population will exceed 100,000, and it should be around 150,000 by the year 2020.

As the Indian comedian Charlie Hill used to say, "They call us a vanishing race, but when's the last time you saw a pilgrim?"

Along with the population growth, there has been considerable movement of off-reserve people. Today, about 55% of First Nations people don't live on their reserves; instead, they have moved into the cities or out of the province.

But now we are feared for our large numbers. The concern that we will overwhelm the rest of the population looms as an ever-present threat. Attitudes of tolerance and understanding appear to be hardening in the ageing white population, placing our people in a precarious position. Will our bright young people become the victims a bunch of cranky old white folks?

We have the opportunity to revitalise and enrich this province, but instead, population growth is seen negatively. Do we have to use the "r" word to describe this hardening attitude? Is this province sliding into the self-destructive swamp of racism? To all those out there who decry our rapid growth, I say, "Too bad." This is the new reality for Saskatchewan, and we are here to stay more than any other group.

I suspect that as our standards of living and levels of education improve, our birth rate will drop off to reflect the rest of the country's birth rates.

In any event, we will have to survive through cooperation and understanding on both sides. When the day comes that we form the majority in Saskatchewan(and it will), I hope that we have a better and more tolerant attitude toward each other.

Make It a Fight Worth Having

Language is a weapon, and its effects can have overkill, just like any destructive force. When words are overused, they lose meaning and become common.

The Friends of the Lubicon once won a court case in Ontario that allowed them to continue with their consumer boycott against Daishowa, a pulp and paper company logging within the disputed territory of the Lubicon First Nation. However, in bringing down the judgement, the court ruled that the group was to cease using the word "genocide" in connection with the issue.

"Genocide" is one of those loaded words that are thrown around a little too carelessly. It means "the systematic killing of a people" and came into usage following the Second World War. The Nazis were found guilty at the Nuremberg trials of systematically killing over three million Jews – they were found guilty of genocide.

"Genocide" is a very serious word, and to use it carelessly debases the language and cheapens it.

Another word that gets tossed around with abandon is "racist" (or "racism"). It is also a loaded word, and it can be used to describe the repressive apartheid policies of South Africa or racial divisions in the American Deep South. It can also be used to describe a broad spectrum of racial discrimination. The problem with using a word like "racist" is that it quickly brings discussion to a halt. It's like calling someone "fat and ugly"; the conversation is over.

The use of the "r" word is a card that should be played selectively and only when one really means it. Otherwise, the word will lose its serious meaning and its strength when it is truly needed.

A few years ago, the National Chief of the Assembly of First Nations, Phil Fontaine, used the "r" word and got into hot water with the Reform Party. He called the party's continuing comments regarding the Stoney Band Administration "the worst kind of racism." Over several months, the Reform Party had launched a scathing attack on First Nations administrations, and Fontaine was clearly sick of it.

The Reform Party wrote to the National Chief, demanding that an apology be placed in *The Calgary Herald* and that Fontaine retract his statement. If he didn't, the veiled threat was that they would see Mr. Fontaine in court.

Fontaine, of course, refused, and the wheels of justice pointed toward a court battle with the Reform Party. But the Reform Party's ham-fisted response works to the advantage of the Assembly of First Nations, which can truck out all kinds of negative examples in court.

In politics, an accusation is only as good as the denial. When Nixon was backed against a wall with Watergate, he went on record, stating, "I am not a crook." This famous statement had the effect of convincing the public that he was indeed a crook. The Reform Party would make the same public relations blunder by dragging the Assembly of First Nations into court to prove that it is not a racist party.

The AFN prepared a list of statements and strategies used by the Reform Party over the years that reveal its negativity about First Nations.

Whether the Reform Party wins its suit or not is not at issue. The party stands to be humiliated for its attitude toward First Nations, which will stick to its image for years to come.

In politics, they say that when they laugh at you, you're finished. The public laughed at Joe Clark, and he was toast. The Reform Party is a good source of fodder for First Nations politicians. Some guy will take pokes at the party and receive a laugh and a round of applause. The Reform Party has become a joke in Indian country.

But as First Nations people, we should thank the Reform Party for its tactics. It has united First Nations as nothing else has since the 1969 White Paper, and we're thankful for that.

We're Not like Peas in a Pod

One constant source of amusement for First Nations people is the attempt to lump all of us together and make us fit into the same mould.

The most recent example came from the Ontario Provincial Police one summer when they announced that they had sent observers out to British Columbia to gain information on the crisis at Gustafson Lake to use for the occupation at Ipperwash Provincial Park.

Why did they do this? Both groups were very different as were the issues. Gustafson Lake did not have broad support in the First Nations community while Ipperwash held the First Nations public's sympathy and support.

Ipperwash was land that held a burial ground, and it had been seized for use as a military base during the Second World War. The war ended over fifty years ago, and Eastern Europe had been liberated. It was high time that the land was returned to the First Peoples.

If the police and government officials had taken the time to examine the issues and see the people involved as individuals rather than as another bunch of Indians, Ipperwash could have been negotiated peacefully.

Unfortunately, ignorance is usually the case. First Nations people are seen as a monolithic group that somehow marches in lockstep.

During the Oka crisis, the media scoured the land for a groundswell of Indian opinion that would lead to some kind of national revolution. Some groups held marches in sympathy and a few blockades were even thrown up. But action in sympathy just doesn't compare with a real grassroots protest. Once again, the herd refused to stampede.

Other issues, such as mercury pollution and solvent abuse, have been identified by the media as national issues, only to turn out to be local and confined to scattered communities.

The Canadian public must understand the reality that the Aboriginal community in Canada is as diverse as Europe or Africa. There are over 600 individual First Nations in Canada that speak in over 50 languages. Each First Nations community is made up of a close-knit group of families, and this is reflected in each community's personality. The culture and history of each community is unique.

It's true that there are some universal similarities, and these are often overlooked. Indian religion is similar from coast to coast. The belief in the Almighty or Manitou is universal, and the interpretation of the spirit world may vary, but the principles remain the same. There is also universal respect for the wisdom of the elders.

In the past, the First Nations were united for negative reasons. There was universal hatred for Indian Affairs, and in 1969, when the Trudeau Government brought down its infamous White Paper on Indian Policy, the First Nations united in condemnation. The government made the blunder of uniting the First Nations as no one else could.

The First Nations have outgrown Indian Affairs, which is now seen as irrelevant or harmless. The challenge for politicians on the national scene is to foster the development of a positive common cause among the First Nations. The problem, though, is that after generations of being in a mode of constant opposition, it is almost impossible for some leaders to shift gears and become proactive instead of reactive.

The old ways die hard. The other day, I received a call from an eastern reporter who told me that Ovide Mercredi was proposing a training centre for non-violent protest, and "how was it going over in Saskatchewan?"

I said that was the first I had heard of it, and it was probably not a burning issue out here. He sounded genuinely confused and couldn't see why it wasn't the centre of our attention.

He hung up and continued his search for someone who would give him the comment he wanted.

For all I know, he's still looking.

Big Bear's Heart of Darkness

One of the classics of English literature is Joseph Conrad's novel *Heart of Darkness*. It was the first book I read in my English 101 class, and I'm sure it's a regular in many introductory English classes. It is the story of the timeless fear that we all have of the unknown, but it also carries a deeper and more disturbing message.

The story details Marlow's journey up the rivers of the Belgian Congo. He is in search of a member of a company and is feared to have "gone native." Marlow's journey becomes an odyssey back to a time of fear and violence. He arrives at his destination to discover his worst fear: Kurtz, the object of his search, has indeed become part of the native community.

Kurtz participates in unspeakable rituals and practices. These are never explained, and we never know what the horrific acts are. This ambiguity serves to fuel the reader's imagination and fears. The reader is left with the impression that the practices of the "primitive" people are pure evil.

This was the attitude of the imperial countries of Europe when the book was written. Europe (especially England or the colonizer's country of origin) was considered pure and holy. Europe thought itself the centre of the civilized world, and imperialism included the act of saving uncivilized wretches from themselves.

People spoke with conviction and candour about being an imperialist in much the same way as today's businessman will speak in favour of the free market system. Imperialism was a part of how the world ran, and most people saw nothing wrong with it.

Heart of Darkness was adapted to a screenplay in the movie *Apocalypse Now*, taking place during the Vietnam War. However, the movie is unclear whether it was the war or the people of the jungle that made Kurtz a monster. The book makes it clear that he is a good man turned mad by evil, primitive influences.

Heart of Darkness is a disturbing book because of its racist theme. The Aboriginal people of the world were seen as evil. This was shown in stories of the cannibals of the South Seas, the wild men from Borneo, Fuzzy-Wuzzies, and so on.

We were called "savages" and "barbarians," thus allowing the government and the churches to subjugate and convert us. If the strengths and humanity of our people and colonized people everywhere were expressed and understood, colonialism would have been less successful. The legacy continued after the occupation, and people of the colonies were seen as primitive and undeveloped.

The attitudes of colonialism persist. A few years ago, missionaries travelled into the Amazon rain forest in search of a new tribe. The missionaries spread both the word of God and influenza. The resulting epidemic decimated the tribe.

The story must now be told from the other side.

In 1998, I was a part of a production team filming the story of Big Bear, which was made into a four-hour miniseries. *Big Bear* is the antithesis of the theme of *Heart of Darkness*.

Big Bear feared the Europeans – not as individuals, but for what they could do as a civilization. He saw the end of his freedom, and the end of his food source, the buffalo. He saw strangulation for his people on reserves, living in little mud huts. He prophesied that European civilization would take his children, and that the language and culture would come under attack.

He avoided signing the treaty. Instead, he continued to pursue his old way of life. He attracted people from other bands who shared his scepticism about a new life on reserves. He was a holdout, and so the government went after him.

The story of Big Bear is the story of one man's humanity and ideals in the face of the colonial machine. He is the "primitive." Big Bear saw the imperialists for what they were, and he feared them. They were *his* heart of darkness.

Afro-American History Parallels Our Own

February is Black History Month and the First Nations can claim a role in Black history throughout the Americas.

When the Americas were first colonized, the Spanish and French fought with and enslaved its indigenous people. Columbus forced the Indigenous people on the island of Hispaniola to work his gold mines. The island now contains the countries of the Dominican Republic and Haiti. Columbus quite literally worked the Indians to death. Indians succumbed easily to the white man's diseases and died by the thousands. However, because the Indians knew the land, they could easily escape into the forest.

The Spanish continued to enslave the Indians across the Caribbean and later on the mainland. By and large, however, Indians made poor slaves because they kept dying or escaping.

The Aztec, Mayan, and Inca civilizations, and others, had highly developed farming cultures. So, the Spanish confiscated the land and turned the Indian farmers into the equivalent of feudal serfs, a more sophisticated type of slavery.

When I travelled in South America a few years ago, I was taken aback by the Incan fields terraced into the sides of mountains. All the best land was still owned by the Spanish, who live in the cities as absentee landlords.

The Spanish basically ruined Indian civilization in South America, Central America, and the Caribbean. The Spanish openly and freely practised genocide as they moved across the Americas. When the indigenous people couldn't be used as slaves any more, the Spanish turned to Africa and began to import Africans as slaves. The Black slaves had nowhere to run, and they were less susceptible to diseases such as measles and small pox.

The French also practised slavery in their colony of Louisiana. They imported slaves from Africa and captured the local Indians. At one time, there was a flourishing trade of Black and Indian slaves between Louisiana and New France.

Any wealthy Quebec family simply had to have a slave. Slave ownership was a symbol of status and wealth. The French also captured and enslaved a few of the local Mohawks, Algonquians, and other tribes.

The same held for the Loyalists who travelled north to Canada following the American Revolution. These people brought their slaves, many of whom eventually helped to form the black communities in Ontario and Nova Scotia. Also, Blacks who fought for the British in the Revolutionary War were granted land and asylum in Canada.

The Indians and Afro-Americans have a shared history, which brought the two groups together. In French Louisiana, and later other southern states, black slaves who escaped from bondage could seek sanctuary in the local Indian villages.

The Indians were able to stand up to the slave hunters and turn them away from their villages, but they were no match for the army and the government, which forcefully relocated southern tribes such as the Cherokee. The Cherokee endured the Trail of Tears on their forced march to the Oklahoma territory.

The resentful and land-hungry Americans pushed the tribes westward, and the relationship between the two groups was destroyed. But their long-lost friendship comes alive again when Mardi Gras rolls around. Many of the Afro-American participants in the Mardi Gras parade create beautiful Indian costumes with a wealth of feathers and beadwork. In keeping with the Mardi Gras theme, they at first appear artificial and grossly overdone, but their history is real.

This practice began over a century ago in order to honour and remember the Indian people who risked their lives to give them freedom.

We share a parallel history with Afro-Americans, and that shared experience continues. We have both felt the stings of racism, poverty, social upheaval, and other injustices. But we can both look with pride to a history where we persevered and grew together.

Learning from "The Kids"

One winter, I worked with a class at Saskatoon's Pleasant Hill School to develop a video drama. The topic was supposed to deal with racial discrimination, and the kids taught me a few things in the process.

Racism is one of those things that I have a problem with. I spent my childhood on the reserve, and later we moved to La Ronge. There I was just one more kid, and we didn't worry what race we were. Back then, La Ronge was a blend of Indian, white, and Métis, with no group dominating another. We didn't see a difference, at least one that mattered.

When I was fourteen, we moved to southern Alberta, and I got my first dose of redneck racism. I wasn't prepared for it, nor did I know how to react. I still don't know how to react to racism because it's irrational and based on fear and hatred.

But I've grown used to the double standard that permeates our lives. A friend of mine from Africa pointed out that while a stone building with a thatched roof in Scotland was called a "cottage," in Africa it was called a "hut." I replied that in Canada if you see a white man running down the street, he's jogging; if you see an Indian running down the street, he just stole something. It would be funny if it weren't true, but a friend of mine was running to hockey practice and the police stopped him. He looked suspicious running down the street with a big bag, and, after all, he was an Indian.

A drunken white man is a good old boy and a drunken Indian is, well, a drunken Indian.

Back to Pleasant Hill: the students were in grades seven and eight, and they had already seen a lot of life – a lot more than I had seen at that age. Life in the cities is hard for young Indians. It is a life of poverty, slum landlords, removal from your roots, and, yes, racism.

In Saskatchewan, many of the complaints brought before the human rights branch come from First Nations individuals. We live in a society that has targeted Indians as the race of preference when it comes to discrimination.

Young Indian people growing up in the city are cut off from their family support on the reserve. Grandparents are only seen a few times a year and do not fill the traditional role of teacher and leader. The burden then falls on the parents, and often just the mother who is under stress and strain with city life and its complications. Young people are often on their own when it comes to working out the more complex issues of life.

We asked the Pleasant Hill students to write a story about their experiences with racism. We used their stories to develop our script. This is where my eyes were opened. I expected stories about discrimination against Indians, but new stories emerged. The stories were about Indian kids picking on white kids at bus stops and malls. They saw racism as something they were *practising*.

Their story is called *The New Kid*, and it's about a new student who attends their school. He's white, and he becomes the focus of abuse from a few of the other students. The kids work it out through discussion and bringing in a student mediator.

These young people live in a world where they are the majority. They live in an urban ghetto, and white people are the outsiders. Often, the Native kids are the ones doing the discriminating.

Some may see this as "reverse racism." This term is a white liberal expression, and it indicates one group getting back at another. I see the term "reverse racism" as a cop-out. Racism is racism, no matter who practices it. Racism isn't the exclusive property of white people.

These young people saw their racism for what it was and were willing to address it. I was impressed with their maturity, but felt a chill for the reality of their situation.

In Saskatchewan, we have developed urban ghettos on the comparative scale of the black ghettos in American cities. We can no longer claim the moral high ground when it comes to issues of race. But is it too late? Not as long as we are willing to talk about it, and not as long as the young people are there to show us where we go wrong.

Racism, by Any Other Name

> - *What do you call an Indian driving a Cadillac?*
> - *A thief.*

Unfortunately, too many people have preconceived ideas about other races. The information one hears on the news or sees in the entertainment media somehow becomes fact before logic and decency have a chance to take hold.

If you loved *The Godfather* and are a fan of *The Sopranos*, then obviously most Italians are gangsters. All Asians are masters of the marshal arts, and, of course, all Blacks are drug dealers. These statements are as illogical as concluding that since the members of the Ku Klux Clan are white, all whites are dangerous racists. It's a leap that defies logic, but many people unquestioningly make it every day.

It's a leap that governments and police forces are now making with frightening regularity. Anyone who is dark-skinned and swarthy is the subject of searches and harassment, especially at the border and in airports. It's called "racial profiling," and it's the latest sanitized buzzword for institutionalized racism.

Ethnic and religious profiling has become an issue since the terrorist attacks of September 11, 2001. Following the attacks, the United States' attorney General Ashcroft ordered the detention of 1,200 men of Arab descent. None was connected to terrorism, and not a single terrorism charge was laid. Today, Canadians of Middle-Eastern descent are searched and fingerprinted at the border by American customs inspectors. Respected Canadian writer Rohinton Mistry cut short his book tour of the United Sates because he could no longer stand the humiliation of being searched and harassed at U.S. airports. Mr. Mistry is originally from India, but these days, anyone with a skin colour other than white is suspect.

In Toronto, neighbours reported that a number of visitors started showing up at a Muslim home. When the police went to investigate, they discovered that there had been a death in the family and people were simply paying their respects. Even so, they questioned the family for several hours.

Muslim people are profiled as violent and bent on the destruction of the western world, but how many people have really bothered to study or read up on the religion? Instead, people are content to accept information from the media and the stories told around the water cooler. The basic tenets of the world's religions are essentially the same, calling upon followers to lead a good life, help humanity, treat people with respect, and pass beliefs on to the next generation.

Fundamentalists of all stripes are a big part of the problem. Christian fundamentalists such as Pat Buchanan and Jerry Falwell are capable of sowing as much hate as Bin Laden and his group. No religion is free from its nutty fringe groups. The mistake comes in assuming that the evil few are like the majority, who are actually good and decent people.

We Canadians can't look south and wag our finger without it pointing back to us. During the Second World War, Canada was all-too-quick to round up Japanese Canadians and place them in camps. It was one of the worst examples of racial profiling in our history.

As Indian people, we have had our share of troubles with racial profiling, both with the bureaucratic system and the police forces.

There are two kinds of racial profiling: one is fostered by society and the other is actively practiced by government agencies. When I was in high school, Indian kids weren't considered university material, and we were channeled into technical programs. It took determination to go against the system and demand access to a university education.

When my kids were in elementary school, some of their fellow students believed that since we were Indians, we must be on welfare. That's the type of profiling that comes from the home. Where else do these things get discussed?

Law enforcement officers still tend to practice racial profiling as a matter of course. A friend of mine was surprised to hear that the police in Alberta were looking for him. Apparently, they were looking for a longhaired Aboriginal man, and he filled that description. I don't know if you've noticed, but there are an awful lot of longhaired Indian men out there.

Another friend was travelling on the Yellowhead Highway near North Battleford when he was pulled over by the RCMP. After he gave them his driver's license and registration, he asked why he was stopped since he wasn't breaking any laws. The reply was that many young Indian men in the area didn't have their licenses, so they routinely stopped cars driven by Indian men.

Racial profiling and just plain racism are as common as grass in this country's police forces, and the situation is allowed to persist because the majority believes that certain races are prone to certain behaviours. When I was researching this column, almost everyone I spoke to could recall an incident where they or their friends were stopped by the police only because they were Indian.

The majority of Canadians simply want to get on with their lives without a lot of fuss; however, the fear and panic of September 11, 2001 has become the enemy of logic. Attitudes are hardening, and racism based on fear is increasingly the order of the day.

Remembering "Indian Summer"

How time flies. It was over fifteen years ago in 1989 that Canada woke up to the Oka crisis. Over the following months, the Mercier Bridge in Montreal was blocked, Aboriginal people from across the country went to the Mohawk community of Kanesetake, and we emerged a different people. The Indian summer of 1990 was a watershed for Indian people, and Canada realized that we were serious about protecting our land and our rights.

The Oka crisis was a combination of determination on the part of the Mohawks, and stupidity and bumbling on the part of the government of Quebec and the town of Oka.

Oka is a pretty little town up the Ottawa River from Montreal. In the 1980s, it was invaded by upscale yuppies from Montreal who loved the country life and commuted in their luxury cars. They had no appreciation of the history of the area, and they assumed that they could do what they pleased. And they needed to expand the golf course from nine holes to 18. Without this, their lives weren't complete.

The Mohawk community of Kanesetake borders the town of Oka, and they shared a beautiful pine forest. This pine forest is some of the last old growth pine in the province. The people from Kanesetake also had a graveyard located in the pines and for years had considered the pines a part of their land. In fact, the pines had been Mohawk territory and were part of a land grant dating back to the 1700s. Over the years, the land shrank and the rights of the Mohawk were either ignored or abused.

In 1990, the Mayor of Oka supported the expansion of the golf course on land claimed by the Mohawk people, and construction was planned.

A small group of Mohawk people from Kanesetake held a vigil to protect the land, and when the police attacked in a predawn raid, they were ready for them. The resulting battle left one Quebec policeman dead. The course of history was changed forever.

Oka is an event that is burned into the collective memory of Aboriginal people. People can remember what they were doing when they first heard of the attack and subsequent battle. And we can all remember the summer of confrontation and confusion that followed.

A new breed of leaders came forward. They were people with nothing to lose, people who weren't afraid of confrontation. The Uncle Tomahawks panicked. Indian people from across the country made a pilgrimage to Oka. The traffic congestion was so bad that people couldn't even get close to the community.

My wife is Mohawk from Akwesasne, and we have relatives in Kanesetake and Kanewakee outside Montreal. We had an inside view of the "crisis." My wife's aunt, who lives at the bottom of the hill where the warriors set up their blockade, refused to move and remained home for the duration of the crisis.

We have other relatives in Kanewakee who suffered from trauma caused by the pressure of helicopters flying overhead and of living in a community under attack. They told us that it felt like being in a war zone.

Later, the army moved in and for the third time in Canada's history, troops were deployed for a domestic issue. The first was when the militia was dispatched in 1885 for the North West Rebellion, the second was during the Quebec crisis of 1970, and the third was for Oka. It's very telling when a democratic country uses an army against its own people, but it is even more telling when Aboriginal people are put down by military force. There is a large degree of racism shown when the government uses its own army against a small number of protesters.

Following the Oka crisis, the Canadian government used the American strategy and charged everyone who had even the remotest connection to the blockade. This strategy was designed to break them financially and to set an example for others. The strategy backfired as support poured in, and people were found not guilty or charges were thrown out of court.

The Oka crisis left deep scars on Mohawk communities. The golf course remains at nine holes, but the land dispute is still unresolved. Race relations are tenuous at best, and the standard of living remains lower in the Mohawk communities than in the white communities. The Oka crisis was also a black eye for Canada at a time when it was sanctimoniously criticizing South Africa for racist policies toward its Aboriginal people. But across Canada, Aboriginal people benefited with greater awareness, a sense of pride, and the knowledge that individuals must stand up for their rights.

Oka was a turning point in our history. It defined us as a united people, and it showed the country that we weren't willing to take it any more. Oka defined us for the coming century.

Tom Longboat: A Legendary Athlete

The name Tom Longboat draws immediate respect in Indian country. Each year, the top Aboriginal amateur athlete in Canada receives the Tom Longboat Award, and through this Longboat's name lives on.

Longboat was an outstanding athlete, but his battle against racism makes him stand out as an even greater hero.

Longboat was born in 1887 on the Six Nations Reserve near Brantford, Ontario. His father died when he was young, and his mother was left to raise four children by herself. He was a member of the Onondaga Nation, and his Indian name was Cogwagee. He would use his Indian name throughout his life, never turning his back on his people or his heritage.

Tom was often seen running on the reserve. He loved to run long distances, and at 19 he entered the Hamilton Bay race. He was an unknown, and so the odds on him were 60 to 1.

Throughout his life, Tom had to deal with the rampant racism of the time. If he didn't win, he was a "lazy Indian." If he won, though, he was a "the speedy son of the forest." The newspapers called him "Injun" or "Heap Big Chief."

So it was no surprise that when he competed in his first race, a local reporter described him as "a pathetic figure in a pair of bathing trunks with cheap sneakers on his feet, and hair that looked as if it had been hacked off with a tomahawk."

Coming within a shadow of the course record, Tom went on to win the race. A few days later, he won the 15-mile Ward Marathon in Toronto, and several months later, he won the Boston Marathon with a time of 2:24:25. His record would stand until the course was changed and made easier.

Tom had an enormous reserve of strength, pacing himself so that during the last mile of the marathon, he would gain speed and sprint to the finish. This would leave his competition in the dust, demoralized.

Tom was a hero in Canada following the Boston Marathon. He was hot property and was under contract to Tom Flanagan, the owner of the Irish Canadian Athletic Club. For a while, Longboat's career continued to flourish, but the strain began to show. Flanagan was domineering and manipulative.

In 1908, the New England Amateur Athletic Union stripped Longboat of his amateur status. The accusation was that since he didn't have a job and was allegedly supported by the Irish Canadian Club, he no longer held amateur status. He was banned from returning to Boston to defend his title. However, he was able to be a part of the Canadian Olympic Team to participate in the 1908 Olympics in London, England. Unfortunately, he collapsed at the 19-mile mark while he was in second place. The speculation turned to drugs, and the manager of the Canadian Olympic Team even mused that it must have been a drug overdose. Some speculated that Longboat was drugged so that the bookies could rake in a huge windfall. Others pointed to the exceptional heat on the day of the race as being the main factor.

In the end, Longboat left his condescending manager, and did quite well on his own, in spite of Flanagan's dark threats that he would squander his winnings and end up in the gutter. After all, he was only an Indian.

Longboat went on to win the most famous race of his career in 1908 at Madison Square Gardens. It was a two-man race against Dorando Pietri, the great Italian runner. They raced on a circular track for the full distance of the marathon. The two ran beside each other for the first 25 miles, with Pietri taking the lead. However, in the last mile, Longboat surged ahead in his trademark style. Pietri couldn't keep up, and he collapsed on the track.

For their trouble, Longboat and Pietri were each guaranteed a quarter of the gate, which amounted to $3,750.00 apiece.

In 1916, when Longboat was 29, he joined the army and went to Europe. He was a member of the 107th Pioneer Battalion in France, and he had the dangerous assignment of running messages and orders between units. During this time, he also raced in inter-Battalion sports contests. He was wounded twice, and once he was even declared dead.

Longboat survived the war and returned to Canada in 1919. He returned to his roots and married a woman from his reserve. For the last 20 years of his life, he worked as a garbage collector in Toronto. The Canadian public largely forgot him, but his fame lived on with his own people.

Longboat died in 1947 of pneumonia brought on by diabetes. He was buried on Six Nations. The funeral service was conducted in the Native spiritual tradition, a tradition he held to throughout his life.

Today, Longboat remains a special hero to Indians across Canada and on both sides of the border. People mention his name with respect and take pride in his legacy.

Edward Ahenakew: Our Martin Luther King

First Nations resistance and political organization are not recent under-takings; they go deep into our past. One of our unsung heroes of the past is Canon Edward Ahenakew (1885-1961). During his lifetime, Ahenakew saw his people begin the early stages of political development, and he played an important role in that development.

Canon Ahenakew was the first formally educated member of the Ahtaka-koop Reserve. He went to Emmanuel College in Prince Albert. Emmanuel College was a boarding school established in the 1880s to train teachers and pastors for the Church of England. In 1903, Ahenakew graduated with his senior matriculation and taught school on the Muskoday Reserve. Later he decided to go into the ministry, and in 1912, he convocated from Emmanuel College, which by then was a part of Saskatoon's new University of Saskatch-ewan.

After convocation, Ahenakew moved to the Onion Lake Reserve and served the people there for several years. In 1918, a worldwide influenza epi-demic was brought home by soldiers returning from the Second World War. Indian people were especially hard hit, and Onion Lake was no exception. He described the scene: "the church was piled high with bodies. On the reserves so many people were dying that mass funerals and burials were being held." The epidemic took a terrible toll. By 1920, the Indian population was at an all-time low; according to the Indian Department's annual report of 1920, there were "about 105,000 Indians in the whole Dominion of Canada."

In these tragic times, Ahenakew decided to study medicine to be of greater use to his people. He took a leave of absence and moved to Edmonton to study medicine at the University of Alberta. This was before the days of educational assistance, and so Ahenakew paid his own way with the help of a small stipend from the woman's auxiliary of the Anglican Church. He was forced to drop out after three years because his poverty led to malnutrition. He left medical school, exhausted and sick.

Ahenakew returned to Saskatchewan, and after a period of convales-cence, he returned to the ministry. He moved to Fort a la Corne, now the James Smith First Nation east of Prince Albert.

During the 1930s, the League of Indians was formed to speak on behalf Indian people nationally. It was started by a Mohawk named Frederick Ogil-vie Loft. Loft was from the Six Nations Reserve in Ontario, and he was a veteran of the First World War. The organization was short-lived, but it sowed the seeds for future Indian organizations. Loft was branded an agitator by the Indian Department and placed under police surveillance.

In 1932, Edward Ahenakew was elected vice-president of the League of Indians for Western Canada. He travelled to Ottawa as a part of his duties and met with senior officials of the Department of Indian Affairs. The reception was hostile, and the League's representatives were treated like criminals. The government complained to the church, and at a 1933 meeting of the League in Poundmaker, Ahenakew tendered his resignation. He was replaced by John Tootoosis.

The Bishop had told him to attend to his duties and not meddle with the affairs of the state, but Ahenakew remained a spokesman for his people. He lived on the James Smith Reserve until his retirement in 1955. He lived in poverty and never married, devoting his life to his work and to his people.

Ahenakew was a prolific writer, and following his death, his manuscripts were discovered and printed in a book called *Voices of the Plains Cree*. He chronicled the old stories because he feared the past would soon die and that young people would lose their history.

Edward Ahenakew was the first in a series of political and spiritual leaders who worked within the church to help their people on a broad level.

The early organizers had no source of finances. They had to pay their own way. Also, at that time, only members of the clergy received any advanced education. Like the early leaders of the civil rights movement in the United States, they used the resources of the church to further the progress of their people. Edward Ahenakew was our Martin Luther King.

Chapter 2

Our Home and Native Land,
Thank You Very Much

On Canada Day, Remember That Canada Was Built on the Treaties

Canada Day is our national holiday, and while we may not go nuts with the same passion as the Americans do three days later on Independence Day, we nevertheless have much to celebrate.

There are many yardsticks for determining a nation's greatness, but I look to European pickpockets who prize a Canadian passport above all others. A Canadian passport commands the highest price on the black market. Forget the separatists, forget the grumpy old men in the Conservative Party, and forget all the prophets of gloom. The thieves know who is number one.

So how did we become number one? Whom do we thank?

Our history is unique in that with the exception of the conquest of Quebec, Canada was expanded and developed by peaceful means. And the treaties with the First Nations set us apart as a special place.

The role that the First Nations played in the history of Canada is seldom seen in a positive light, but, in reality, the First Nations in the west played a pivotal role in the establishment of Canada as a nation.

The year 2001 is the 125th anniversary of the signing of Treaty Number Six, which ceded large tracts of Alberta and Saskatchewan to Canada. In 1876, two significant events occurred in Indian country. First, the Battle of the Little Big Horn took place, and second, Treaty Number Six was negotiated and signed in Canada.

The Canadian government was worried about the peaceful settlement of the west. In *The Treaties of Canada with the Indians*, Lieutenant Governor Alexander Morris writes that "the gravest of the questions presented for solution . . . was the securing of the alliance of the Indian tribes and maintaining friendly relations with them."

Americans were waging a genocidal war against the Indian Nations within their boundaries, and it was spilling over into Canada. American traders were entering the country illegally, and in 1873, there had been a massacre of Assiniboine people in the Cypress Hills.

Also, Sitting Bull would seek asylum in Canada, and later the Nez Pierce, under the leadership of Chief Joseph, would try to make it to safety in Canada.

The American philosophy of Manifest Destiny was in force and the Canadian West was filling up with settlers. Earlier, the Americans had fought a war with Mexico and gained the territories of Texas, Arizona, New Mexico, and California. They were now casting greedy eyes on the land to the north.

President James Monroe had earlier stated that the boundary between the United States and Canada should be set at the 55th parallel of latitude. The pressure was clearly on Canada to secure the West before it was lost to the United States.

The numbered treaties began in the so-called Northwest Angle, which was the territory between the western shore of Lake Superior, Fort Francis, and present-day Winnipeg. Treaty One and Treaty Two were located in southern Manitoba and contained different terms than Treaty Three or the Northwest Angle Treaty.

Treaty Three set the pattern that the other numbered treaties would follow.

It was established that the leaders of the First Nations would speak for their people in negotiations, and the leaders would be regarded as heads of state. The warriors and the Northwest Mounted Police held equal status. The treaties were therefore international in character and were made in the name of the Crown, and so should stand up to the vagaries of future politicians.

It was also made clear on both sides that what was negotiated in the future would apply to all. Therefore, Treaty Six may have the medicine chest clause that assures health care, but it was added to future treaties and applies to all because of the spirit of the negotiations. The numbered treaties are incremental and apply equally to all.

However, as an emerging nation that wasn't yet a decade old, Canada received an enormous land base that was assured to remain Canadian. At the time, the westward expansion of the United States posed a real problem for Canada. The Americans were eyeing the western Prairies with greed and a belief in their Manifest Destiny. It was crucial that Canada secure this vast land mass.

After the negotiations were concluded, the Chiefs received red treaty coats to wear on official occasions and to reflect their rank as leaders and representatives of the Crown. They also received a large silver treaty medal and a flag. At that time, Canada still used the flag of Great Britain, the Union Jack. With these symbolic gifts, the treaty negotiators extended Canadian sovereignty over the ceded land. The Chiefs would represent the Crown, and they would fly the flag. This meant that the Americans would have a difficult time taking the Prairies since they legally belonged to Canada.

At the time, the West was sparsely settled and American whiskey traders were moving in. The Cypress Hills Massacre was a result of American fur traders importing genocidal tactics. The First Nations feared the Americans and chose to remain in Canada. Sitting Bull knew of the protection the Crown afforded, and he sought sanctuary in Canada following the Battle of the Little Big Horn.

The First Nations to the south of us fared much worse. Treaties were negotiated at gunpoint, and genocide was the alternative.

Once, I met a group of Aboriginal health educators who'd been to the States to see what programs were being developed and implemented there. Their reaction was, "Thank God we live in Canada." Apparently, there were no innovative programs, and health and education were poorly funded. Schools and clinics were housed in old buildings and budgets were low. It made them thankful that we live in a country that provided meaningful programs in spite of complaints from our leaders.

In the United States, services are provided to Native Americans with an attitude of largesse. There are no treaties of substance, and the country's constitution provides no protection as Canada's constitution does to its First Nations people.

For a brief time, Canada sought an alliance with the First Nations to secure a land that would some day be the envy of the world. The early Chiefs saw themselves as allies with the Crown and Canada, and the government treated them as such. As the West opened to settlement, though, it became apparent that this alliance would change.

The First Nations were partners in the development and establishment of Canada as a country. The First Nations could have made a treaty with the United States, but the choice was Canada, a decision that many more people would also make in the future.

Is 125 Years Such a Long Time?

In the summer of 2001, the 125th anniversary of the signing of Treaty Number Six was commemorated at Fort Carlton, one of the locations where the original treaty signing ceremonies took place.

Treaty Six was negotiated and signed at Forts Carlton and Pitt in Saskatchewan. Later, in 1889, an adhesion was signed for the Lac La Ronge and Montreal Lake First Nations at the north end of Montreal Lake.

My First Nation, Little Pine, signed an adhesion to Treaty Six at Fort Walsh in 1879 along with Chief Lucky Man. They were an independent and difficult group, traits that exist to the present day. Later, Chief Big Bear and his people also signed Treaty Six, but the events of the North West Rebellion overtook them, Big Bear was sent to jail, and the band members were dispersed among the Cree reserves in the Battlefords area and Alberta.

And it isn't as though the treaties are that old. In the 1950s, the Saulteaux and Witchekan Lake First Nations signed adhesion to Treaty Six and received reserve land. The Treaty Land Entitlement Agreement of 1992 recognized the land still owing to First Nations under the terms of Treaty Six.

But I have always wondered about the two solitudes that exist around the treaties: while the First Nations revere them and use them as the basis of their political and historical relationship with Canada, the other side virtually ignores them.

It wasn't always this way. The 50th Anniversary or Jubilee of Treaty Number Six in 1936 was a major event. It was held on the Mistawasis First Nation and attracted a large group of dignitaries and speakers. Apparently, there was even a guy there with a bi-plane selling rides.

My father attended the Jubilee. He told me that Grey Owl, the famous writer and naturalist, was in attendance among the dignitaries. When Grey Owl spoke, he used Cree, but every Cree speaker there knew that he spoke with the accent of someone who had learned the language. Nobody pointed this out, and they let him go on playing Indian.

In 1976, we commemorated the Centennial of the signing of Treaty Number Six. This time, the Beardy's First Nation was the host. Once again, the dignitaries and their spear-carriers showed up, and copies of the original treaty medals were handed out to the present-day Chiefs.

These gatherings have never been viewed as celebrations because the treaties were never fully implemented and we gave up so much. Instead, the milestones have been regarded as commemorating the past and honouring the future.

But the treaties are not old, molding documents. They are a part of Canada's national fabric. They are woven into the Constitution. Section 35 affirms existing Aboriginal and treaty rights. The Supreme Court has recognized this, and has pointed out in its decisions that the treaties must be given a "broad and liberal interpretation." In other words, where ambiguity exists, the decision must favour the First Nations.

The treaties read like the colonial documents that they were. The British were famous for promising one thing and doing another; it's how they built their empire.

The text of the treaties promises peace and friendship, a schoolhouse on the reserve, land for families, and other economic and social rights. However, because the treaties were written over a century ago, they're silent on important issues like resource revenue sharing and First Nations governance. Naturally, they also lack consideration of advances in technology over the past century.

Over the years, our leaders have maintained that the treaties cannot be translated literally. Instead, they must be interpreted in their broader spirit and intent. In this way, the text of the treaties makes sense in a modern-day context.

In addition, our leaders have maintained that the treaties between the First Nations and the Crown are international treaties between sovereigns. This, of course, is disputed by the Canadian government, but recourse to international courts, tribunals, and organizations like the United Nations still exists. These are not routes that many First Nations leaders want to take because of the time and expense involved. Instead, the Canadian government must get on-side and educate the public about their legal and historical obligations. Inaction is leading to ignorance and misunderstanding.

As a result of the government's resistance, we have ongoing battles with fishermen on both coasts as First Nations fishermen try to exercise their fishing rights and make a living for themselves and their families.

In Saskatchewan, we have a situation where only Indians living on reserves have treaty rights. The federal government has successfully dumped the off-reserve First Nations people on the Province, in spite of the federal government's constitutional responsibility for First Nations people regardless of where they live.

So now we have over 125 years of history behind our treaties. I wonder what the future will hold, and whether the treaties will continue to grow and define our relationship with Canada. The First Nations know which way to go; now it's up to Canada.

It's Jurisdiction, Stupid

"It all boils down to jurisdiction," a First Nations politician once told me. He was pointing out that while the Supreme Court was recognizing our rights, the federal and provincial governments were silent on the implementation of those rights.

Treaty and Aboriginal rights are part of the Charter of Rights and Freedoms and have been recognized by the Supreme Court. The issue now is that our rights must be implemented.

When the Charlottetown Accord was negotiated, First Nations self-government was recognized as a legitimate order of government in Canada. However, for a variety of reasons, the public defeated the accord in a referendum. Self-government slipped off the table and has not been seriously discussed since.

We can expect conflict over fishing rights on the East Coast and other issues to continue if First Nations self-government and jurisdiction are not recognized.

First Nations jurisdiction refers to the government's ability to enforce laws in areas that directly affect its lands and peoples. Instead of having self-government, First Nations governments have been restricted to self administration, and the result has been stagnation in social, economic, and political development. Self administration is a form of neo-colonialism and is designed to turn our Chiefs into modern-day Indian Agents rather than political leaders.

The imbroglio involving the East Coast fishery is an example of what can happen when rights are recognized but no positive follow-through occurs, and there is a failure to recognize First Nations' right to govern their people and control their lands and resources.

However, no government is truly independent or sovereign. In the modern, integrated world, all governments must work together to arrive at equitable solutions. The problem for First Nations is that this has not been happening. We are constantly left out of important policy-making processes.

For example, in the area of health and social services, millions of dollars are transferred to the provinces from the federal government. The province takes the money and spends it, but what input do First Nations have over what is essentially their money? Health and social services were promised under the terms of the treaties, but we only control a very small portion of the total amount.

First Nations entrepreneurs are developing at a rapid pace economically, but the lack of jurisdiction to tax, license, and regulate has left First Nations governments on the sidelines. For example, there is legislation that allows for federal and provincial corporations, but there is nothing that recognizes the rights of First Nations to create legislation that would recognize corporate law under the jurisdiction of First Nations.

Also, with increased economic activity, our governments must have the ability to raise revenue through corporate and individual taxation. Instead, the federal and provincial governments insist that only they have these powers, and so we have situations like the battle over the Ochapowace First Nation's decisions to impose its sales tax and to eliminate federal and provincial taxation.

In Saskatchewan, First Nations have been gaining a much larger land base through Treaty Land Entitlement and other land claim settlements. This new land base will make First Nations among the largest landholders in the province, which will necessitate the need for legislation and joint planning. When First Nations have gained land in urban areas, the civic governments will have sat down and negotiated in good faith. They recognize the need to work with First Nations governments because, in many ways, we represent the future.

I have yet to see a First Nation that will work in isolation with its planning and not take into consideration the outside community. Shared jurisdiction may well be the way of the future, but we must have serious recognition of our jurisdiction first.

First Nations are rapidly gaining in economic and political stature. In the future, it will be incumbent upon governments at all levels to work with First Nations and give honest recognition to their jurisdictions.

Yahoo, Delgamuukw!

On December 11, 1997, Santa Claus came to Indian country in the form of a Supreme Court decision in favour of the right to Aboriginal title for the Gitxsan and Wet'suwet'en First Nations. The case known as Delgamuukw (pronounced *Del-ga-mook*) made history across Canada and especially in British Columbia. It left radio and television news announcers sputtering to pronounce the names and it left politicians and bureaucrats gasping for breath.

The Gitxsan-Wet'suwet'en case has been a long-standing issue for years now. In 1982, when Aboriginal leaders and the First Ministers met for the first time, the issue of Aboriginal title was raised. Prime Minister Trudeau smugly asked what was meant by "Aboriginal title" for the First Nations. James Godsnell, an elder and former Chief for the Gitxsan, rose to the occasion, replying, "Lock, stock, and barrel. We own it all!" Trudeau asked, "You own it all?" Godsnell stated emphatically, "We own it all."

This exchange was one of those defining moments in First Nations history. Godsnell wasn't prepared to lower his sights in the face of the Prime Minister's condescension. Trudeau's attitude was typical of the general reaction to Aboriginal title. The attitude from the government was that Indians were a conquered people and should just shut up and assimilate. This attitude persists in various forms today. Godsnell's assertion "Lock, stock, and barrel" is basically the same conclusion that the Supreme Court reached. The First Nations have a constitutional right to own their ancestral lands and so can use them as they wish.

This Supreme Court decision has put the Government of British Columbia in a tailspin that should result in serious negotiations with most of the First Nations of British Columbia. The province has never been surrendered by the First Peoples. Only a portion of the northeast part of the province is covered by Treaty Number Eight.

I don't feel particularly sorry for the Government of British Columbia or its people. The issue of Aboriginal title has never been addressed, and successive provincial governments have failed to negotiate in good faith. They have preferred instead to shove the First Nations out of sight, out of mind, and to leave it to the next generation to deal with land claims.

As we all know, some things can't be ignored to death. Toothaches, taxes, that funny sound in your engine, and the rights of the First Nations don't go away. They fester, get worse, and must be dealt with sooner rather than later.

British Columbia is now going to have to negotiate seriously, and sooner rather than later. The settlement will only get bigger the longer the government demurs.

Another major outcome of this decision is the importance given to oral testimony. In a previous decision on the Gitxsan-Wet'suwet'en, the Provincial Court of British Columbia had poured scorn on the oral history presented by the elders to establish their occupation of the land in question. The Supreme Court ruled that it was a mistake not to consider oral history. The decision written by Chief Justice Antonio Lamer stated: "Had the trial judge assessed the oral histories correctly, his conclusions on these issues of fact might have been very different." The decision also recommends negotiations rather than another trial.

This is arguably the most important Supreme Court decision in the history of the relationship between the First Nations and Canada. The effects of this decision extend beyond the two First Nations, the First Nations of British Columbia, and other parts of the country which lack treaty relationships with Canada. All First Nations will benefit, even those with treaties.

Contrary to popular belief, the treaties did not extinguish all of our Aboriginal rights. We still maintain our culture, language, religion, and the right to govern ourselves. We also never negotiated away mineral rights to the land. These rights are probably our most important economic rights, and they weren't part of the treaty negotiations. They remain a part of our rights as First Nations, and now they must receive the attention and respect that all Aboriginal rights should.

The acceptance of our oral tradition and the recognition of our right to our ancestral lands will open new doors to negotiation. The Supreme Court has made a major decision that will take us into a very interesting future.

"Activist Judges" Are Doing Politicians' Jobs

Canadian courts are now making decisions that politicians should have recognized and made years ago. The courts have shown leadership and responsibility where no political will or backbone existed in Parliament.

Decisions regarding land claims, boarding school claims, and jury selection have come under careful scrutiny by the courts. Our detractors, including the political right, like to refer to these learned jurists as "activist judges," implying that they have a political agenda. Comments like these are an example of prejudice, and reduce the quality and importance of the judges' carefully considered decisions.

The Supreme Court opened up land claims with the historic Delgamuukw decision that in effect states that Aboriginal title is based on continuous occupation. This historic decision has sent resource development in British Columbia into a nosedive. In B.C., there are no treaties or agreements with the First Nations. Past provincial governments have arrogantly taken the land and resources without any concern for Aboriginal people.

Now the chickens have come home to roost, and British Columbia has to negotiate with the First Nations in good faith. Our elders have told us that if you want to get the White Man's attention, you have to hurt him in his wallet.

Meanwhile, in New Brunswick, a lower court ruled that Aboriginal people had a treaty right to timber on Crown land. Close to 80% of New Brunswick is Crown land, and so this decision in effect gives New Brunswick First Nations access to almost all of the province's timber. The case was overturned in provincial court, but it now appears to be headed to the Supreme Court. And with the precedence of the Delgamuukw decision, it may well be decided in favour of the First Nations.

Delgamuukw could have an impact on Saskatchewan, too, as the FSIN negotiates resource revenue sharing. The FSIN takes the position that the treaties granted the shared use of the land, and that the land was needed for agriculture only. Issues such as minerals, water, and forestry were to be discussed "later." Of course, "later" never came.

Meanwhile, the British Columbia Supreme Court has ruled that victims of boarding school sexual abuse must be compensated for their suffering. Students at the United Church boarding school at Port Alberni were victimized by a sexual predator who assaulted dozens of young boys. He was hired by the school as a dormitory supervisor who was, in the words of the Judge, a "sexual terrorist."

This landmark decision will cost the churches and government millions before it runs its course. It currently stands as a provincial decision only, but it has set an important precedent and other provincial litigation will surely follow.

Meanwhile, Indian Affairs in Saskatchewan continues to pay out compensation to victims of sexual abuse at Gordon's School. In light of the British Columbia decision, the Department has to get serious and pay out real compensation, not just hush money. It's likely that these settlements will be revisited, and proper compensation will have to be paid.

Recently, the Supreme Court also ruled that potential jurors can be questioned about their racial biases. This decision will have a positive impact on Indian people facing criminal trials. The Supreme Court ruling referred to the case of a British Columbia man whose conviction was overturned because his lawyer wasn't allowed to question potential jurors. In its decision, the Supreme Court said that when widespread racial bias is shown, it is reasonable to permit lawyers to question potential jurors about their views.

Like it or not, there are people out there who don't like racial minorities, including Indians. In a democracy, people are entitled to a fair trial, and that includes everyone.

Leadership in this country is not coming out of Parliament, but down Wellington Street at the Supreme Court. The courts are making decisions on issues that the politicians have been avoiding. The Courts are now forcing the governments to act, and to live up to their responsibilities.

Alliance Platform Ignores the Constitution

The Reform/Alliance/Conservative Party has had a very negative and divisive party platform, and its Aboriginal policy has been called "racism of the worst kind" by the Assembly of First Nations. The so-called "new ideas" of the Alliance are anything but new. If the Alliance ever runs the country, it will be devastating to the First Nations.

The party platform trumpets "equality for all Canadians," and avoids recognition of treaty and Aboriginal rights. This is because the party does not want any special rights for any group of Canadians, including Quebec, the First Nations, or any other group. Any rights for First Nations are called "race-based rights." This specious term ignores the fact that treaties were signed with nations, and our treaties are agreements between nations. Calling our rights "race-based" cheapens our treaties and creates an impression of unfairness.

Our treaties, now included in the Charter of Rights and Freedoms, have legal weight. The Canadian Constitution and the Charter of Rights and Freedoms stress group rights over individual rights, but the Alliance has failed to let this stand in the way of its one-sided philosophy.

Group rights have been central to the history of Confederation. Quebec has its own civil code, and legislation exists to protect the French language and culture. Also, an equalization payment to the poorer provinces recognizes group rights to fiscal equality. We are not a nation where each person and group stands alone. We are a diverse nation where the rights of groups take precedence over individual rights.

In addition to treaty and Aboriginal rights, affirmative action programs (such as employment equity that reflects the composition of society, and initiatives like the Federal set-aside program for Aboriginal business) would disappear, and we would continue to fall behind the rest of society. Equality to the Alliance really means "white power."

Another weasel word that the Alliance likes to use is "accountability." Now everyone wants accountability. It's like motherhood, but the devil is in the definition. First Nations people want their leaders to be accountable to them, and to spend money properly and meet their community's needs. This extends to the Alliance seeing accountability as First Nations being accountable to government regulations and spending priorities. The Alliance sees our leaders as Indian agents administering their own poverty.

Combine the Alliance's definition of equality and accountability, and self-government disappears. Theirs is not new thinking. It is reactionary thinking in the face of the rising political and economic power of the First Nations.

This is what appears to be at the heart of the matter. We are a rapidly evolving nation within Canada. Our people are becoming more politically aware, we are developing institutions, and land claims are rapidly expanding our economy. But the Alliance is capitalizing on people's fears without taking a positive leadership role. In recent years, a population explosion, rapid development, and rising expectations in the First Nations community have come about. Our people are competing for jobs and business like any other group. The problem is that we are perceived as not doing it fairly because of our treaty rights and affirmative action programs.

The base of the old Reform Party was western and rural, the area most affected by the rapid changes in Indian country. The members elected in these constituencies have shown that they are by and large reactionary, grumpy old men who prefer to complain and fan the fires of discontent rather than embrace change. It's a dangerous game because it will only serve to turn people against each other.

This was made very clear when the Alliance began harnessing the discontent brought about by the Supreme Court decision on fishing rights for the Mig'ma people in Atlantic Canada. The Alliance has targeted the constituency of Saint Mary's Bay in Nova Scotia as fertile ground to plant their seeds of racism, and to win a seat in the process. Rather than accept change and a Supreme Court decision, they prefer to drive wedges between people, creating animosity and hatred.

But one of the most crippling policies in the Alliance philosophy is the decentralization of government services to the provinces. Under an Alliance government, there would be wholesale decentralization of programs and resources to the provinces. The federal government would have few strings on this funding, and the country would become a loose confederation of semi-independent states. This wouldn't be good for the country, but it would be even worse for the First Nations.

For years, the First Nations leadership has fought against the transfer of federal responsibilities to the provinces. The federal White Paper of 1969 was a thinly veiled attempt to dump the responsibility for the First Nations on the provinces, and it united Indian people as no other initiative has before or since. In 1969, the Liberal Party backed down and shelved the unpopular policy. The background to our opposition goes back to the Treaties, the British North America Act, and The Royal Proclamation of 1773. Today, the Canadian Constitution includes these important documents, but it seems that means little as the Alliance continues to capitalize on people's fears and prejudices.

First Nations people are undergoing a period of rapid change. We are committed to education and economic development, our people are becoming urbanized, and our population is growing faster than any other group's in society.

The Alliance policies are racist and negative, and they ignore the Constitution. They will harm race relations and the progress of the First Nations. This is a time when we must pull together and cooperate.

Louis Chicken: A Northern Leader

Louis Chicken was a leader of the Dene people in the far north of Saskatchewan. He was a Chief, an elder, and a citizen of the Black Lake First Nation. He died at 87 after a lifetime of service to his people.

Louis spent the first 40 years of his life as a hunter and trapper. The Black Lake First Nation traditionally occupied the northeast corner of Saskatchewan and part of the Northwest Territories. Until recently, the Black Lake community was isolated, and there was little contact with the outside world.

When he was about 40, Louis was asked by his people to be their Chief. At the time, traditional self-government consisted of families who lived in small groups throughout their traditional area. Louis accepted the challenge and was Chief for over 20 years. He fought for treaty rights to education, better health services, and improved living conditions. He spoke no English and all business was conducted through interpreters.

Louis also found out that the Band did not receive its full allotment of land under the terms of Treaty Number Ten. He worked to have that shortfall recognized, and in the early 1970s, the land between the communities of Stony Rapids and Black Lake was transferred to reserve status. The recognition and subsequent settlement of the Black Lake Treaty Land Entitlement was an important step in the recognition of outstanding Treaty Land Entitlement for the rest of the province. The previous Premier, Ross Thatcher, had gone on record stating that the Indians would not receive another square inch of land.

Traditionally, the Dene people owned the land in that part of the province and still travelled freely over it, but Louis foresaw the day when the land would be claimed for mining or settlement. He worried that his people would be pushed aside. The new reserve was surveyed and set aside, and it is also named after him.

In 1969, the Federation of Saskatchewan Indians formed a Council of Elders or Senate. Eight men were selected by the Chiefs to form this important body, and the Dene Chiefs selected Louis to represent them. The Dene First Nations occupy the far north of the province from La Loche to Black Lake and south to Patuanak on the Churchill River.

The Senate was originally established to provide the Chiefs and the FSIN Executive with a body of elders who were former political leaders. These advisors would provide valuable counsel and maintain the focus on the treaties. The FSIN was established to protect treaty rights, and the Council of Elders was required to review political positions and tactics.

Over the years, all the other original senators passed away. Louis was the last of the original group, but becoming an elder did not mean retirement.

Louis attended all of the Chiefs' meetings and spoke out on the issues. He also continued to be a community leader in Black Lake and spoke regularly to the children in the school.

I attended an elders' conference at La Ronge several years ago, and Louis was there. He spoke of the need to educate young people and of the role that elders must play in the preservation of the language and culture. He loved young people and saw the need to educate them to save the language and culture for future generations.

A year ago, Louis addressed the Chiefs at their winter assembly. He knew that his time would soon be up, and he stated that this would be the last time that he would speak to them.

When Louis Chicken passed away, it represented the end of an era. Today, the Chiefs speak English and don't need interpreters. Louis didn't carry a cell phone or run a big administration. He spoke from his heart, and he spoke for his people.

Chief Gordon Oakes Led by Example

Chief Gordon Oakes was a leader whose influence went far beyond his small community.

Chief Oakes had retired, but because he had been Chief for so long, and because his influence continued, he was still regarded as a Chief even when his son Larry had taken on the responsibility.

For over 30 years, Gordon skillfully led his people through a time of rapid change. The Nekaneet First Nation had been isolated and ignored by the federal government since Chief Nekaneet insisted on living in the hills.

After the treaties were signed and the reserve system was put in place, the Cypress Hills were considered off-limits for reserve settlement. The First Nations were moved north to Battleford or east to the Qu'Appelle Valley. One of the Cree Chiefs, Kahkewistahaw, moved to The Crooked Lake area of the Qu'Appelle Valley. One of his headmen was a man named Nekaneet. Being forced away from the hills did not sit well with Nekaneet, and he received a message in a dream that he was to return to the hills and protect them for future generations. The Cypress Hills were considered a sacred place where all Nations could gather in peace. No tribe or Nation held ownership of the Hills, which were seen as neutral territory.

Taking some followers along, Nekaneet left his home in the Qu'Appelle Valley and traveled back to the hills. They settled on the northern slope and remained there for several generations.

Indian Affairs tried to move them, but after repeated failures, they gave up and granted them a small amount of land. They weren't regarded as Treaty Indians, and they were bureaucratically classed as an "historical curiosity." They were left alone, and, as a result, they kept their language, culture, and religion, unlike most Saskatchewan First Nations who fell under the yoke of the boarding schools.

It was into this world that Gordon Oakes was born in 1933. His Father was Abel, and his mother went by her Cree name Ma-ca-no. When he grew up, Gordon was a cowboy, a ranch hand, and a worker for the Department of Highways. In the 1960s, the band held elections, and Gordon was elected Chief. Over the years, the band's population had grown, but there was only a limited amount of land. Chief Oakes was one of the first Chiefs to research and demand his Treaty Land Entitlement. His band was still considered an historical curiosity, but he was eligible for land.

Throughout the 1970s and '80s, Chief Oakes lobbied the government and worked with the FSIN on behalf of Treaty Land Entitlement. When the agreement was finally signed in 1992, Nekaneet was not part of the original agreement, but a separate one was signed later, taking into consideration the First Nation's unique status.

When the federal government sought a location for a women's healing lodge as part of the replacement for the old Prison for Women in Kingston, Ontario, the Nekaneet Band put in a proposal which was picked as the best choice. The Band and the town of Maple Creek worked together to make the lodge a reality. The beauty and healing power of the location and the strong traditions of the people combined to make it the best bid. At the time, it was a controversial choice, but over the years, it has been a godsend for many troubled women.

Gordon and his wife Jean worked as elders in the lodge and played an important role in its formative stages when their leadership was needed most.

Over the years, Chief Oakes and the Nekaneet people have protected and fostered the Cree culture. Nekaneet hosts an annual conference of traditional healers from across North and Central America. The conference is an outstanding success and draws people from across western Canada.

Gordon was well-known across Indian country as an elder, a leader, and as a man who lived his culture. In the end, his health deteriorated, and he fell victim to diabetes and kidney failure.

Chief Gordon Oakes was a good man who lived a good life and worked hard for his people. His legacy will be an expanded land base and the recognition he earned for his people for their unique role in Saskatchewan history.

Len Marchand Was a Political Trailblazer

In 1969, when I was working for the Alberta Native Communications Society in Alberta, I covered a meeting with the Alberta Chiefs. Len Marchand, the first Status Indian to become a Member of Parliament, spoke to the gathering. Afterward I interviewed him and asked him why he didn't cross the floor and sit as an independent after the government brought down the disastrous 1969 White Paper on Indian Policy.

I was a fresh from university and ready to change the world. Len replied that he felt he could do more inside the system than outside it. At the time, we agreed to disagree, but in retrospect, I realise that if he had crossed the floor, he would have been seen as a one-trick pony and become nothing more than a memory.

As it turned out, Len had a distinguished career as a parliamentarian, a cabinet minister, and a senator. Over the years, we became friends and we continued to bump into each other at functions and on the street in Ottawa. One day, he called me up to let me know that he had just announced his resignation from the Senate. It was with some sadness that we reflected on his remarkable career.

Len's life is full of firsts. He was the first Indian to graduate from Vernon High School. He was the first member of the Okanagan Band to convocate from university. He was the first Status Indian to work as an assistant to a cabinet minister. He was the first Status Indian to be elected to the House of Commons and the first to be appointed to the Federal Cabinet.

His interest in politics began back in the late '50s and early '60s when he worked for the North American Indian Brotherhood. This organization was the early version of the Assembly of First Nations and lobbied the federal government on national issues.

He said, "I worked with leaders such as George Manual, John Tootoosis, and Walter Dieter. We lobbied for better education, self-government, and the federal vote." He told me, "I was 27 years old before I could vote in this great land."

In 1968, Len was elected to the House of Commons where he sat as a Liberal representing Kamloops-Caribou, British Columbia. In 1972, he was appointed Parliamentary Assistant to Indian Affairs Minister Jean Chretien, and in 1976, he was appointed Minister of State for Small Business. He was later appointed Minister of the Environment in 1977. "Environment was what I really wanted," he told me. "I had a master's degree in forestry, so I couldn't be snowed by the bureaucrats. I knew the language."

He was also a friend of Prime Minister Trudeau. Once, on a trip to Cuba, Trudeau introduced him to Fidel Castro. "Len's a Native Canadian," Trudeau said. "They want the country back, and sometimes I would like to give it to them."

In the election of 1979, Len was defeated in his Kamloops riding. For five years, he worked as an administrator with the Nicola Indian Band at Merritt. It was a rewarding time for Len because he was working at the local level, addressing local issues.

In 1984, Trudeau appointed Len to the Senate. He represented British Columbia and later was the First Nations Senator. He had been preceded by Senator James Gladstone from Alberta and Senator Guy Williams from British Columbia.

Over the years, the "Native caucus" on Parliament Hill steadily grew. Aboriginal MPs included Wilton Littlechild from Alberta, Ethel Blondin Andrew from the Northwest Territories, and Elijah Harper from Manitoba.

During his last year as a senator, Len came down with the flu, and it hung around for several months. One morning, he arose at 5:00 a.m. to catch a 7:00 a.m. flight to Ottawa. He said, "I decided that I didn't need this any more." Rumours that he was ill travelled around Parliament Hill. The press reported that he was too sick to carry on. "Those guys think I have one foot in the grave!" he joked.

In spite of the distance he had to travel, Len maintained an impressive work record. From August 1990 to December 1997, he maintained an 89% attendance record, including work as chairman of the Senate Standing Committee on Aboriginal Affairs.

Over the years, Len has been a good soldier: he has paid his dues and worked hard for his people. He also remains active by continuing his work assisting the veterans with fundraising for their proposed monument on Parliament Hill.

He says, "There are lots of good leaders out there, and I know that we will have more members in Parliament. We must never be marginalized again. We must participate in all aspects of Canadian life." He also predicts, "In the next century, we will have a Prime Minister; I know it."

Chapter 3

Education: Fighting for the
Little Red Schoolhouse

Some History

The other day, my little girl gave me a form to fill out for school. It was a class project to find out about the schools her parents had attended.

I told her that I began my education in a one-room schoolhouse on the Sandy Lake Reserve. It contained grades one through four with two years allotted to grade one for English instruction. Grades five, six, and seven were in another building, and high school meant going away to boarding school.

We were punished if we threw a piece of crayon on the 45 gallon drum that had been converted to a wood stove sitting in the middle of the room. That was a favourite trick because it created a stink and smoked up the room. If you rode a horse to school, you had to take care of it. And, of course, there was always a pack of dogs outside waiting for its owners.

This was Indian education in the 1950s.

And we were the lucky ones. On other reserves, children went away to boarding school starting in grade one. The old boarding school experience separated families, ruined childhoods, and created a nasty legacy that remains to the present.

Later, the government began a policy of integrated schools, meaning that children were bussed miles each day to a school in a local town. Sometimes the town's population was actually smaller than the reserve's, but it was a one-way policy, and no facilities were planned for the reserves.

In the 1970s, the Federation of Saskatchewan Indian Nations challenged this racist policy, and the Chiefs adopted a policy of Indian control of Indian education. Across the province, the parents pulled their children out of local schools and placed them in temporary schools on the reserve. These schools were usually old buildings or portable classrooms, but ultimately the parents were in charge, and so education became meaningful.

In one spectacular instance, an Indian student was accused of having lice.

The accusation turned out to be false, and the incident sparked a school strike with a temporary school being established on the reserve. Of course, there was fallout. Integrated schools in local towns suddenly became half empty and teachers were laid off, but the original process was so flawed that this type of reaction was inevitable.

The Chiefs' Policy of Indian control made education a priority across Saskatchewan. An education task force in 1969-70 called for institutions to support Indian education.

The first institution to be developed was the Saskatchewan Indian Cultural College (SICC), which creates curriculum materials and catalogues, and distributes First Nations resource material. The Cultural College also served as an incubator for the Saskatchewan Indian Community College, which has evolved into the Saskatchewan Indian Institute of Technologies and the Saskatchewan Indian Federated College (SIFC). The SIFC became the First Nations University of Canada, located on the University of Regina campus.

The Saskatchewan Indian Cultural College continues its developmental role. As well, a First Nations museum is currently in the works, intended to preserve and make history more accessible to schoolchildren.

Indian education grew from the day school and boarding school experience to the First Nations'-controlled institutions we have today. When I look back to my days in the one-room schoolhouse, I don't think we could have imagined such a promising future.

Education Is Our Priority

A recent poll conducted among First Nations people on reserves indicates that education is a number one priority. The survey was the third national survey of First Nations people living on reserves. It was commissioned by the Department of Indian Affairs and was based on a national sample of 1,507 telephone interviews.

While education has been the priority since the 1960s, almost half the people surveyed said that the quality of on-reserve education was worse than that received by other Canadians. Also, while education was seen as the most important priority, interviewees felt that culturally relevant education and the preservation of language and culture in the schools was necessary.

Social issues like drug and alcohol abuse and psychological issues were also seen as priorities. These findings point to one conclusion: Aboriginal people are very concerned about their children's future. Our people see that education is the key to a healthy, positive future.

Our people who grew up in the boarding schools vowed that their communities would grow and develop with proper education. In 1972, the Federation of Saskatchewan Indians produced a paper called *Indian Control of Indian Education*. This was no hasty document, but the result of an education task force that spent two years studying Indian education in Saskatchewan. Indian education was found wanting; it was not in First Nations' control, and it lacked meaningful cultural content.

Saskatchewan's Chiefs adopted the policy, and it later became a national policy under the National Indian Brotherhood (the forerunner to the Assembly of First Nations). The result was a series of school strikes across the province. Parents pulled their children out of integrated schools and demanded that they have a school on the reserve as promised in the treaties. This was needed if our people were to progress.

The school strikes created chaos in the Department of Indian Affairs as its carefully laid-out policy of integrating Indian children into off-reserve schools was called into question. It was also the policy of the Department of Indian Affairs to offload federal responsibility for Indian education to the provinces. The policy backfired badly, and the turmoil of the school strikes was the result. Indian Affairs was forced to provide temporary schools on reserves, and these portable classrooms and trailers became a common sight.

At that time, no institutions would support further development of First Nations education. The FSIN received funding for a cultural education centre, and it became the focal point. The Cultural Centre was located in Saskatoon on the University of Saskatchewan campus, and it was a beehive of activity, with committed First Nations educators and political animals joining forces to advance the cause.

I remember that Ida Wasacase from the Ochapowace First Nation was put in charge of academic programming and the development of a post-secondary institution. That was her job description. She would eventually head up the Saskatchewan Indian Federated College in Regina.

Osborne Turner from the James Smith First Nation was put in charge of skills training, and his work resulted in the development of the Saskatchewan Indian Community College, which later became the Saskatchewan Indian Institute of Technologies. All this work didn't fall under the mandate of a cultural center, and the rules were routinely bent and broken, much to the dismay of the funding agency, the Department of Indian Affairs. It was poetic justice that the very department that funded the boarding schools and was pushing for integration also held the key to our future education plans.

Education was the Chiefs' priority, and the effects of that priority were felt in the development of a series of educational institutions, including the First Nations University of Canada, the Saskatchewan Indian Institute of Technologies, and the Saskatchewan Indian Cultural Centre. These institutions have grown to be a major force in First Nations education in Saskatchewan and across the country. The First Nations University even has an international program that reaches out across North and South America to provide exchange programs for students and teachers.

The band-controlled schools were the institutions that drove the larger institutions. I remember in 1981 attending a graduation in Pelican Narrows for 50 students who received their teaching certificates. The Federated College held an extension program to assist the Peter Ballantyne First Nation to develop its own teachers. Some went on to teach in the band schools and others came south to complete their degrees. It was an example of a program that catapulted the community into controlling its own education program.

Today, modern schools have been built on reserves, realizing the dream of Indian control of education. I recently visited the new school on the Cowesses First Nation, and I was impressed with the care and detail that went into its construction. For example, the students provided artwork that was incorporated into tiles and placed in public gathering places in the building. Even more impressively, Indian students are now being taught by First Nations teachers.

Evolving to where we are today has required that we have had to bend the rules and give priority to our own people. Affirmative action programs have benefited our people on individual and community levels. Individuals who oppose these programs must not realize the positive results at the local level.

Affirmative action is based on the democratic principle that those who are furthest behind should be helped the most. In the long run, when all groups have an equal chance to advance, the entire society will benefit.

Two examples of affirmative action with long-term positive effects are the University of Saskatchewan's Native Law Centre and Aboriginal Access to Nursing Program. These programs have led the way in the education of much-needed Native lawyers and nurses.

A person's choice of career is most often the result of positive role models. A student may like a teacher and say to him- or herself, "I could do that job." As a result of positive role models, we have an educated workforce where most have chosen teaching, social work, administration, or the RCMP as their professions. This is an excellent first step, but now we also need to look seriously at the sciences, health care, engineering, and other non-traditional careers.

Thirty years ago, Native leaders in Saskatchewan made education a priority. Today, we lead the nation in university graduates and reserve-based education programs. Our post-secondary institutions turn out graduates who make contributions across the country, but there remains much more to do. We must constantly work to increase the quality of our education system and raise the education level of our people. Then we can work in both a First Nations environment and the general society.

While Indian control of education has been a success, it is also a race against time, considering our population growth. Back in 1972, there were around 40,000 First Nations people in Saskatchewan. In the year 2000, there were about 100,000 Native people here; by 2011, 204,000; by 2021, 250,000; and by 2041, 400,000.

Today, one third of students entering grade one are Aboriginal. Thirty-eight percent of the province's total student enrollment is First Nations, including university and trades training. Close to half of the regional budget of Indian Affairs is allotted to education.

The education of Saskatchewan's First Nations people is important for the province's future. The population is shifting toward a First Nations majority, and we must be prepared to work in the emerging reality. In the future, we will see First Nations people in all walks of life working here.

Loss of Languages Alarming

Aboriginal languages are facing extinction, and the results are unprecedented. We are experiencing a loss of an important part of our distinct culture at an alarming rate.

A report from Statistics Canada brought out this sad message. In the year 2000, only three out of the 50 Aboriginal languages in Canada were considered secure from the threat of extinction. These three are Cree, Inuktitut, and Ojibway. In Saskatchewan, we have both Cree and Ojibway. On the Plains, the Saulteaux are members of the Ojibway nation. Both Cree and Ojibway are part of the Algonquian language group. In Saskatchewan, the Dene or Athapaskan language is still spoken in the home, and its chances for survival also appear good.

The key to the survival of a language is its "viability," or chance of being passed to the next generation. For this to succeed, the language must be spoken in the home and used in daily conversation. When English takes over, the Aboriginal language is submerged and fails to be passed along.

Today, about a dozen Aboriginal languages are close to extinction. In some cases, the language is retained only by a small group of elders. For example, in the year 2000, the Kutenai language had only 120 speakers remaining, and there were only 145 Tlingit speakers left alive.

The Statistics Canada report points out that this is a tragic situation for the First Nations. Our languages took centuries to develop, and now they may disappear in a only few generations. The percentage of Aboriginal people whose home language was their mother tongue declined from 76% in 1981 to 65% in 1996. The average age of a person with an Aboriginal mother tongue went up from age 28 in 1981 to 31 in 1996, indicating the ageing of the population still speaking the language.

Loss of a language is a major blow to a culture. In fact, in many cases, the culture ceases to exist when its language is lost. The oral history in the mother tongue disappears; the grandparents can no longer speak to their grandchildren, and the sense of humour and descriptive nuances change. What we end up with is a pan-Indian culture that, while it is distinct, has the English language at its base.

How did we end up in this sorry situation? There are four answers. The first answer is easy: the boarding school experience led us to believe that our languages were substandard and archaic. Children who attended boarding schools learned the language at home, but they weren't allowed to speak it at school. The result was a stunted development of the native language, where young adults spoke like little children. However, with a few years back on the reserve, their language skills grew.

The second answer is that with the migration to urban centres, the language of the home has become English. In the cities, families are often on their own, grandparents are back on the reserve, and the family unit that would normally speak the native language has been broken up.

The third (and hardest-to-accept) reason for the current situation is that we did it to ourselves. Like any parents, Aboriginal parents want what is best for their kids, and so Aboriginal parents felt that teaching their children their language would hold them back in school. In fact, a second language is a great learning tool rather than a hindrance. Experience has taught us that bilingual education is preferable for young people. They start out in their own language and then gradually switch to English. In doing so, they become educated in two languages and wind up speaking both much better. This is a strange irony of bilingualism; people who speak two or more languages tend to speak both better than those who are unilingual. However, many Indian young people today speak neither English nor their Aboriginal tongue properly.

The fourth reason for the loss of native language, and the greatest existing threat, is television. The great killer of Aboriginal languages was welcomed into our home. It was revered and given a place of honour, and we (like all Canadians) would sit and watch it for hours. The television has done more damage to our languages than any other government policy or piece of technology. It permeates the home, English becomes the language of everyday interactions, and we ultimately pay for it with the loss of our language and culture. It's our version of pay TV, and the price has been too high.

In fact, television has made English the operating language in the home. Parents don't communicate with their children in their first language any more. English has taken over, and television was the Trojan horse that let it happen. We welcomed the television into our homes, we went into debt to get one, and if we didn't have one, we went and visited the neighbours. In the end, it ate away at our language and culture, giving us little in return.

In the 1960s, Newton Minnow, Head of the Federal Communications Commission under the Kennedy administration, declared that television was a "vast wasteland." He was right on the money, but he was roundly condemned by the television industry at the time. For example, when the script for *Gilligan's Island* was written, the wrecked boat was deliberately named " The Minnow."

To give Minnow credit, over the years the television has largely been a wasteland with only sporadic flashes of brilliance. It was also there for the first moon landing, Diana's funeral, and the tragedy of September 11th. However, it has helped in the Americanization of Canada with the proliferation of American programming and the saturation of American culture. Television is a window on the world, but whose world is it, and whose language is being spoken?

In the case of First Nations, although television has served as a source of communication and as a doorway to another culture, it is more than a benign wasteland. It has attacked, and continues to attack, language and culture, introducing foreign values into First Nations society. In many homes of all cultures, the television has become the one-eyed babysitter. Children are placed in front of it in the hope that they will become interested in something and stay out of trouble.

A few years ago, the Aboriginal People's Television Network was inaugurated, and it was felt that some help was in store for Aboriginal culture and languages. But the issue is too great for one national institution. If we look at the concentrated effort the government undertook to preserve and strengthen the French language, then we must realize that a massive effort is needed to preserve Aboriginal languages.

So what can we do to save our languages?

Political cartoon character Pogo said, "We have met the enemy, and he is us." We must first recognize the problem, and then work to solve it. And recognizing it is the most important part. Indian parents are not unlike many immigrant parents in that they want their children to do better than them. They see English as the language of education, business, and so on. They don't see that Cree, Saulteaux, or Dene will help their children in the future. This is a tragic mistake that their children and the children of future generations will pay for dearly.

First Nations schools are now teaching the languages, and some are practising bilingual education. But in the cities, there is a vacuum in First Nations culture and language. Multicultural councils hold "Saturday schools," where language and culture are taught to children by volunteer teachers. First Nations parents should look at and adapt such a concept.

Grants and programs alone will not preserve our languages, though. Parents must teach their children, visit elders and grandparents, and work together to make the languages viable again.

Aboriginal languages could survive in a fossilized form, like Latin. They may be taught in schools and used in prayers, but their souls will be lost if they aren't used in daily life. We shouldn't continue to let our beautiful languages be reduced to the status of museum pieces instead of the living, thriving languages they once were.

An Indian University: Why Not?

In 1996, the Saskatchewan Indian Federated College (SIFC) in Regina celebrated its twentieth anniversary. The SIFC is now considered the flagship of post-secondary education in Canada, but getting there wasn't easy.

In 1972, the Federation of Saskatchewan Indians released a report as a result of a two-year task force on Indian education in the province. The report was an exhaustive examination coordinated by Rodney Soonias from the Red Pheasant First Nation, who now practises law in Alberta.

The report examined all aspects of Indian education and concluded that the best way for Indian people to benefit from education was to take control of it themselves. This message was taken to a Chiefs' meeting, where a strong endorsement was received to adopt a policy of Indian control of Indian education. This was to be a major battle cry of the 1970s.

Previously, Indian education had been the function of the Department of Indian Affairs, and they had created a sorry legacy. The Department's policy was to abdicate their responsibility to the church-run boarding schools, and, later, to dump Indian students on local municipalities by providing money for integrated schools. Both policies failed because they were one-way streets with no parental or community involvement.

The early 1970s was a period of unrest and school strikes. Parents refused to send their children to school off the reserve and insisted on control of their educational programs.

The institution that became the focal point for the implementation of this policy was the Saskatchewan Indian Cultural Centre. The Cultural Centre, an institution of the FSI, was able to receive relatively stable funding, and it became the developmental institution for the policy of Indian control.

The education task force called for the development of a post-secondary academic institution, and the late Ida Wasacase was hired to develop the idea.

The first discussions were with the University of Saskatchewan, which couldn't accept the idea of an independent institution, and so discussions fell through. Meanwhile, the President of the University of Regina, Dr. Lloyd Barber, was sympathetic and worked with FSI officials to develop a college with federated status with the U. of R.

Lloyd had an interesting position in the scheme of things. His position was unique because he had an inside view of Indian country. He had been appointed Indian Claims Commissioner as a part of the terms of the 1969 White Paper on Indian Policy. The First Nations leadership had roundly rejected this policy, and Lloyd was caught in the crossfire. He was rejected and ignored as a part of the political climate of the day. He sat in his office in Regina and watched the tumbleweeds roll by.

The FSI Chief, Dave Ahenakew, and Sol Sanderson, his Executive Director, met regularly with Barber and briefed him on the issues. He was on side for the establishment of the Federated College.

In 1976, the Federated College became a reality.

In the early days, the college was a crazy place, with lots of freewheeling and political brinkmanship. There was no established funding, and Indian Affairs resisted at every turn. It finally took the political muscle of the FSI to force a funding formula.

The college became a magnet for pioneers and innovators. At one time, the staff of the College was the most international of all the University of Regina's faculties and departments. We had people from Jamaica, Barbados, and Hong Kong. The staff members that passed through the college were of a calibre that they went on to succeed in their future professions. For example, Glenda Simms went on to head the Status of Women, and Gerald MacMaster went on to head up the First Nations Art Department of the Museum of Civilization in Ottawa. Gerald is now an art curator with the National Museum of the American Indian in Washington, DC.

Over the past twenty years, starting with the first graduate, Piapot's Sharon Carriere, the college has graduated over 1,450 students.

The march of progress is a strange procession. It is headed up by the dreamers and pioneers, followed by the builders who make the dream a reality, and finally come the administrators and bureaucrats who make an institution permanent.

The SIFC began as an idea and existed in rented space that was begged, borrowed, and stolen from the University. The Federated College has now undergone major change. The name has been changed to The First Nations University of Canada, and they occupy an exciting new building on the Regina Campus.

But a university cannot be seen as merely an edifice; it is a living centre of free thought that must first exist in the hearts and minds of the staff and students. The college leaders must keep this in mind as they head into the future

Boarding School Genie Out of the Bottle

It just gets worse. The boarding school genie is out of the bottle and the accusations and lawsuits are flying. It is an issue that will not go away.

There has been a steady parade of lawsuits directed at the churches and the federal government. Accusations and charges of physical and sexual abuse have made the news with regularity, but these charges are only the tip of the iceberg. In fact, the whole boarding school system was fundamentally flawed.

The theory was that if a generation were removed from the evils of their families and culture, they would embrace Christianity and become just like white Protestants and Catholics. The solution to the "Indian problem" was to get rid of the Indians.

These were not the upper-class boarding schools like Eaton, Harrow, or Upper Canada College. They were designed to destroy a culture, not preserve it.

It's hard to imagine, but during the school year, there were only adults and young children in our communities. Like the Pied Piper, buses and trucks scooped away all the school-aged children. Children were yanked away from their parents in tearful separations. The children went away for months of loneliness. If they were lucky, they would come home for Christmas. Some didn't, and they spent the whole ten months away from home.

Some didn't come home at all. Diseases like tuberculosis took a terrible toll on Indian children. In some cases, the children were sent home to die. The boarding school at Delmas was known to send sick children home to their parents in the Battleford area when it became apparent they were about to die.

In the children's absence, communities suffered and became dysfunctional. Loneliness and despair replaced the happiness of family life. Families wasted away. Some turned to drink to cover their pain. The emphasis has been on the children who attended the schools, but the despair of the people left in the community has been forgotten.

Meanwhile, the children were living in unnatural surroundings, learning how to fight and defend themselves. In too many cases, both boys and girls were victims of sexual and physical abuse.

The boarding school system was an abject failure on all fronts.

The government broke the treaties when they turned education over to the churches. They abrogated their responsibilities and turned a blind eye to the resulting damage.

The precedence for the churches' involvement has a long history in Canadian politics. After the fall of Quebec, the French elites moved back to France, creating a vacuum in the Quebec governing class. The British colonial government turned to the churches to run the schools, hospitals, and social programs. As a result, the church operated Quebec institutions until recently.

It had proved to be good colonial practice to turn certain functions over to the churches to reduce the burden on government, so it followed that church-run institutions would be the cornerstone of government Indian policy.

The treaties promised that a school would be built on reserves, and Indians would become "educated like the white man." In Saskatchewan, only a few reserves actually received "day schools." The vast majority only had access to education from a boarding school. This was a serious breech of treaty and was disastrous for all concerned.

A friend of mine once told me that he went to a boarding school that was fewer than ten miles away from his home. He would look out the third-floor window, see his reserve on the horizon, and he would imagine his home. Sometimes he saw smoke coming from the chimney. He would imagine his mother and father. They were so close he felt that he could reach out and touch them. But he spent eight years there, and he only saw his parents during the summer and at Christmas.

He was robbed of his childhood. He was robbed of the love of his parents and scarred for life. He can sue the government like so many have, but he will never regain his life. Canada has a long way to go to repay our people for generations of damage, and I doubt that they can.

Get an Education!

When spring arrives after what seems like another endless Saskatchewan winter, the sure sign it's really here is not the weather, nor the flowers, but the number of kids in my neighbourhood who cut class and stay out of school.

It used to be that everyone had to stay in school until they turned 16, but that no longer seems to be true.

Cutting classes is sometimes fun and most students try it at some time. But quitting school is definitely not cool. Without a good education, you will find yourself in the slow lane of the highway of life. Today, we are looking at lifelong learning to stay in the fast lane. People are continually returning to upgrade their skills and increase their knowledge.

The basis of a worthwhile education is grade twelve. It used to be that someone with grade twelve was considered well educated, but today it's only the first step. This is really scary when I see that our young people are dropping out of school in grades seven and eight. Dropping out is a sure formula for failure later in life, meaning years of upgrading to catch up and many missed opportunities.

A few years ago, education became a priority for the First Nations leaders in Canada and it remains one today. Communities that have embraced education have a high rate of graduation and subsequent enrolment in university and technical training. These communities are well on their way to addressing social and employment problems.

The problem is greatest now in the cities, where over half our people now live. In urban settings, there is little support from the government. Treaty rights to education seem to evaporate at the reserve boundary. Our people are on their own without the help of their friends and family on the reserve. The result is that family becomes isolated and education ceases to be the priority that it should be.

Many families living in the city experience a different kind of poverty in the cities. Many are single-parent families. The mothers are often isolated and lonely. If a mother works or has to go out, daughters often have to stay at home to baby-sit, which seriously affects their education and ability to keep up with homework.

Also, the growth of urban gangs results in increased peer pressure on students to quit and follow the gang. Many times the students can see no future opportunities and gangs provide protection and a sense of belonging. But gang membership leads to drugs, violence, prostitution, and other crimes.

The answer to the high dropout rate begins in the home. Parents must convince their children that education is their ticket out of poverty. As parents, we must get involved in our children's education. Most teachers welcome parents who volunteer in the classroom to provide some individual attention or to assist the teacher in preparing materials.

Also, we must examine the system of heritage schools that the multicultural groups conduct on Saturdays. These schools teach children their heritage, history, and language. They are staffed by volunteers and are a valuable source of pride and understanding for immigrant children. We must look at this example and not always expect the education system to provide everything. We must take the time to volunteer our services and make a heritage program work.

When our children have support from home and the community and knowledge of their heritage, education brings reality to their dreams. It takes on new meaning and will combat the appalling dropout rate.

Career Day Is Payback Time

Every year, our reserve school holds a career day and all the people who received support for their education from the band are obligated to return and make a presentation to the students. And while this is voluntary, the Chief and council will twist your arm until you agree to show up. After all, we received support from our people for our education, and it's only fair that we give something back.

Our schools are where our next generation is incubating. With all the talk of self-government and business development, we need to educate the next generation. All the activity in the world is meaningless if you don't have an educated and informed public. Also, implementation of self-government and the rhetoric of independence strongly depend upon our ability to be educated and economically independent.

My reserve has a variety of individuals in the professions. We have teachers, social workers, businesspeople, and people in commerce and various trades. We also have a pharmacist and two filmmakers. I'm one of the filmmakers, and my niece Thurza is ready to graduate with a degree in filmmaking from Emily Carr in Vancouver.

My reserve has had a day school since the 1920s, and so many of our people were able to stay at home and avoid boarding school. Over the years, the school population grew, and today we operate our own high school, staffed by many of our own people.

Over the years, the Band has turned out a steady stream of graduates. My late Aunt Jean Goodwill was one of Saskatchewan's first Indian Registered Nurses and both my Dad and two uncles attended Teachers College and the University of Saskatchewan.

It must be made clear to our students that while education is a treaty right, it is there for the common good of the First Nation. In other words, our ancestors asked that education be included in the treaties so that our people could adapt to the coming changes.

The treaties call for a school on each reserve. Over the years, this has been changed to reflect the changing times and to include post-secondary education.

Education assistance is given to those who qualify, and the Band administers the program. This assistance exists as part of the treaties, and while it is given to an individual, it is meant for the common good.

A few years ago, educational assistance was a political hot potato, and the Department of Indian Affairs dumped the program on the First Nations. At first, this looked like a cowardly and opportunistic move, and it was, but over the years, it has been made to work in our favour.

Today, our students thank the Band for their education, and our guidance counselors direct the students into a variety of trades and professions. A few years ago, almost all the graduates were in education or social work. Today, we're represented in a much wider range of professions.

That's why we are travelling back to the reserve for career day. We also pay back the debt by working for the band when called upon. A few summers ago, when we hosted the Summer Games, volunteers from across Saskatchewan came back to help out. There is no mileage or per diems given out. Helping out is our way of paying back our debt.

Alex and Albert Bellegarde: Two Brothers Who Were Leaders in Education

In the late 1970s, Saskatchewan Indians mourned the loss of two brothers who had served their people both locally and provincially. Alex and Albert Bellegarde were leaders who served their people at a crucial time in our history. Sadly, they died of cancer within two years of each other.

The Bellegarde family is no stranger to political life. In the 1960s, Wilf Bellegarde, an uncle, was Chief of the Federation of Saskatchewan Indians. He was a veteran who worked with his people locally on the Little Black Bear Reserve.

Alex and Albert's brother, Dan Bellegarde, served with distinction on the executive of the FSIN. His speciality was land claims and he was arguably the driving force in the negotiations for Treaty Land Entitlement. Another brother, Clarence, is Chief of the Little Black Bear First Nation, and Perry, another relative, was Chief of the FSIN from 1995 to 2003.

Albert Bellegarde was a former head of the Saskatchewan Indian Cultural College. His strengths lay in administration, and he once served as the Assistant Regional Director of Indian Affairs. This position had been negotiated by the FSI to get some accountability in the colonial office. This was accountability for people, but not the narrow sense of financial accountability we have today. This was a time when Indian Affairs still ran the lives of Indians. It took someone like Albert to remind the government department that the sun had indeed set on the British Empire.

Albert came back to the FSI and successfully ran for Chief of the FSI. His term came to an untimely end when it was discovered that he had cancer, and, six months after being elected, he passed away.

His brother Alex was a member of the Executive of the Federation of Saskatchewan Indians, and later he was Chief of his First Nation. He was an avid sportsman and served his people well. However, over a year after his brother passed away, he was diagnosed with cancer and died while still in office.

Alex and Albert Bellegarde were leaders when the foundations for the current FSIN were being built. They both played a role in the development of our educational and political institutions. Sadly, they were not able to live to see rapid growth in the provincial, district, and local levels.

But their memory lives on. As Indian people, we believe that the memory of our loved ones must live on. For example, people who have lost family and friends to cancer or diabetes will participate in fundraising events such as the Terry Fox Run. These are private acts of remembrance to keep the memory alive and helping to find a cure.

Each year, the children of the next Bellegarde generation host the Chief

Alex Bellegarde Memorial Golf Tournament. The proceeds go to the Albert Bellegarde Memorial Scholarship Fund. This arrangement is to remember both Alex's love of sports and Albert's dedication to education. The scholarship fund was established in 1985, and so far, ten young people have received assistance to complete their studies.

Chapter 4

Health and Wellness:
A Tough Battle

We Have Our Own Health Care History

Historically, medical care for First Nations people has been much different than for the rest of Canada. We suffered more from introduced diseases and lifestyle changes than any other group in the country. The history of medical care for First Nations people can be placed into three phases: the epidemics, the environmental diseases, and now the lifestyle diseases.

First, the epidemics were imported by European contact. Our people had no resistance to diseases such as measles, tuberculosis, and smallpox. As a result, plagues swept through our nation, decimating our people. This was a phenomenon throughout the Americas and other isolated places, such as the South Sea Islands. The results were catastrophic, with whole communities and tribes wiped out.

Millions of people were killed in the settlement of the Americas, and they were killed in the most inadvertent way: diseases from Europe, such as measles and smallpox, spread across the continent like wildfire.

Epidemics of one form or another have been present in the Aboriginal population right up to the present day. The "Spanish Flu" pandemic of 1918 was especially devastating to the Aboriginal population. The Spanish flu was misnamed since it originally came from Asia and was introduced to Europe by American soldiers, and in turn brought to Canada by returning veterans. Twice as many people died in the flu pandemic as died in the First World War. In Canada, 50,000 people died of the Spanish flu. In Saskatchewan, over 5,000 people died. Poverty and lack of access to hospitals caused a greater percentage of Aboriginal deaths.

Aboriginal communities were especially hard hit. My dad was baptized the same day he was born because his parents feared for his life during the epidemic.

At Onion Lake, Reverend Edward Ahenakew reported in his journal that the church was piled high with coffins, and that families were in mourning throughout the community. Ahenakew was so touched by the tragic loss of life that he enrolled in the University of Alberta School of Medicine and studied to become a doctor. At the time, there was no financial support, and he was forced to withdraw in his second year. Nevertheless, he went on to make a mark as one of the province's great Indian leaders of the twentieth century.

Our people also suffered from tuberculosis long into the twentieth century. Finally, through improved health care and immunization clinics, our people were able to overcome the diseases that had so decimated our ancestors.

In the 1950s, public health care came to reserves. Through immunization programs, many diseases were brought under control. As a child, I recall the nurse making regular visits to the school to inoculate the students. We feared the nurse's visits, but improved public health ultimately saved many children's lives.

Diseases caused by environmental conditions marked the next phase of our health history. When our people were placed on reserves and not allowed to move around, the environment began to deteriorate. First, the water supply became contaminated and people had to rely on slough water. Also, housing was crowded and substandard, and so children suffered from diseases of the lungs and the digestive tract. During this period, infant mortality was at record levels.

Later, in the 1970s and '80s, clean water and improved housing came to reserves, thereby creating a decrease in environmentally caused diseases.

During this period, however, alcoholism became a serious disease among our people. It could be classified as an environmental disease because it grew out of a culture of poverty and alienation. Addictions are still with us, but they have expanded into drugs and now affect our people at all ages. We continue to suffer from a higher degree of alcoholism and drug addiction than the rest of the country.

Finally, we are currently in a third wave of medical concerns from diseases related to lifestyle. Diabetes, heart disease, and various types of cancer are much higher for Aboriginal people than for the general public. Acquired Immune Deficiency Syndrome (AIDS) has also been introduced, and it is having catastrophic effects on our communities.

This third wave of preventable diseases is propelled by social ills and poverty. For example, our rising cancer rate is largely due to excessive use of tobacco, and diabetes has increased over time from a poor diet and sedentary lifestyle. Also, social ills have contributed to substance abuse. Substance abuse has obvious detrimental effects on health, mainly from violence and accidents.

While epidemics, environmental diseases, and lifestyle diseases appear to be three separate phases of our health history, there is some overlap between them. For example, tuberculosis is still with us, but the new strains are more virulent and harder to combat. Tuberculosis is on the rise, especially in Aboriginal communities. Environmental diseases are still with us. Clean water is a universal right in Canada, but some Aboriginal communities still have contaminated water, and the resulting water-borne diseases are rampant. Urban and rural housing is substandard and overcrowded for many of our people, and pathologies are connected to that.

Today, with a rapidly growing population and mass urbanization, our people have a much higher incidence of depression and related conditions. These bring with them their own sets of new issues and problems.

First Nations health history is a long list of neglect, poverty, and abuse. We have a way to go before we can look at ourselves and state that we have a truly healthy population.

Health Care, Yes, but Treaty Rights, Too

In his report on the future of health care in Canada, Roy Romanow has examined Aboriginal health and found it to be in an "appalling state." His solution has been to focus on partnerships between federal, provincial, and First Nations agencies, and on the gradual devolving of Aboriginal health care to the provinces.

This is a dangerous course of action because it will meet with stiff resistance from Treaty First Nations, who see health care as a treaty right and a federal responsibility.

Romanow's proposal of placing funding into a super agency, using culturally sensitive approaches, and delivering programs that meet our specific needs has merit. However, to make Aboriginal people junior partners and transfer the responsibility to the provinces is a non-starter with First Nations leadership.

Romanow forgets that our right to medical care predates Medicare. When our leaders negotiated the treaties, the well being of their people was uppermost in their minds. The negotiations took place at the time of the great plagues that were wiping out whole communities. Our leaders feared what would come in the future, so they insisted that medical care be included in the treaty text. Therefore, the text of Treaty Number Six states, "a chest of medicines shall be provided." This was in 1876, and medical science was still in its formative stages; a "chest of medicines" was considered adequate medical care.

The numbered treaties from One to Ten are incremental. In other words, what one group negotiated applies to all. Therefore, the medicine chest clause that was included in all treaties above Number Six also applies to those that came before.

Also, the treaties are living documents, and so they have evolved over time to include hospital care, nursing stations, immunization clinics, and so on.

When Medicare was first introduced across Canada, the local, regional, and national First Nations leadership opposed it, not because they were opposed to Medicare, but because they were opposed to the transfer of health services to the provinces. Since our leaders considered medical care a treaty right, they were in opposition to the new program.

When Romanow was Premier in Saskatchewan, he was well aware of the concern that First Nations expressed about the transfer of provincial jurisdiction into areas of treaty rights and federal jurisdiction. In his report, however, it would appear that he learned nothing.

With our treaty rights enshrined in section 35 of the Canadian Charter of

Rights and Freedoms, it will be much harder for future governments to deny us our treaty right to medical care. Romanow ignored or forgot our special relationship.

Today, Canada is revisiting the delivery of Medicare for the nation and looking to changes in the future. When this exercise is complete, our treaty right to health care must be protected, strengthened, and considered as a part of any new system.

Diabetes: Our Modern-Day Epidemic

In Saskatchewan, virtually every Aboriginal person can look into his or her family tree and find several close relatives with diabetes. In some cases, one needs to look no further than the mirror to find someone with diabetes.

It doesn't matter if you are an Aboriginal person in Australia, a Maori in New Zealand, or an Indian in the United States or Canada, diabetes is having a devastating effect on original peoples around the world.

What is the reason for this epidemic? Aboriginal populations lived healthy and isolated lives for generations. The coming of the European colonists brought diseases that were swift and deadly. Today, the survivors are faced with diseases linked to the new lifestyle, but which are nonetheless as deadly as the microbes that caused smallpox, tuberculosis, and other contagious diseases.

Is "epidemic" too strong a word? I don't think so. Nationally, the incidence of type 2 diabetes is three times higher in the Aboriginal population than in the general population. In some communities, between half and three quarters of the adult population has type 2 diabetes. In one community, 18% of the population over 15 had diabetes. Clearly, we have a crisis on our hands.

Studies have shown that 8% of Aboriginal people between the ages of 19 and 39 have diabetes, while 50% of Aboriginal people over the age of 60 have the disease. Also, the rates vary from community to community. In most cases, the rates are between 15-22% of the community. In others, up to one third of the population has diabetes. The Pima Reservation in Arizona holds the dubious world record with almost 100% of its population afflicted with the disease.

In the last half of the twentieth century, our people underwent some of the most profound changes in their history. Previously, our people were active, living on trap lines, farming with horses, and doing daily chores like hauling water and chopping wood. The trapping economy slumped badly, and our people were encouraged to stay home so their children could go to school. The horse was replaced by the pickup truck, and simple farming was a thing of the past. A welfare economy has replaced self-sufficiency.

Diabetes is a relatively new phenomenon in First Nations communities. As recently as 50 years ago, diabetes was almost relatively unknown. The epidemic we're currently experiencing has its roots in our contemporary lifestyle. For generations, our people lived a healthy lifestyle, with lots of physical activity and a natural diet of fish and game. People picked berries and preserved them for the winter. They had their own gardens, hunted wild game, and did manual labour. Diseases like diabetes, heart disease, and various cancers were uncommon.

Today, we have an unhealthy diet with starches from foods like bannock and fat from foods like hamburgers and fried chicken. Couple a poor diet with a sedentary lifestyle, and you have a recipe for disaster. Poverty and unemployment also play a role since poor people tend to eat a high-starch diet, and unemployment often breeds a sedentary lifestyle. In the cities it may be necessary to spend more money on the food bill to include more fresh fruits and vegetables. This will not be easy for our families on welfare, but it is necessary.

One theory that makes sense is that First Nations people evolved a "thrifty gene" that allowed us to rapidly store fat during times of plenty so we could survive the lean winter months. It makes sense that those among us that could put on weight rapidly would survive times of famine, and so this characteristic became more dominant over the years. In a tough land, we needed all the help we could get to survive. Unfortunately, when there is no famine the weight stays on.

The extent of the problem has created an awareness and concern throughout the Aboriginal world. Today, Aboriginal groups are organizing and educating their constituents in what is literally a race against time.

In the spring of 1999, the National Chief of the Assembly of First Nations, Phil Fontaine, declared that the first Friday in May would be declared National Aboriginal Diabetes Day.

National Aboriginal Diabetes Day is followed by the annual Sadie's Walk. This annual walk for awareness is named after Sadie Muik, a tireless health-care worker from the Okanagan Valley First Nation in British Columbia. One of her plans was to organize a walking club in her community. Sadly, Sadie was killed in a traffic accident. Her co-workers picked up her dream, and now her legacy lives on in the annual Sadie's Walk. This seven-kilometer walk is held across the nation in Sadie's memory to promote exercise and a positive, healthy lifestyle. The walk is seven kilometers because this was the distance from the accident site to Sadie's office.

In addition to promoting awareness, we have to get serious about our lifestyle. Many men continue to drink alcohol after they are diagnosed with diabetes. As a result, they are subject to blindness and kidney failure. For some reason, men think they are bullet-proof and tend to ignore the reality of diabetes. Today, self-help groups are working with diabetics in the First Nations community. There is a growing awareness and steps are being taken by our people to educate and help those who suffer the affliction.

We need to develop our own approaches to combat this serious health problem. Only through helping ourselves will we be able to address our diabetes epidemic.

Infant Mortality: The Tragic Cost of Poverty

The recent revelation that Saskatchewan has the highest infant mortality rate in the country is not a surprise to health care workers in the Aboriginal community. A study found that in 1994, Saskatchewan had the highest rate of infant mortality in Canada at eleven deaths per thousand, compared with an average of six per thousand for the rest of the country.

Government officials were quick to point out that it was the Indians' fault. They cited examples of poor housing conditions, heavy smoking in the home, and inadequate diet. The "northern and Native" infant mortality rate is double the provincial average, and in small provinces that can skew the overall figures.

That's a quick explanation, but it needs clarification.

Any health professional that has worked with First Nations will agree that the rate of infant mortality is far too high, but the figures represent only part of the story. The mortality rate is the result of serious underlying factors.

A closer look at First Nations morbidity statistics reveals that the majority of infant mortality is the result of two environmentally caused diseases and a third factor that is easily preventable. The leading causes of Aboriginal infant mortality are upper respiratory diseases and gastroenteritis. These are diseases that are caused by the environment and poor living conditions. In other words, they are the diseases of poverty.

Substandard, crowded housing leads to an unhealthy situation where babies catch pneumonia, whooping cough, and bronchitis. A crowded, draughty shack is a recipe for disaster, and yet many of the First Nations and Métis people in this province have no choice but to endure it.

Gastroenteritis is an illness of the bowels caused by waterborne organisms. Many Aboriginal infants are hospitalised for gastroenteritis, and some die as a result of diarrhea and other diseases that can be traced back to the home water supply. This situation has become exacerbated because of the growing population of our communities. Many people still get their water from creeks and even sloughs that are contaminated by dangerous bacteria and other pollutants.

In 1974, the United Nations Habitat Conference held in Vancouver called for clean water for the world by the year 2000. Canadian representatives thought that they were talking about third world countries and heartily endorsed the proposal.

But the third world exists right here at home, and the high rate of Aboriginal infant mortality proves that.

The government has not cut back on the budget of the Department of

Indian Affairs as it has with other departments, but it hasn't been increased to match the rate of growth in the First Nations population. As a result, we have seen the deterioration of services in First Nations communities as population pressures take their toll on capital budgets. The First Nations population has doubled in the past 20 years, and it shows no signs of slowing down.

The third and more easily preventable reason for a high rate of infant mortality in Indian country is the extensive use of tobacco. Women who smoke during pregnancy can seriously damage the health of their babies. Also, crowded conditions in the home support an environment of second-hand smoke that can also do harm to an infant.

Aboriginal people have a high incidence of smoking. Tobacco companies have targeted women as a growth market. While smoking has always been a part of our culture, now it has become an addiction. Once, I heard a woman complain that smoking was the only vice she had, and she wasn't about to give it up. In a world of poverty, depression and addictions are common.

A woman who smokes during pregnancy weakens her baby's health, and she tends to produce a smaller baby. The baby is at a disadvantage, especially when it has to survive in a hostile environment. Weak babies and poor living conditions form a dangerous combination. Our infant mortality rate proves that.

The high rate of First Nations infant mortality is caused by a combination of factors. We can blame our economic situation to a point, but we must look within ourselves for part of the answer.

AIDS: The Disease of Despair

AIDS has been described as a pandemic, a worldwide epidemic, and no group in society is immune. AIDS has now established itself in Indian country, and the results are frightening.

Some estimate that as high as 20% of the 14,000 reported AIDS cases in Canada are Aboriginal. Nationally, we represent about 2% of the population, so our incidence of AIDS is ten times the national average.

One of the problems in arriving at these figures is the lack of information regarding ethnic origin. In some jurisdictions, it is contrary to human rights legislation to identify racial origin.

The information that does exist comes from clinics operating on the frontlines of the inner cities. In Vancouver, for example, a clinic that cares for HIV-infected pregnant women found that 41% of women under its care were Aboriginal.

HIV is the name of the virus that enters the bloodstream and eventually leads to a condition where an individual has no resistance to any infection. This is the stage known as AIDS, or Acquired Immune Deficiency Syndrome. A person may be HIV positive and not even know it; sometimes only when the effects of the virus are felt through persistent infections does a person get diagnosed. Anyone who is at risk can go to a clinic and have a blood test that will identify whether the virus exists.

Aboriginal people are more susceptible to AIDS because of their low socio-economic status in this country. In other words, poor people with little hope of opportunity gravitate to the inner cities and become victims of drugs and poverty.

According to the Canadian Aboriginal AIDS Network, "studies in mainstream society have found that instances of HIV infection occur more frequently where poverty, violence, drug abuse, and alcoholism are present." This is shown in the trends observed by front-line groups working with AIDS victims.

A recent study of intravenous drug users in Vancouver found that there was an alarming increase in the incidence of AIDS cases among Aboriginal peoples. In B.C. and Alberta, studies have shown that 15% to 26% of newly diagnosed HIV positive cases are Aboriginal.

And our people tend to be contracting AIDS at a younger age. Thirty percent of all newly documented Aboriginal cases are young people under 30. Some are as young as 19 and 20.

In some cities, the clientele using needle exchange services ranges from 25% to 75% Aboriginal. We have a disproportionate number of people in federal and provincial institutions. The incidence of Aboriginal men in provincial jails is about 60%, and the incidence of women in provincial jails is as high as 90%. These institutions can be breeding grounds for AIDS, and so once again, more of our people are at risk.

While the major incidence of AIDS is in cities, the fact is that we are a highly mobile group. We are like a bunch of homing pigeons. We travel between our reserves and the inner cities, and this means that even the most remote Aboriginal community is not immune.

Fear, homophobia, and lack of education have created a siege mentality in some Aboriginal communities. There are horror stories of individuals being barred from their home reserves and told to go and die elsewhere, without community and family love and support.

Some leaders refuse to admit that their communities have a problem. They feel that if they ignore the problem, it will go away. But AIDS is not a problem that will simply go away. It has a strong foothold in our communities, and while the incidence of AIDS in Saskatchewan is relatively low, our people living on the West Coast are at higher risk, and they will bring it home.

We are looking at a situation that has the potential to get worse. The rapid spread of this disease, the conditions of poverty, the despair that plagues some communities, and the lack of education and understanding are all combining to form a disaster in the making. Here in Saskatchewan, we have groups, such as the All Nations Hope AIDS Network, that are working to educate people in the community, and to prevent the spread of the virus.

AIDS is a symptom of our poverty and place in Canadian society. Our leaders must become more aware, demand more programming to educate our people, and confront the serious problem of intravenous drug use. We must not let groups of our people fall by the wayside. We must help each other and work together to eradiate this modern-day epidemic.

We're Depressed: Is It Any Wonder?

A report on the state of the health of off-reserve Aboriginal people reveals that we are not only less healthy than the rest of Canadians, but we are also more depressed.

The report concluded that off-reserve Aboriginal people had health problems that were 1.5 times more prevalent, including diabetes, heart disease, high blood pressure, and arthritis. The report also found that urban Aboriginal people suffered depression about 1.8 times higher than the rest of the population, and 13.2% of those surveyed indicated that they had experienced major depression in the past year.

However, even when socio-economic factors such as education, work status, and household income were taken into account, the incidence of depression was still 1.3 times the general population. Clearly, something else is at work here.

The full explanation for our depression can't be found in the cold light of statistics. But the statistics serve to highlight a situation that has persisted in First Nations communities for generations.

Our people are depressed and the root cause is that many of our people are sick at heart. There are intangible facts understood only by Aboriginal people, and the problems exist both on and off the reserve. Our history lives within us, and it drags us down.

Aboriginal Canadians are not like other Canadians. We have been jerked around by the system for generations. For example, for decades here in Saskatchewan, children were taken from their parents and placed in boarding schools. The Indian Act regulated every aspect of our people's lives. My father told me how he and his father had to go see the Indian Agent to get permission to sell hay off the reserve and how demeaning that was. Today, welfare and unemployment continue the soul-destroying process.

This lack of control and responsibility has led to the breakdown of families and communities. Our people have suffered from depression for generations only it hasn't been properly diagnosed. We have instead been labeled as "lazy", and as drunks and criminals. Poverty, alcoholism, and crime are the symptoms of a greater problem and stem largely from depression. Poor people don't or can't see a doctor when they feel low, and so they self-medicate with alcohol, drugs, or both.

I remember taking part in a survey in Edmonton in the 1970s, where the Indian Association of Alberta was trying to get a snapshot of the state of urban Indian people. It was determined that people moved to the city for employment, post-secondary education, and access to better health care. Many of the people interviewed were older people with chronic health problems who moved to the city to be closer to better health care. At that time, it was defined groups that moved to the cities for specific reasons.

In the 1980s and 90s, however, the major population shift occurred, and now over half of First Nations people live in the cities. It has been a major demographic shift and federal, provincial, civic and First Nations governments have done little to address it.

When a group of people experience rapid change and lose control of their lives, the results are personal and catastrophic. A friend of mine, an academic and a thinker, described a group of people who lost their land, moved to the cities, and fell into a world of poverty and alcoholism. It sounded as though he was talking about Indians, but he was actually talking about landless peasants who were forced into British cities during the Industrial Revolution. It made his audience stop and think because in most cases those peasants were their ancestors.

British cities during the Industrial Revolution were a mess of slums, open sewers, and rampant alcoholism. It took decades to clean things up, and many of the problems still exist.

Meanwhile, governments have failed urban Aboriginal people. The federal government in particular has failed its treaty obligation to First Nations people. It has wrongly and conveniently maintained that once Status Indian people leave the reserve, they are no longer a federal responsibility. However, the Corbiere case has determined that off-reserve Indian people maintain their political rights, so it follows that off-reserve Indians also keep their treaty rights.

Our people living off the reserve are left in a jurisdictional void, and it's part of the cause of our poor mental and physical health. This is a serious issue that will only grow and not go away if the federal government doesn't address it. It will ultimately be very costly to the system.

Tuberculosis Is Not Gone, and It Is Not Forgotten

Some of my earliest memories are going to the Sanatorium in Prince Albert with my parents to visit family members and friends with tuberculosis. I still remember my fear that I might catch it.

The first half of the twentieth century was the time of the tuberculosis epidemic for First Nations. Any individual who survived that era can look at an old family photo or class picture and recognize those who passed on before their time because of tuberculosis.

At the time, there was no cure for the disease other than plenty of bed rest, and sometimes patients would spend years in "the San." These were especially hard years for Aboriginal people because the distances from home would be so great. It would take considerable effort for families to make the journey. Also, the separation from the language and culture contributed to the sense of loneliness and despair. People from the Far North were especially vulnerable; because there were no facilities close to their communities, they would spend long periods away from home.

It was therefore with some concern that I learned that Saskatchewan's Aboriginal community currently has the highest rate of tuberculosis in the country.

Eighty-seven percent of all TB cases in the province are Aboriginal compared to 60% in Manitoba and 28% in Alberta. Nationally, Aboriginal people are four times more likely to contract tuberculosis.

Over the past century, Aboriginal people were settled on reserves and came in to contact with an increasing number of outsiders, resulting in a tuberculosis epidemic that is still with us. A Health Canada report states that the incidence of TB in Aboriginal communities varies inversely with the length of contact with the European settlers and higher rates occur in those areas last exposed. The report states that the incidence of tuberculosis increases from east to west and is higher yet in the north, reflecting the western European migration and the later contact in the north.

On the plus side, while drug-resistant strains of TB and HIV co-infection are a potential threat, they have not yet become a significant problem in the Aboriginal population.

What are some other reasons for the high rate of TB in Saskatchewan? First, statistics more often reflect the high proportion of Aboriginal people in Saskatchewan, which is the highest in the country. In Saskatchewan, First Nations and Métis people account for about 20% of the total population, and anything that affects us will be shown in a higher proportion than in provinces like Alberta, where the Aboriginal population is about 5% of the total population.

However, tuberculosis is a reflection of poverty, unemployment, and poor housing in many First Nations and Métis communities.

At a time when we represent a large part of the province's future work force, the fastest growing segment of the economy, and are a group with special issues like the tuberculosis epidemic, we were conspicuously absent from the provincial government's spending plans. In the budget speech of 2003, we were not mentioned. It's as if we don't exist.

Of course, the Province will argue that it includes First Nations and Métis in all its spending estimates, and rightly so, but we need some special programming if we are to attack the issues that are unique to us.

And it's not as if we are not making a contribution. The Saskatchewan Indian Gaming Authority provides the Province with millions of dollars annually. We pay sales tax, property tax, and all the sin taxes. Federal transfers take into consideration federal responsibility for health, education, and equalization payments. We also have institutions like the Saskatchewan Indian Federated College, the Gabriel Dumont Institute, and the Saskatchewan Indian Institute of Technologies looking for partnerships with government. But the government response has been zero.

Saskatchewan benefits from the Aboriginal population, but we get little in return, as we are finding out, with the highest rate of tuberculosis in the nation. The Saskatchewan government must start to address the serious issues that we face as a people, and, as a result, all Saskatchewan residents will benefit.

Jean Goodwill: A National Icon

My aunt Jean lived a life of service, both to her people and to the health profession. Over the years, she obtained recognition by receiving an Order of Canada, an honorary degree from Queens University in Kingston, Ontario, and a National Aboriginal Achievement Award.

While her public achievements brought her national fame, her family remembers another person. Shortly after she was born, her mother died, and she was adopted by my grandparents. She was cared for with love and nurturing like any member of the family. As a little girl, she struggled with her health, catching tuberculosis and spending several years at the Sanatorium in Prince Albert.

After her time at the Sanatorium, Jean went to Saskatoon where she got her grade twelve at Bedford Road Collegiate. Following that, she studied to be a nurse at the Holy Family Hospital in Prince Albert. In 1954, she graduated, becoming one of the country's first Indian Registered Nurses.

My grandmother was a midwife, and she delivered many babies on the reserve. Jean followed her example after graduation, moving to La Ronge where she and a nurse's aid provided primary health care to the community. The first year she was there, she delivered over fifty babies, removed numerous fishhooks from kids and tourists, and attended to a wide variety of other health needs.

She once told me that her work as a public health nurse was an exhausting and frustrating experience. Most health problems in Indian communities were caused by poverty and poor living conditions. No amount of work on her part would change that. Political action and changes to government policy were needed.

Jean's career as a frontline healthcare worker gave her a lifelong appreciation for the need to improve First Nations living conditions, and, in return, our community health. She worked for the Department of Indian Affairs, the Department of National Health and Welfare, and, in 1979, she was appointed special advisor to Monique Begin, the Minister of Health. Her appointment followed a period of turmoil between the Minister of Health's office and the country's First Nations. Her job was to work with the Minister and the First Nations to improve health programs. She approached the problem in her own quiet way, and her legacy lives on with greater understanding between the two groups.

Jean was an organizer, working at both the political and educational levels to bring about change. She was a founding member of the Native Women's Association of Canada, a past president of the Indian and Inuit Nurses Association of Canada, and a past president of the Canadian Society for Circumpolar

Health. She also worked with the University of Saskatchewan, helping to develop the Indian and Inuit Access Program to Nursing, and with the Health Sciences program at the Saskatchewan Indian Federated College. She wanted Indian health professionals who were not only trained professionals, but who also shared her passion and understanding for their people.

She and her husband, Ken Goodwill, lived in Ottawa for a number of years. Ken also worked for the federal government in various capacities with Secretary of State and Treasury Board. In recent years, Jean and Ken retired from the civil service and moved to Ken's reserve, the Standing Buffalo Reserve near Fort Qu'Appelle. Ken worked for the band council in various capacities while Jean became a lecturer and teacher at the Saskatchewan Indian Federated College in Regina.

Eventually, health problems began to plague Jean. She had a fall at their home and suffered a badly broken leg. Later, her tuberculosis made a return and flared up in the glands in her neck. This was followed by the leukaemia that eventually killed her.

Referring to her early life, my father told me that when someone struggles so hard to live, there must be a reason for it. My aunt had both a hard life and a good life, and she never stopped working for her people. Her life had a purpose, and she made the most of it.

Everett Soop: He Truly Broke the Mold

Everett Soop was one-of-a-kind. Over the years, we crossed paths at school, at work, and by just showing up at the same place. Soop spent most of his life in a wheelchair, but he refused to let his disability hold him back.

Back in the late 60s and early 70s, *The Kainai News* was the hottest Indian newspaper going. It was produced by a group of dedicated young idealists on the Blood Reserve in Southern Alberta. Soop was a cartoonist and columnist, and his work was the first thing we looked for when we opened the paper.

At that time, political organizations were just getting off the ground, and the word was out that you didn't criticize your leaders in public. The same prohibition is still out there today. But Soop believed that sacred cows make the best hamburger, and so the Chief and Council on the Blood Reserve came under Soop's mocking pen without mercy.

Following a band election, Soop made a cartoon of a donkey being led into the council chambers. The caption read, "But the people elected him." The cartoon was hilarious, but the council thought otherwise. Each council member took it personally, and demanded a retraction. Soop, of course, loved the attention.

Soop had been diagnosed with muscular dystrophy in his teens. The doctor told him that he would be in a wheelchair when he turned 20 and probably wouldn't live to see 30. When he told me this, he was over 30 and still walking around.

Soop used his health as a secret weapon. In a bar once, a member of the Band Council approached him and tried to start a fight over some column or cartoon. Soop replied, "Are you going to try and beat me up in front of all these people? Me, a poor cripple? That will make you look like a big hero." The man backed down.

Aboriginal societies have the trickster, one who tells the truth for the good of the nation. That was Soop's role. He told it like it was.

Soop had no favourites. He picked on everyone. Once, he created a cartoon of an Indian chopping a branch off a tree. Underneath, a man in a suit was busy trying to nail the branch back on. The branch was labeled "Indian Affairs Branch." Another cartoon showed a Chief with a bunch of arrows in his back, captioned, "My people are behind me."

And he just plain had a sense of humour. One cartoon he did showed an older couple hitting the pow wow trail in their Volkswagen Beetle. They had tied a travois behind it, and the caption was, "maybe next year we can afford a trailer."

I was once editor of *The Native People*, the publication of the Alberta Native

Communications Society. We were the northern equivalent to *The Kainai News*. For a while, Soop worked for both papers. In a staff meeting, he appeared to be taking copious notes. Following the meeting, he showed me his handiwork: he had made a caricature of each person at the table.

But Soop was a man of many facets. He finally put his money where his mouth was and ran for council on his reserve. He was elected, and for two terms he held the education portfolio. The Blood reserve is the largest reserve in Canada, and had a population of about 6,000 people at that time. Education was and still is a priority, and Everett took on his new task like a man with a mission.

As a council member, Everett was incorruptible and steadfast in his resolve to work for the people who elected him. He took that attitude into his work with people with disabilities. He was a member of the Alberta Council of Persons with Disabilities and the National Aboriginal equivalent.

He turned his wit and communication skills on the public and on governments who ignored or avoided people with disabilities.

In 1999 Soop was given a Lifetime Achievement Award from NAJA, the Native American Journalists Association. This award was recognition from his peers, which always has special meaning.

Sadly, over the years, Soop's health deteriorated and he was confined to a wheelchair. He developed diabetes and his muscular dystrophy progressed relentlessly. He valued life because it was such a struggle for him. He was disabled living in the land of cowboys where physical ability is the mark of a man. He stood out, fearless and steadfast for his people. He was a pioneer, and he will be missed.

Chapter 5

Our Veterans Changed Our World

The Postwar Watershed

I was a child of the 50s. I was a part of the postwar baby boom that enjoyed the legacy fought for by our parent's generation. For First Nations people, the Second World War was a major political and social watershed.

Indian people have a strong warrior tradition. The warriors who protected the people and kept the peace always had a special place within our community. The veterans filled that important role following the Second World War. Up to that point, we had few heroes, and the old colonial system liked it that way.

First Nation soldiers signed up in record numbers. In some reserves, every able-bodied young man signed up, glad to get away and go on a great adventure. Others were glad to get away from the boarding schools. It was a journey they would never forget. Many would not return home, but those who did would forge a new world for the last half of the twentieth century.

Our veterans' involvement in the Second World War was a life-changing experience, the likes of which they would never repeat for the rest of their lives. When our soldiers were overseas, they received respect and equality that they hadn't experienced before. The return for most was especially hard; they had to go from the excitement of the front lines to a backwater community where nothing seemed to change.

When I was a kid, I remember the veterans as brash men who spoke English well and sometimes drank too much. They tended to work off the reserve and were the first to have cars or pickup trucks. And while the rest of the world may have forgotten them, they remained our heroes. Every year when we would hold our pow wow, a veteran would carry the flag in the grand entry, and at the end of the day, they would take part in the flag-lowering. This was in keeping with our tradition of warriors as the protectors and peacemakers. The veterans always had a special place in Indian country.

This tradition continues today. On special occasions when flags are used, such as at the opening of the Saskatchewan Chief's Legislative Assembly, the veterans carry the flags and are accorded a place of honour.

The war stories of the veterans are famous. They fought on the front lines and were respected by their fellow soldiers. Some were captured and forced to spend years in prisoner of war camps. A Saskatchewan soldier, Henry Beaudry, was fighting in Italy when the Germans captured him. He was sent to a prison camp in Yugoslavia, and, later on, he and another soldier escaped. They traveled across Europe behind enemy lines. They hid during the day and traveled at night. Finally, they reached allied territory. It was Henry's hunting skills and knowledge of living off the land that saved them.

When the Korean War started, many Indian veterans signed up for another hitch. This was largely because they couldn't adjust to life back on the reserve. They missed the action, the travel, and the respect. The British Commonwealth's most decorated war hero was Tommy Prince from Manitoba. He also signed up to go to Korea because adjusting to civilian life had been difficult for him. As one veteran told me, "We fought in Europe, and we were heroes. We came back to Canada, and we were Indians all over again."

The generation of Indian men that travelled to Europe, the Pacific, and, later on, Korea was the first generation to leave the cocoon of the reserve and see the world. They brought back stories of heroism, valour, and pain. The people on the reserve had no way to relate to these stories. FSIN Senator Allen Bird from Montreal Lake First Nation served in Korea with Tommy Prince. Prince was fearless, and, in Allen's words, "Tommy scared the hell out of me. I feared him more than the North Koreans."

Some veterans had seen too much, and they grew old overnight. They became lost to their people and turned to alcohol, suicide or ended up in jail. To this day, some of the veterans I know are still haunted by what they saw and did.

Today, we know this suffering as "post-traumatic stress disorder," but back then it had no name other than "shell shock." In the white community, veterans were not so isolated, and people more often understood what had happened. In the Indian community, a veteran would suffer in silence, isolated and alone. They were lonely heroes who were brave warriors on the outside but deeply wounded within.

A friend of mine told me that when he came back home, he didn't feel right sleeping in a house; because they had been out in the open so much, a structure was considered an unsafe place to be during war. Therefore, he slept outside in the barn in winter and a tent in the summer. He finally got over it on his own, but I used to wonder how many other veterans suffered like him. The war created hardships for all who were there, and many veterans of all races had a tough time getting back to civilian life. Our veterans had additional issues to face.

Others were able to shake it off and get on with their lives. Because they had been off the reserve for several years, they spoke good English. They translated for the older Chiefs and in later years they would assume leadership.

The veterans were the ones who would make changes. Throughout the 1950s, our people organized. There are stories of a veteran standing up and challenging the Indian Agent. They called the agents "little Hitlers" because of the way they ran the reserve and other people's lives. On the provincial and national scene, our people arranged meetings and built awareness. The first leaders of these organizations were veterans because of their self- confidence and ability to speak English.

For example, the first leaders of the National Indian Brotherhood were Walter Dieter and Omar Peters, both veterans. On the provincial level, the veterans also took a lead role in political organizing. The Second World War was an important watershed in creating the political gains we have today.

In Saskatoon in 1946, the Chiefs and supporters met and formed The Union of Saskatchewan Indians. The late John B. Tootoosis was elected as its leader. The veterans played an important role in the formation of the Union. Later, in 1959, the Union evolved into the Federation Of Saskatchewan Indians. By then, the veterans were able to assume leadership positions, and during the sixties, the veterans who served in leadership included David Knight (he's the guy the crescent in Silverwood is named after), Wilfred Bellegarde, and Walter Dieter. These men are deceased now, but the contributions they made live on in Indian country. David Ahenakew, a Korean veteran, served as Chief of the Federation of Saskatchewan Indians and later National Chief of the Assembly of First Nations.

While other veterans received education, housing assistance, and grants for farming and small business, our veterans only received a meager allowance of $1,400.00. This program was handled by the Department of Indian Affairs and was subject to abuse and personal animosity. Many veterans received nothing because they were outspoken or considered unworthy by the Indian Agent.

Earlier, after the First World War, large pieces of some reserves were surrendered for soldier settlement. Our veterans were not eligible for land, but our people were expected to give it up to other soldiers.

Canadian soldiers all wore the same uniform and fought in the same war, but they weren't considered equal when they got home. While the non-Indian veterans had education assistance, housing, land grants, and other benefits under the Department of Veterans Affairs, our veterans had to receive their benefits from the paternalistic Department of Indian Affairs. This was a major mistake on the part of government because it segregated and isolated our veterans. Had they received their benefits from the DVA like all other veterans, organizations such as the Canadian Legion could have helped and demanded equality for the soldiers who all fought in the same war. As a result, our veterans received far less that they were entitled to, and in some cases were allocated only a small plot of land on the reserve with small cash grants closely monitored by Indian Affairs.

This was in keeping with the Department's paternalistic policies. During the war, the soldiers' pay was sent to the Indian Agent who gave it out in small amounts to the wives. The Department's policy was to assume that the women would squander the money. Once again, our people were treated like children.

Over the years, the treatment of our veterans has been a piece of unfinished business. Our veterans never received compensation for the shabby treatment from the government, nor did they receive equitable recognition for serving their country.

In 2002, our veterans and their descendants received a settlement with the federal government. This has been a long-standing grievance, and so many of the veterans who fought for justice are not alive to see it. The offer consists of a maximum amount of $20,000.00 for each veteran or surviving spouse. This settlement has been controversial because the veterans expected more. However, in the end, most seem prepared to accept it. There are very few veterans left. They led a hard life, which is shown in the number who died young.

But our veterans left us with an enduring legacy. They fought for our freedom, and, for a brief moment, they enjoyed real equality. They were the first generation to leave the reserve and compete in the outside world, and they brought back the warrior tradition. We should remember them every day, but especially on November 11th.

Veterans' Benefits

The Second World War may have come to an end over 50 years ago, but some unfinished business remains to the present. Issues have been in the public eye for some time, such as pensions and proper recognition for the Merchant Marine and compensation for Japanese Canadians who were held in detention camps. However, the treatment of Indian war veterans remains an issue that has not been dealt with, and it has not received the public attention it deserves.

During the last war, Indian men and women joined up in greater numbers per capita than any other Canadian racial group. And this was in spite of the treaties that were signed with the Federal Crown. The treaty negotiations included the statement that Indians would not be subjected to "enforced military service." Instead, our leaders agreed that they would support the war effort to safeguard our treaties.

In Ontario, the Six Nations Reserve declared war on Germany and the axis powers as an independent gesture of support to the Crown. On some Saskatchewan reserves, such as Muskeg Lake and Peepeekisis, virtually every able-bodied young man joined up.

Indian soldiers were there at Dieppe, D-Day, and the liberations of France, Holland, and Italy. Indian veterans distinguished themselves and their people, but to the rest of Canada they remain unknown.

Henry Beaudry from Saskatchewan was captured as a prisoner of war in the Italian campaign, and he was transferred to a prisoner of war camp in Yugoslavia. While there, he became friends with a Russian soldier from Mongolia. The two didn't speak the same language, but they were both outsiders and their friendship grew. They escaped and travelled across Europe to safety in Switzerland. This story is the stuff of legends, but it's largely unfamiliar to Canadians.

When Native veterans returned home, they found that they were not to be dealt with by the Department of Veterans Affairs like other Canadians whom they fought beside, but they would instead have to beg for their benefits from the Department of Indian Affairs. Our people paid their dues, but they returned to the same old system that they left. The freedom they fought for would not be theirs back home.

Other veterans went on to university and trades training, received low-cost mortgages, and qualified for veterans' land grants. Indian veterans received a small cash settlement of about $2,500.00. The Indian Agent held this money, and the veteran had to beg for it, unlike non-Indian former soldiers. For example, non-Indian veterans could apply for and receive farmland. If an Indian veteran wanted land, the Indian Agent would have to take it from an existing farmer on the reserve. Of course, this caused problems on the reserve.

Ironically, following the First World War, reserve land was taken by the federal government to fulfil its obligation for veterans' land grants. Numerous Saskatchewan reserves lost about half their land base so that non-Indian veterans could have a land grant. On the other hand, if Indian veterans wanted equal treatment, they would have to enfranchise and lose their treaty status.

As Indian people, we respect and revere our warriors. The brave men and women who joined the forces 60 years ago were the warriors of their generation. They deserved better benefits than they received.

Enduring Landmarks: Geo-Memorial Project Honours the War Dead

The list of the war dead in Saskatchewan is close to 4,000, an enormous number when you consider the size of our province's population. Canada lost about 42,000 young men and women in the Second World War. The First World War cost Canada an astounding 55,000 lives.

In 1947, the Saskatchewan government began the Geo-Memorial Project and undertook the process of naming lakes, islands, bays, and other landmarks after soldiers killed in the war. Saskatchewan has a lot of geography, but in 1947 much of it was unnamed. It is crucial that we remember those who made the ultimate sacrifice, and landmarks are a fitting way to keep soldiers' names alive.

Some of the soldiers were First Nations men killed in Europe during the Second World War. What follows are the accounts of four men whose names live on in Saskatchewan landmarks.

Harvey Dreaver from Mistawasis died in Belgium during the Battle for the Leopold Canal. Joseph Okemasis was from the Muskeg Lake First Nation and was killed in action in Italy at the Moro River south of Rome. Harvey Dreaver was the son of Mistawasis Chief Joe Dreaver who fought in the First World War and received the Military Medal. The Military Medal was established in the First World War and awarded for acts of bravery. Chief Dreaver had two brothers who fought in the Battle at Vimy Ridge. One was killed in action, and the other was wounded and later died. In spite of this tragic history, Chief Dreaver took fourteen young men to sign up in Prince Albert. Three of them were his own sons, including Harvey.

Harvey Dreaver, L27547, joined the Regina Rifles and served in D company. In 1944, Harvey, a Lance Corporal, landed on a French beach as part of the D-Day invasion. Over half his company was killed when their landing craft struck a mine. Only 120 men made it ashore. They joined the rest of their regiment, cleared the beach and headed inland taking the village of Reviers, capturing 35 prisoners. He was promoted to Platoon Sergeant and provided impressive leadership in several decisive battles early in the campaign, including the fighting at Ardenne which was one of the Regina Rifles' most famous and costly victories.

On October 6, 1944, Harvey Dreaver was at the battle of the Leopold Canal to open the port of Antwerp in Belgium when he was shot in the head by a sniper. He is buried at the Adegem Canadian War Cemetery in Belgium, and he left behind his widow Louise and a daughter Doris. The Belgian Government awarded him with the Belgian Croix de Geurre avec Palm. Later, back home in Saskatchewan about 100 kilometers north of La Ronge, Dreaver Lake would bear his name.

South of the Mistawasis First Nation is the Muskeg Lake First Nation. At one time these two reserves touched, but today they are several kilometers apart. Ironically, the land was surrendered for soldier settlement following the First World War.

Joe Okemasis grew up on this reserve with his parents Andrew and Jane. On October 14, 1941, when he was seventeen, he left the Saint Michael's Residential School at Duck Lake and headed to Prince Albert where he enlisted in the Saskatoon Light Infantry.

Two years later, Private Joseph Okemasis L2987 and the Saskatoon Light Infantry were in the midst of some of the toughest fighting of the war. In September 1943, the Allies had landed in Southern Italy, and the Canadians were part of the campaign working their way north in the mountainous terrain. The fighting was fierce with the Germans moving into deep river valleys and counterattacking relentlessly.

South of Rome at the Moro River, the Germans dug in, and fighting was at close quarters with huge losses. On December 7, 1943, Private Okemasis was killed in action. He is buried along with about 1,600 fellow Canadians who died in the battle at the Moro River Canadian War Cemetery close to Ortona. The Italian campaign has not been as well known as the northern campaign that began on D-Day. But the battles were fierce.

The battle of the Moro River resulted in the deaths of 2,119 Canadians, including Private Joseph Okemasis. Saskatchewan honoured Private Okemasis by giving his name to Okemasis Lake about 100 kilometers east of Stony Rapids in Northern Saskatchewan.

Thomas Bear, L2944, enlisted in the Princess Louise Fusiliers and was killed in Italy on January 13, 1945 at age 26. He was the son of Magloire and Marguerite Bear who lived on the Flying Dust First Nation.

In early 1945, the Allies were completing the long and dangerous Italian campaign. The Italians had surrendered, but the German army, while in retreat, was fighting a rear guard action. In May 1945, the Allies reached the border, and the Italian campaign was over.

Thomas Bear is buried in northern Italy at the Ravenna War Cemetery, which is not far from the Adriatic Coast. Today, Thomas Bear's name is preserved in the name Bear Island located on Wayow Lake in the northeast part of Saskatchewan.

Maurice Bellegarde, L64684, was the son of Moise and Margaret Bellegarde who lived on the Peepeeksis Reserve. Peepeeksis was a community with one of the highest rates of enlistment in the country. Practically every young man on the reserve signed up and joined the armed forces when war broke out in Europe. They also had an impressive record in World War I and

Korea. Today, they continue the tradition with both men and women serving in the armed forces.

Maurice Bellegarde was a member of the Regina Rifles, otherwise known as the Farmer Johns. The Farmer Johns were tough and battle-hardened, landing in Normandy on D-Day as one of the assault battalions and fighting through France, Belgium, Holland, and Germany.

Maurice Bellegarde was killed in Belgium on the third of November, 1944. His grave is in Belgium at the Adegem Canadian War Cemetery. Maurice Bellegarde is remembered in Bellegarde Bay which is part of Wapiyao Lake also in the northeast corner of Saskatchewan.

La Ronge's Doug Chisholm, a bush pilot who has photographed most of Saskatchewan's landmarks named after the fallen soldiers, has published these in a book, *Their Names Live On*. He told me that Bear Island and Bellegarde Bay are located quite close to each other. The two lakes are located about eight kilometers south of the Northwest Territories border and about 120 kilometers north east of the town of Stony Rapids. The two lakes are about six kilometers apart.

The threat of war will never go away. We have enjoyed six decades of an uneasy peace since the Second World War, but the regional conflicts and peacekeeping can be just as deadly. While we honour our war dead, we must continue to pray for peace, honour our veterans, and remember those who died for their country. Time dims the memory, but the names of the fallen will be remembered in Saskatchewan's maps.

The Start of the New Generation

To me, Remembrance Day didn't always hold the significance it does for me now. When I was first elected to the FSIN Executive Council in 1976, one of my duties was to work with the veterans and help them organize. I soon got to know the veterans as a bunch of crazy guys who teased each other without mercy, enjoyed life, and to me they didn't seem to take anything too seriously.

The Second World War was a serious watershed for our people. It broke the isolation and ignorance of the old reserve system. Our men and women came back changed people, and they, in turn, would change our world forever. One day, they had been marching triumphantly through Holland, heroes in the eyes of a thankful nation. A year later, they were back on the reserve dealing with the small-minded, vindictive Indian Agents. They had changed, and it couldn't be business as usual. They say you can't go home again, and the veterans had to change their home to fit their vision. They began a life-long crusade to liberate their own homeland.

The First Nations political movements had started before the war, but after the war, the veterans picked up the pieces. In 1946, they assisted in the formation of the Union of Saskatchewan Indians, which evolved into the Federation of Saskatchewan Indians in 1958.

While working with the veterans, I also learned that they didn't like to talk of the horrors of war. They wanted to remember the good parts. They had all lost close friends, some had been wounded, and still others had spent time in prisoner-of-war camps. They carried their hurt silently and close to their hearts.

There was Albert Noname from Piapot who had been at Dieppe, and Joe Ewack from White Bear who had been taken prisoner and held for several years inside Nazi Germany. Henry Beaudry from the Mosquito Reserve was captured in Italy, and transported to a prisoner-of-war camp in Yugoslavia where he escaped and travelled to Switzerland. These were men who had seen more suffering and action in a few years than many do in a lifetime.

The veterans had spent their lives organizing the political organizations, and under the leadership of the late Henry Langin, they had formed the Saskatchewan Indian Veterans Association. Henry had joined the army in 1940 and saw the entire war. Other veterans, such as Gordon Ahenakew, David Knight, Edwin Pelletier, Doc Swanson, Boss Daniels, Allen Bird, and Howard Anderson, joined him. Howard remains active in the organization and has served as its leader.

Over the years, the veterans held a number of functions. One year at their annual convention, we were able to lobby Ottawa and have the Parliamentary

Secretary to the Minister of Veterans Affairs, Gilbert Parent, attend the banquet and give the keynote speech. Gib later went on to become the Speaker of the House of Commons. The veterans warmly welcomed him, and his wife received a few whistles when she was introduced.

Another time, when they held the November 11th Commemoration at Fort Qu'Appelle, a Soviet Union diplomat who happened to be touring the country joined them. The media never found out, and he was regarded as just another old soldier.

Many of my old friends are gone now. As a postwar baby, I learned about the war from my parents and the veterans. November 11th has become a sad time for me. I remember the vets and what a great bunch of characters they were. They were the first generation to leave the reserve. In doing so, they propelled us into a new era of peace and political change. Most of all, though, they were crazy guys, and I loved them for it.

Chapter 6

Indian Urbanization:
Migration to a Better Life?

Federal Policies Have Failed Our Growing Population

There is a crisis facing western Canada, and it's bigger than the agriculture crises, the economy, or any other problem. It's the future facing urban Aboriginal people. If things continue on their present course, both Aboriginal and Canadian societies will face future disaster.

I don't think I'm overstating the issue. Over the past couple of decades, the population of Aboriginal people has grown quickly, tripling since 1970. Aboriginal people are also leaving the reserves in record numbers. In 2004 there were about 117,000 Aboriginal people in Saskatchewan. The 1996 census determined that 50% of Aboriginal people across Canada live in urban areas, and of that number, 65% lived in cities in the western provinces.

A recent study done by the Canada West Foundation looked into the socio-economic condition of urban Aboriginals and came up with facts that are no surprise, but which are nevertheless cause for both concern and hope.

First of all, urban Aboriginal people are much younger than the rest of the population. In Saskatoon and Regina, 41% are under the age of 14. This is currently putting considerable strain on the school system, but in the long run, the percentage of young people represents a future workforce for an ageing general population.

In fact, population research done by the Aboriginal People's Television Network indicates that 70% of the Aboriginal population in Canada is under the age of 28. This research was based on the 1996 census. Such a young population creates a number of issues that must be addressed. For example, in Saskatchewan Aboriginal admissions to adult provincial correctional institutions are 76% of the total and 63% of those on probation are Aboriginal.

On the employment front, 25% of Saskatoon's Aboriginal population was unemployed, compared to 6.8% for the general population. In Regina, there was a 26.6% unemployment rate compared to 6.4% for the rest of the population. Naturally, this shows up in employment figures. The percentage of the population 15 years and over with an income of less than $10,000.00 was 51.3% for Aboriginal people in Saskatoon, compared to 27.3% for the rest of the population. In Regina, it was 47.6% for the Aboriginal population and 24.2% for the rest of the population.

This has created a new area of policy issues that must be addressed if our people are to adapt and prosper in a new employment environment.

The federal government is the culprit in much of this issue. The feds have shirked their responsibility and followed a policy of dumping urban Aboriginal issues on the provinces and municipalities.

The federal government's responsibility dates back to the Royal Proclamation of 1773, the treaties, and the British North America Act. For example, the BNA Act states that the federal government is responsible for "Indians and land reserved for Indians." It doesn't state where the Indians are supposed to *live*, only that the federal government has a constitutional responsibility.

Recently, John Corbiere from the Batchewana First Nation in Ontario went to the Supreme Court to argue that as an off- reserve member of a First Nation, he had the right to participate in elections. The Supreme Court agreed, and he and other off-reserve First Nations people now have the right to participate in elections. Now that we have the right to vote, don't we also have the right to receive some services from our First Nation? This is the next battle, and we should win it.

Over the years, the Department of Indian Affairs has chronically under-funded our First Nations governments and their institutions. This was by design and has contributed to the evacuation from the reserve. In return, Indian Affairs has given precious little to the provinces or municipalities to compensate.

The federal government is the deadbeat dad of the First Nations, and it's time they got serious about urban Aboriginal people.

Urban Problems Are Close to Home

Several recent events within my family have caused me to do some soul-searching to examine the present state of our young people.

My dad's cousin recently celebrated her eightieth birthday. She lives by herself in Saskatoon and is still quite independent. The other night, two boys around age ten dropped by to see her. She knew them, and she got up to offer them something to drink. When her back was turned, they grabbed her purse, cut the phone line, and headed out the door. Fortunately, they didn't get much money, but she was out her identification, a few dollars, and her telephone.

Recently, my niece was downtown during the day with a friend when they were attacked by three girls. They said they wanted to beat up some white people, and when my niece told them she was an Indian, they proceeded to jump on her friend. It was only after some people driving by stepped in that they ran away, but they left the two girls battered and bruised.

Both of these incidents left deep emotional scars on the victims, and left us questioning what's happening to our people when they commit such cruel and senseless acts. Why do little boys rob from their elders? Why are girls attacking total strangers because they appear to be white?

Years of poverty and neglect have produced a crisis within the cities. It will only lead to more violence and to organized crime. We are losing a large part of our Indian Nation to a new culture of urban crime and poverty. These people will soon be Indians in name only.

How do we turn this around?

We need to import our elders, organizers, and other leaders to the cities to broaden the cultural and social revival into a moral and ethical revolution. Physical poverty can be addressed through jobs and improved social services, but poverty of the soul can destroy us.

We can't accept the old bromides that all our problems stem from white people, boarding schools, Indian agents, and any other convenient excuse that comes along.

Violence and theft against your own people are not the white man's fault, nor are they any kind of political statement. They are merely the actions of criminals.

But we can't fall into the revenge trap that leads to the creation of more experienced criminals. The criminal gangs in Winnipeg, for example, have moved into the jails and are active in places such as Stoney Mountain Penitentiary. Gang activity only reinforces criminal activity and creates its own culture. We have to develop new programs that address the needs of our young people in trouble with the law. A trip to jail or a juvenile institution is seldom a deterrent; the young offender only comes out more streetwise and less "Indian."

The strongest deterrent to crime is peer pressure, and that comes from an organized movement to strengthen the cultural and moral fabric of our communities.

Back on the reserve, people who got drunk in public used to be ignored and tolerated, but now they are subjects of scorn and derision. The result has been a movement toward sobriety and a more mature attitude to alcohol.

People in the cities enjoy a certain amount of anonymity, though, and can continue to drink and carry on with impunity.

We must address the problems in our cities soon; otherwise, we will see the formation of a new group of Indian people that has no culture other than the culture of poverty. These people will have no knowledge of the wonderful world that can be theirs within the First Nations family.

And our people will continue to fall prey to each other, wasting their time and effort going after each other. We can't afford to turn our backs on our own people. These people are our relatives and friends, and they are a part of our great circle.

Urban People Now Have Voting Rights on the Rez

The status of urban Indians has been a divisive and negative issue in Indian country, but it is purely artificial. Its roots lie in the federal government's historical policies, and its reluctance to live up to its constitutional obligations.

The federal government stopped living up to its constitutional responsibilities years ago by refusing to recognize responsibility for off-reserve Indian people. Once we leave the reserve, the federal government fails to recognize our treaty rights.

Also, band elections conducted under the Indian Act did not grant off-reserve Indians the right to vote. The Supreme Court has recently overturned this injustice in the Corbiere case. First Nations governments are now including all of their members, regardless of place of residency.

Interestingly, this decision overturns years of government policy that refused to recognize off-reserve Indians. It will cause considerable changes to First Nations elections over the coming years. First Nations can no longer ignore their off-reserve band members. In Saskatchewan, this policy has been under attack for years, and the majority of First Nations now conduct their elections under the section of the Indian Act that allows for the "Custom of the Band." When First Nations exercise this right, they most often include all members of their First Nation, regardless of place of residence.

If First Nations must now recognize their off-reserve members, it stands to reason that the federal government must recognize its constitutional responsibility for all Indian people, regardless of place of residence. This will free the provincial government from providing services for off-reserve Indians and place the responsibility squarely on the shoulders of the federal government.

Now a third party has emerged on the scene in the form of CAP, the Congress of Aboriginal People. This organization had its heyday during the constitutional talks. The federal government granted it a seat at the table in an effort to reduce the clout of the Assembly of First Nations.

It was openly stated that CAP represented the non-status and Indian people living off reserves. In fact, this was the majority of the First Nations people, but they had no membership list or infrastructure to reflect the size of the organization, nor did they obtain a groundswell of sympathetic support in Indian country. At the time, the Congress of Aboriginal People wasn't even listed in the Regina or Saskatoon phone books.

Unlike CAP, First Nations organizations such as the Assembly of First Nations and the Federation of Saskatchewan Indian Nations have strong infrastructures and networks of institutions. Most Indian people don't consider themselves members of CAP. We consider our roots to be with our First Nation, which in turn is represented by the Federation of Saskatchewan Indian Nations.

In Winnipeg, where CAP does have a presence, the urban Native programming includes all Aboriginal people and ignores the treaty rights of the First Peoples. On the surface, it may sound fair that all people are treated equally, but it must not be forgotten that our relationship with Canada exists through the treaties and the federal government.

In Saskatchewan, Indian people have been moving into the cities in record numbers. Saskatoon and Regina have the majority with over 20,000 in each city. In reality, these are the province's two largest reserves. Prince Albert has a smaller population, but it is overall about one-third Aboriginal.

First Nations people in the cities come up against a host of issues, including employment, housing, access to services and racism. People don't like to hear the "r" word, but I know from first-hand experience the subtle and not-so-subtle racism that our people face on a daily basis.

We need to extend the jurisdiction of our Chiefs and Band Councils into the cities to include First Nations-led programming and development. Also, with Treaty Land Entitlement, we are able to purchase land in and around urban areas. This land holds potential for economic development, housing, and the creation of new reserve communities.

It is only when we take control that we will see a real change for our urban people, and now, with the Corbiere decision, we can expect more urban activity.

Social Inequities Have to Be Addressed

Two significant events illustrate what is happening in Indian country: while institutional and business development is increasing at a record pace, the social dysfunction of another part of Indian society is also moving at a record pace.

In Saskatoon, Canada's first Aboriginal bank, The First Nations Bank of Canada, formally received its letters patent and approval from the Canada Deposit Insurance Corp. It was an historic occasion that brought the Prime Minister to Bay Street for the official launch and all the accompanying hoopla.

Meanwhile in Winnipeg, Ted Hughes, a retired judge and conflict of interest commissioner for the Province of British Columbia, tabled his report on the riot at the Headingly Correctional Institution in Manitoba. In his report, Hughes urged the Manitoba provincial government to "bring to national attention" the social inequities that have led to the disproportionate number of Aboriginal people languishing in Manitoba jails. The Headingly Institution was a powder keg of racism and discontent with 70% of the inmates being Aboriginal.

Over the past two decades, we have seen a social revolution in Indian country as more and more people have moved off the reserves and headed to the cities. They were originally looking for a better way of life with a job, decent housing and improved health and social services. Instead, they have found ghettos, poverty, racism, and a loss of identity.

The loss of identity is arguably the worst of the social ills. Indian people living in urban ghettos are separated from their extended families back on the reserve, and so the young lack role models. The resulting loss of self esteem makes the young easy prey for the ravages of drug and alcohol abuse. It then becomes a short hop to petty crime, youth detention, and jails or a penitentiary.

Material poverty is one thing, but poverty of the soul is a poverty that can last for generations.

A large part of the blame for the plight of urban Indians can be placed on the federal government. First, reserves were treated as nothing more than human storage bins for a country that saw no place for the Indian population. When the bins overflowed, and the people moved to the cities, the federal government declared that they were no longer a federal responsibility.

The First Nations leaders fought for the portability of treaty rights, but they were met by an uncaring government. The federal government move to disenfranchise off-reserve Indians was penny-wise and pound-foolish because now they are paying the price.

The social, criminal, and racial problems growing in the western cities are a product of this neglect and callous disregard for the rights of our people. In Saskatchewan, half the First Nations population now live off of the reserve, and many are alienated from their homeland, their culture, and their language. The result has been the growth of urban gangs, rising crime rates, and a deep sense of powerlessness among the youth.

This sense of powerlessness manifests itself in the usual ways. The other night I dropped by the corner store and noticed the young people hanging around. They were dressed in baggy clothes and displayed the same attitude that poor urban blacks have in the States. They were loud, abusive, swore a lot, and didn't care what people thought of them.

They want to stand out and be somebody, even though in this society they have few of the skills required to succeed. These kids have very little in common with their cousins back on the reserve.

Power is a basic human need. People who don't have it act as if they do. If they don't have it, they will take it. People with no power cannot be kept down indefinitely; if they want something, they will get it, even illegally.

While one part of First Nations society builds for the future, another part faces a bleak future.

Working for a New Beginning

The new battleground for First Nations organizing and social activism is now in the Saskatchewan's cities. Over half of the province's First Nations population now lives off-reserve, and this is resulting in a whole new range of social and cultural issues.

Regina has over 30,000 Aboriginal people, mainly concentrated in the inner city. Problems with housing, poverty, substance abuse, and unemployment have festered for years, and are now reaching critical proportions.

In 1993, a number of women founded an organization that would address these issues. Ivy Kennedy was one of the driving forces behind the organization Women of the Dawn.

In First Nations culture, the dawn represents the start of a new day, and each new day is seen as a gift from the Creator. By calling their organization Women of the Dawn, Ivy and her supporters capture the feeling that they represent a new beginning. They have now built up an organization that works with men, women, youth, and families. One of their first projects was to set up a computer-training program for 24 women. The computer-training program has been an outstanding success with 85% of the graduates finding long-term employment. So far, they have held four classes and trained close to 100 women.

Ivy had worked in Alberta as an AIDS outreach worker, and knew that social services in Calgary consisted of driving people to the city limits with a stern warning not to come back. "We saw the affect of cutbacks in Alberta, and we knew that the same thing would happen here," Ivy told me. "Our aim was to take Indian women and train them so they could get off welfare."

The Women of the Dawn also operates a counselling service and assists families, inmates, and people suffering from substance abuse. Prostitution is an issue related to poverty and drug addiction. The Women of the Dawn has a special program to work with prostitutes, helping them to get off the street and into drug rehabilitation programs.

"We have a five-point strategy and work with the Police to charge the pimps and johns. In the case of child prostitution, we want them charged with child abuse – a much more serious charge," Ivy told me.

Part of the organization's philosophy is to work to present role models to Aboriginal youth. In the inner cities, there are few positive role models, and many youth feel that success in education, business, or sports is out of their reach. This alienation is one of our greatest enemies because it results in a sense of hopelessness that leads to crime and substance abuse.

For three years now, Women of the Dawn has sponsored the annual

Saskatchewan First Nations Awards, where they recognise Aboriginal achievements in eleven fields of endeavour, including sports, politics, business, journalism, and social work. The awards have been an outstanding success, and last year over 800 people attended. The awards ceremony has taken on a life of its own and now takes over six months of hard work to organize.

The Women of the Dawn continues to work with its people. Its work is both frustrating and rewarding, but through dedication and perseverance, the job is getting done.

Living in the City, Freedom Is a Gift You Give Yourself

Indian society is developing into three distinct groups: those who are moving forward and strengthening their cultural, economic, and educational positions; those who are sinking ever-deeper into the trap of welfare and despair; and those who are rejecting the middle class dream and developing a distinctly First Nations society.

This split is especially noticeable in the cities.

While there's a large group of off-reserve Indians who hold jobs, attend university, and generally make a contribution to the advancement of Indian society, there's also a significant group trapped in the violence and social chaos of the inner cities. Theirs is a life of welfare, exploitation by slum landlords, violence, and substance abuse. It's a world where pimps and drug dealers exploit children, and where the children themselves eventually form gangs and repeat the cycle of exploitation.

As First Nations people, we are living during a period of great paradoxes. We have more people in university than ever before, businesses are springing up all over, and there is a rapidly growing middle class. Couple this with the healing movement and the cultural revival, and things look pretty good. But our urban young people are turning to drugs, violence, and gangs to survive.

Over 280 Indian elementary students left Saskatoon schools last year, and they continue to leave every year. A similar situation exists in Regina. The students just seem to disappear, and nobody bothers to look.

These children aren't from my neighbourhood; they're from the inner city. Some may have moved away, others may have simply stayed home, and others drop out and become street kids.

There is a lot of hatred out there, and it's boiling over with mindless violence, crimes against our own people, and the more recent formation of Indian gangs. While one segment of our society is forging ahead, another segment is falling deeper into poverty and the culture of poverty.

One holiday season, the Saskatchewan Indian Cultural Centre held a very successful pow wow at Sask Place. There were over 6,000 people in attendance, but there were few inner city people. Many had no way to travel out of town to the venue, and, besides, they were too busy lining up at the food banks.

Years of poverty and neglect have produced a ticking time bomb within the cities. It will only lead to more violence and organized crime. We are losing a large part of our Indian Nation to a new culture of urban crime and poverty.

Poor people have to sacrifice a lot to survive. Often, this is their culture and belief system. This isn't done consciously; it just happens. It happens as a result of the constant struggle to survive, dealing with welfare agencies and the police. The culture becomes a culture of poverty that exists for day-to-day survival. These people will soon be Indians in name only. Once this happens, it becomes even harder to crawl out of the welfare trap. People in the welfare trap are made far too dependent upon others, making them lose their ability to make their own decisions. They become dependent on the state.

As Indian people, we are at an important crossroads. History has taught us that meaningful change comes from within, and so we must look to each other for help and support.

This is where the third group comes in. On the surface, this group appears to be the same as low income people, but their culture and spirituality are very rich. This group's members are not out to pursue the middle-class dream, but they are after their own personal spiritual goal.

Many of these people suffered from addictions in the past, and their quest for a better way of life led them to the spiritual path or Red Road. This is a growing group within Aboriginal society, and for the most part, they are invisible to the general public.

This third group's members have taken the important step of looking within themselves for the answers. Freedom is a gift that you give yourself. Nobody else can provide it. We can't simply blame our problems on white people, boarding schools, Indian agents, or anything else. We have to take ownership of our lives.

I do agree that many of our current social problems have their roots in the boarding schools of yesterday. Children didn't learn how to parent at boarding school. And the boarding school violence and sexual abuse were transplanted to First Nations communities.

But once we understand the roots of our dysfunction, than we are compelled to address it.

The pain the parents endured is now inflicted on the next generation. Many of today's children face a much worse situation than their parents who went to boarding school. They are a lost generation that faces violence and exploitation that the boarding school generation could only imagine.

It is correct that most of our problems stem from colonialism, but there comes a point when the colonized peoples must take ownership of their problems and their lives, and forge ahead in their own new direction.

Sustaining people in limbo on welfare has been the colonial approach to our people. People in the welfare trap have been made far too dependent on others, and so they lose their ability to make their own decisions. They become dependent on the state.

As Indian people, we are at an important crossroads. We must look to each other for help and support. Meaningful help comes from within, and that is where we have to look.

The Indian and Métis organizations have been preoccupied with economic development, casinos, and constitutional change, somehow believing that one of these will be our panacea. In the meantime, our inner-city people continue to deteriorate, and the social problems take on new and frightening dimensions.

Jim Buller: A Pioneer Actor

Saskatchewan has provided the country and the world with more than its share of prominent people. And the same holds true in Indian country. One of our unsung heroes is Jim Buller, a First Nations person raised in Saskatoon. Jim is revered within First Nations artistic circles as a pioneer and as the founder of the Native Theatre School in Toronto.

Jim's father, Solomon Buller, came from the Sweetgrass Reserve east of the Battlefords. He received an education at Saint John's College, married a Métis woman from the Red River Settlement, and in the 1920s moved to Saskatoon where he worked for the CNR. Jim was born and raised in Saskatoon. The Buller family was probably the first Indian family to live permanently in the city.

Jim attended Bedford Road Collegiate, where he was active in the drama club and played bass drum in the high school's band.

My father attended the Saskatoon Teachers College on Idylwyld in 1939 and 1940, and the Buller household was a sanctuary for homesick Indian students. Dad was a regular guest at the Buller's for Sunday dinner. Solomon Buller would laugh at his son, telling my father that the Indian Agent used to get after them for wasting their time playing their drums, and now his son was busy practising his drums.

Jim Buller graduated from Bedford Road before joining the army to fight in the Second World War. Following the war, throughout the 1940s and '50s, he held a number of jobs. He eventually ended up in Toronto, where he got a job with the Ontario government. He worked for the provincial Indian Affairs office, where he became exposed to the poverty and despair on reserves for the first time in his life. This experience touched him deeply, and he vowed to do something to create change.

Buller saw his experience in the theatre as a tool for change. He believed that by telling the stories of his people, he could enlighten the uninformed public, and in the process, he could create an Aboriginal theatre community. He worked with a Native theatre group, and it became the hub of the Native acting community, the same way his parent's home had served homesick Indian students.

In 1975, I met Jim Buller at a premiere of a CBC drama special at the Bessborough Hotel. Jim played a part in the drama, and it featured several other Aboriginal actors. Jim's parents were present, by now quite elderly but still active.

Jim was very excited about the prospects for his recently established Native Theatre School. The school had been his dream for some time, and it was now a reality. Over the years, the school has turned out a steady stream of talented actors. Denis Lacroix, Gary Farmer, Kennetch Charlette and Shirley Cheechoo all got their starts there. Other graduates have gone on to teach at well-known institutions, such as Ryerson in Toronto or the National Theatre School in Montreal.

After such successful features as *Dances with Wolves*, *Pow Wow Highway*, and *Black Robe*, the word was out in Hollywood that Canada was the place to cast for Indians, with special interest placed on the Native Theatre School.

Today, Canadian Aboriginal actors are in demand throughout the industry, and a growing body of original work is evolving from writers, directors, and the actors. Series such as *North of Sixty*, *The Rez*, and television movie specials rely heavily on talent from the Native Theatre School. Live theatre, such as Tomson Highway's acclaimed *The Rez Sisters*, included cast members who were the alumni of the Native Theatre School.

The success of the Native Theatre School is the result of one man's dream, a dream to tell our stories and educate the nation. Jim didn't live to see the full extent of his dream, but he knew the direction it was headed. Today, a new generation of Aboriginal actors is working to keep Buller's dream alive.

Healing Through Theatre

Today's urban Native youth are experiencing a lifestyle unique to our history. They grow up divorced from their roots on the reserve, and they face racism and loss of identity. Furthermore, they must carry the continuing burden of the boarding school experience, even though the painful history of the institutions is largely unknown to them.

Kennetch Charlette, an established Aboriginal actor and a graduate of the Native Theatre School in Toronto, decided to develop a drama troupe of Aboriginal youth. The idea came to him in a discussion with Gordon Tootoosis and other cast members on the set of *Big Bear*. I was one of the production's producers, and when Kennetch mentioned his idea to me, it didn't sink in at first. I had a million other things on my mind, and his idea wasn't a priority at the time.

Kennetch's idea was that the process of telling their stories on stage would empower the young people and help them to act on some of their issues.

The Aboriginal Healing Foundation, established as a result of the Royal Commission on Aboriginal Peoples, provided an opportunity for funding. Kennetch and his partner, Donna Heimbecker, collaborated and put forward a proposal to develop a drama troupe made up of urban youth. They would focus on the residual effects of the boarding school experience. Today's young people bear the wounds of the old system and many don't even know why. They have inherited the problems from their parents.

The boarding schools are now only a bad memory, but their negative effects live on. Sometimes we don't even recognize that we are still living in fear, dependence, and self-loathing, the subjects that the boarding schools taught the best.

When the Native theatre first started, Building a Nation (BAN), an urban Native counseling and support agency, sponsored the program. BAN also provided elders, to lead the talking circles and provide optional ceremonies.

The program was ambitious. It was compressed into two months and the participants, young people between the ages of 13 and 23, worked every evening from five until nine o'clock. All this and they began the whole process from a standing start. It was a major undertaking: the script had to be written, the group had to grow and work together, and lines and stage directions had to be memorized.

The theatre introduced the participants to well-known professionals, such as Gordon Tootoosis, Joe Welsh, Andrea Menard, Ian Black, and Chester Knight. They served as role models and instructors. Floyd Favel from CBC's *Dead Dog Café* was brought in to direct.

The script was an exercise in collaboration. Deanna Kasokeo interviewed each of the participants for his or her story. The stories were painful accounts of physical and sexual abuse, loss of language and culture, loss of identity, abandonment, foster homes, and the many pains of racism and loneliness in the city. The participants' stories make "reality television" look pretty shallow.

It became clear that these young people were suffering the multigenerational effects of boarding schools. Their parents and grandparents had carried the pain of their past with them, and had fallen short as caregivers. Today's generation still carries the scars.

The result is *Truth Hurts*, a play that reveals the pain and suffering that today's youth must carry.

Floyd Favel, the play's experienced director, saw the play as an important way to develop new talent and to exorcise the demons of our past. Following the play's premiere, he told me that the success of the play empowered the young people: "They are experiencing success, and the result of their hard work."

Opening night went off without a hitch, or none that the audience was aware of. The story is a powerful one: a group of young people gather together a year after the suicide of a friend. They discuss his suicide and what led to it. They also discuss their lives. Truths and secrets are revealed, and their lives are laid bare.

The audience reaction was positive, and after the cast made their final bows, their smiles and their hugs said it all. "These are kids that don't get much recognition, so a night like this will be remembered for a long time," Floyd Favel told me.

Chapter 7

Social Studies for First Nations

The Welfare Trap

O nce, when talking to an acrobat who came from a long line of circus performers, Princess Margaret said, "One tends to do what one's family does." Now that's fine for royalty, circus performers, and the professional classes, but what happens when families fall into the welfare trap for generations? Welfare has the ability to sap a person's strength, lower expectations, and create a climate of hopelessness. Is it still fine to do what one's family does?

Welfare has become a serious problem in First Nations communities, and it's a serious challenge for the leadership. While everyone agrees that welfare is not a good thing, when a band council tries to control spending and shorten the welfare roles, they go up against an electorate that may not agree.

The Department of Indian Affairs knew a bad thing when they had to administer it. Welfare was the first program they dumped on the Band Administration. It was a pain-in-the-neck to administer, but as any good neo-colonialist knows, you simply turn the colonized into little images of you and continue with the old system.

Welfare is a relatively recent program for First Nations. It basically began in the postwar period around the late 1950s. Earlier, Indian people didn't need a cash economy. We were able to hunt, farm, trap, and conduct other forms of economic activity to sustain ourselves. Welfare was known as "relief" at that time and consisted of food rations handed out several times a year. Life on the reserve was relatively simple. People built their own houses, heated them with wood stoves, and they hunted for food. They lived a subsistence economy.

But life changed as the cash economy took hold. Oil, heat, groceries, and electricity all required a steady cash income. Also, the reserve population grew rapidly, and the demand for farm land outstripped the reserve boundaries.

This placed pressure on reserve governments to care for their people through welfare payments. The treaties clearly state that Indian people will receive assistance during times of hardship, and this has been interpreted as welfare.

While welfare was not meant to be a permanent state, Indian Affairs saw it as a cheap way to deal with the "Indian problem." Welfare meant warehousing people and placing them on a shelf. Welfare meant avoiding job creation and meaningful economic development that would have cost more money in the short term.

Welfare was cheap in the short term, but extremely expensive in the long term. It is expensive because it not only costs us in dollar terms, but it also costs us in human terms. It has ruined whole generations.

The Lac La Ronge Band in northern Saskatchewan led the way in economic development by joint-venturing with existing companies and accessing contracts in resource development. Then they went on to lead the way in welfare reform. Employable people who receive welfare must either take training courses or actively seek work. This may not sound like a revolutionary move, but in Indian country, it represents a serious attempt to address the issue.

Welfare reform is a touchy topic for most First Nations leaders. When the majority of voters are on welfare, and the reserve economy is based on welfare, people tend to want to hang on to what little they have rather than take a chance on reform.

Over the years welfare became known as "social assistance," "income support," and other weasel words that meant welfare. In the end, it remains the same.

Dealing with welfare and its problems is the sad reality of First Nations self-government. We remain dependent on the federal government for program funding, yet it sets the rules and priorities. "Self-government" is really "self administration."

Welfare remains a significant part of First Nations' income off the reserves, too, and so as more people move from the reserves to the cities, the problem is now moving to the provincial economy.

There will always be people who need support from the state: the elderly, people with disabilities, single women with large families, and others. We must open our hearts to those less fortunate, but we must not allow the welfare state to take over our culture and destroy us as a people.

The time has come for the leaders to address the issue, just as the Lac La Ronge Band's leaders have. And the government must provide training funds and other meaningful support for economic development.

Child Care: No Middle Ground

Aboriginal child care is a divisive topic because while the welfare of the child is crucial and must be considered, the group rights of Aboriginal people must also be considered.

Arguments about Aboriginal child care often become emotional because immediate issues must be addressed before long-term consequences are considered. To understand the problem, one must examine the history of Aboriginal child care in Canada.

The role of Aboriginal parents continues to be belittled and ignored. This began over a century ago, when the children were removed from their parents and placed in boarding schools. It was generally felt that the parents would be a bad influence on their children since many of them were "pagans." Even when the parents converted to Christianity, it was believed that the children were better off in boarding school where they could be kept free from the negative influences of their parents and the community.

We were considered a doomed race with no future. Not only did we as a people have no future, but our culture and way of life was also considered obsolete, and the sooner it disappeared, the better.

The boarding schools were an abject failure, and their historical contribution was generations of parents who had little knowledge about functional parenting. When the children were removed from their homes, the roles of the parents, grandparents, and the communities were disregarded and severed. In First Nations families, the grandparents traditionally played an important role as teachers of religion, ethics, and culture. Within the community, parents watched over all the children as if they were their own. All this changed with the social engineering of the boarding schools.

In Saskatchewan, we had boarding schools in one form or another for almost a century. The government-run industrial schools were established in the 1880s, followed by the church-run boarding schools, and later they were administered by tribal councils. The last school closed in 1984.

Then it comes a no surprise that in the 1960s and 70s we had the "big scoop." Child welfare agencies picked up Aboriginal children at will and placed them in non-Aboriginal foster homes. When they ran out of homes in Canada, they sent them off to the United States and Europe. Today, there are Aboriginal children living in foreign countries who are divorced from their past and their cultures, and who are still searching for their identities.

Uprooting children from their culture has proved to be a tragedy. When the Royal Commission on Aboriginal Peoples was conducting hearings across the country, it came to Stoney Mountain Penitentiary. One of the commissioners asked how many of the inmates had spent time in foster homes. To the commission's surprise, over half of the inmates held up their hands.

This is telling proof of the failure of child welfare in the past, and of the damage inflicted on people's lives.

There has been a steady stream of adopted children searching out their pasts and coming back to their roots. The return is often not easy. The adopted have sometimes found themselves at graveyards mourning a parent they never knew, or they have returned to a living parent who is filled with guilt and shame. In the Aboriginal world, family ties are strong, and, in most cases, the children are welcomed back into the community and introduced to their biological grandparents and other relatives.

There are many tragic stories of the journey home. Young people find their roots and then discover that they just don't fit in like they thought they would. They have lost the language, they don't share the same history as members of the rest of the family, and they may have an accent that is foreign. Many adults who search out their roots continue searching for the rest of their lives. They mourn a lost childhood, the loss of their culture, and the fact that they are set apart in a world that is neither Aboriginal nor white.

Newton stated that "for every action there is an equal and opposite reaction." He was speaking in physical terms, but the statement is also true in social situations. Today, Aboriginal adoption agencies are asserting their jurisdiction and demanding that Aboriginal children not be adopted into non-Aboriginal families. This policy is being criticized by the media, the courts, and child welfare agencies. They see a child in need, but not the system that has failed us.

But when you take the long view, it is obvious why the pendulum has swung back in the opposite direction. Aboriginal groups are now developing their own child care and adoption agencies. These agencies have a philosophy that places group rights and First Nations political rights ahead of the liberal thinking that the rights of the child are paramount. Of course, the rights of the children are important, but the rights of the group are also important and must be a part of the solution. Indeed, children's rights cannot be separated from community and political rights; they are interconnected.

The treatment of Aboriginal children is Canada's shame. The country gave up on our people and tried to submerge us in the greater society. The results of this have led to the situation we have today. Instead of concentrating so much on the individual, the answer ultimately lies in working toward healthy communities that will eliminate the need for adoption altogether.

Davis Inlet: A Tragedy Caused by the Federal Government

The tragic events in Labrador's Davis Inlet fly in the face of the Canadian sense of "peace, order and good government." To understand the situation, though, one must look at the history of the community and its people.

The press reports the current events and presents a snapshot of each day's unfolding story. But like the family album, when you view the snapshots together, they tell the story of the family.

For the past two years, nothing but bad news has come out of this community. The name "Davis Inlet" has become synonymous with social breakdown and tragedy. The people are not seen as individuals, but as members of a seemingly dysfunctional community.

This bad habit of the news media of coming into a community and always covering the bad news creates a climate of shame and distrust. This does not help the community to address its problems; it turns their home into a circus. And this is what has happened in Davis Inlet.

The real story is both unique and all-too-common. The problems at Davis Inlet began when the government decided that the people would be better served if they were placed on an island. This was for the benefit of the government and not the people. The North is full of artificial communities designed by and for bureaucrats. The people are treated like cattle with no regard for their historical ties to the land.

The people at Davis Inlet lived in benign neglect until their children were photographed high on gasoline fumes and wanting to die. This shocked Southern Canada, and suddenly Davis Inlet was on the front pages and a household word. There was no shortage of public support and people wanting to help, but in the end, it was up to the community to help itself.

This situation is not unique. All across this country, there are communities digging themselves out of the excesses of welfare and alcohol and the accompanying social problems. Good will and sympathy are not enough.

About 15 or 20 years ago, we underwent a similar change here in Saskatchewan. The reserves were beset with social problems, and the school dropout rate was appalling. The parents and leaders took it upon themselves to control their education system and to develop a reserve-based education system. The movement was largely driven by women who were determined to see a better future for their children.

When Indian affairs resisted legitimate change, the parents pulled their children out of the joint schools located off-reserve and demanded "Indian control of Indian education."

This was an act of civil disobedience from people who would never ordinarily break the law, but it was a necessary part of our development. There comes a time when people must say "enough is enough" and do what must be done to create change. In this case, civil disobedience was an act of empowerment.

The RCMP and the Courts have been denied access to the community of Davis Inlet, and this may worry some, but it is an act of empowerment by the people and part of the process that will help the community to recover.

And all First Nations people may end up owing a debt to the people of Davis Inlet if they gain recognition of the right to administer their own justice system. They are fighting for self-government and the fundamental right to control their own destiny.

The Indian people of Saskatchewan played an important role in the fight for of Indian control of education that has benefited all First Nations people. The people of Davis Inlet may leave their own valuable legacy for all our benefit.

Northern Enlightenment

Some names have negative connotations. "Edsel," for example, is equated with "failure." For years, the "Toronto Maple Leafs" meant "mediocre," and here in Saskatchewan, "La Loche" whips up the image of a welfare trap at the end of the world.

For a long time now, La Loche has taken a bad rap from the news media as a place of despair and dysfunction. News crews have flown in and out the same day gathering shallow and negative stories.

A few years ago, southern journalists discovered northern communities. The end result has been a bunch of stories about places such as Davis Inlet in Labrador, Shammatawa in Manitoba, Ogdensburg in Ontario, and of course, La Loche. The stories were biased and tainted with no small amount of WASP culture shock. Also, these communities don't buy advertising space, so there is no downside to humiliating them.

I don't want to sweep problems under the rug. Everyone will agree that these and other communities are suffering from high unemployment, grinding poverty, and devastating drug and alcohol abuse. But there is another side. There are real people living in these communities, and they live real lives. A visit to La Loche will confirm this.

I spent a few days in La Loche recently and discovered a whole new side to the community. They were holding a hockey tournament, so I walked over to check it out.

I walked up the hill past the spiffy new liquor store, past a collection of trailers that serve as the hospital, and on to the arena. Along the way, I passed people who greeted me. Some stopped to talk and asked why I was in town. I was struck by their friendly and open manner.

La Loche has 12 senior men's hockey teams in town and numerous minor teams. There is a tournament every second week, and the ice is always busy throughout the week. The week I visited, there were also visiting teams from Turner Lake and Buffalo Narrows. The arena complex also houses the studios of CHPN, the local Dene radio station, an affiliate of Missinipi Broadcasting in La Ronge. The game play-by-play is broadcast in the Dene language for those who can't make it to the arena.

The next day, we visited the schools, the town office, and the hospital. The Ducharme School is the elementary school with a student population of 520. There are an additional 70 in the preschool with 35 in each class. Dene is the first language of the children and a healthy sign that in this community, Dene is a living language.

Down the road is Dene High, a high school with 320 students. For the past several years, they have graduated about 25 students each year. This is quite a feat when you look back and see that in 1981 only one student graduated from grade 12. Using their desktop publishing equipment, the students publish their high school paper, *The Howler*, which in 1993 was the winner of the *Saskatoon Star Phoenixs'* Award of Merit.

There are 4,500 people in the village and the surrounding communities, including the Clearwater First Nation located about six miles north of town. La Loche is the largest Dene community in the province.

Sports play a major role in the community. In addition to hockey in the winter and baseball in the summer, track and field events are very popular. In 1993, the high school students sent 25 participants to the North American Indigenous Summer Games in Prince Albert and won 23 medals, 16 of which were gold.

Sure, La Loche has its problems, as has been pointed out repeatedly, but the community continues to attract a group of "outsiders" who put down roots and stay for years. Some of the teachers I spoke to have been there for 15 or more years, and they love it. La Loche is now their home.

The RCMP is also playing a positive role in the community. Three of the constables coach hockey and several others play. The sergeant meets regularly with the village council, and the two groups are working together.

There is always fodder for the pessimists and sensationalizing journalists, but if you open your eyes and see a community for what it really is, you may be in for a pleasant surprise.

FAS and FAE: Irreversible but Preventable

First Nations communities are in the midst of a serious crisis, and it needs to be regarded as a priority. Fetal alcohol syndrome (FAS) is running through our communities like an epidemic.

FAS occurs in the general population in about three per 1,000 live births, and alcohol-related neurodevelopmental disorder (ARND) is three to four times more prevalent than FAS. It is estimated that one Aboriginal baby out of five is born with some degree of (FAS) or (ARND). This is a staggering statistic, especially if one considers that with a provincial population of 100,000, we should have 20,000 people suffering from some degree of fetal alcohol disorder.

The sad fact is that fetal alcohol syndrome and its related effects are completely preventable but utterly irreversible.

In Saskatoon, Judge Mary-Ellen Turpel-Lafond has been branded "controversial" because of her insistence that people with fetal alcohol syndrome/effect be given special programs. But as a youth court judge, Judge Turpel-Lafond has faced a steady stream of young offenders showing the effects of alcohol damage in the womb.

As we learn more about the effects of alcohol consumption during pregnancy, an ongoing tragedy is becoming all-too clear. This country's greatest social problem might well be fetal alcohol effect (FAE) and its close relation FAS.

The condition of FAS is noticeable by a distinct physical appearance. With FAE, individuals lack the physical features, but they can have internal damage to the brain and other organs that is equal to an individual with FAS.

When a woman drinks alcohol during her pregnancy, she can condemn her child to a lifetime of pain, lack of opportunity, and a chance for early death. When she binges, the child drinks right along with her. Alcohol is toxic and does a wide range of damage to the fetus.

Alcohol impairs the growth of the brain and causes learning disabilities, hyperactivity, attention deficit and/or memory deficits, inability to manage anger, and difficulties in problem solving. In addition to brain damage, the child may also suffer from asthma, deafness, height and weight deficiencies, and heart defects.

It is estimated that the birth of one child with FAS will cost the taxpayer more than $3 million. It is also estimated that 60% of prisoners are likely victims of this condition, and the costs of warehousing offenders ranges from $120,000.00 per year for a young offender to $82,000.00 per year for an adult offender. Add to this the costs of missed opportunities, strain on the family and caregivers, and other related costs, and FAS/FAE is an economic black hole. It is estimated that the cost to society of women who drink while pregnant exceeds the national debt.

More important than money, though, is the human cost. Children with FAS/FAE are easily misled, and they have little appreciation of the consequences of bad behaviour. They may get into the revolving door of the justice system, and spend their lives as street people or in some kind of custody. As one FAS web site puts it, "The girls get knocked up and the boys get locked up."

An article published in the September 25, 2000 edition of *Newsmagazine* offered these grim statistics for individuals between the ages of 12 and 51:

- 95% will have mental health problems,
- 60% will have disrupted school experience,
- 60% will have trouble with the law,
- 55% will be confined in prison, drug and alcohol treatment centres, or mental institutions, and
- 52% will exhibit inappropriate sexual behaviour.

For the older adults, it is estimated that:

- 50% of males and 70% of females will have alcohol and drug problems,
- 82% will not be able to live independently, and
- 70% will have problems with employment.

These are grim facts, but they must be addressed. We must acknowledge that in this country we are locking people up because they are mentally ill.

Judge Turpel-Lafond is correct in her concern for those who come before her who suffer from FAS/FAE. What kind of justice system throws people away because of impairment beyond their control? For these impressionable people, prison is the worst environment for them.

A few summers ago, the top news story was the young Aboriginal woman in Winnipeg placed in the care of the state to protect her unborn child. It is a story with no winners and only tragic consequences. A poor, unfortunate woman, at the bottom rung of the social ladder and addicted to solvents, has become the hot topic on the white liberal cocktail circuit, eliciting such questions as,

"If the state can take away her freedom, are we next?"

"Does this mean that if a woman smokes during her pregnancy, the state has the right to take away her freedom?"

White liberals are hung up on the issue of individual freedom, an issue that Indian people living in poverty and an addicted state looked upon in relative terms. Freedom to go to your cottage or fly off to the Bahamas is one thing. Freedom to continue to live in the hell of addictions is another thing altogether.

This is the real issue behind the story. The young woman is a product of years and generations of poverty — an existence that leads to crime, drug addictions, and eventual care in the hands of the state. Grinding poverty leads to a loss of identity and hope. The result is a person with low self-esteem who is easy prey for addiction and the corresponding lifestyle.

Addictions workers agree that solvent-addicted individuals lose all contact with reality and are extremely hard to rehabilitate. There are a number of very good centres for alcohol addiction, but there are very few resources for solvent abusers. Solvent residue may stay in a person's system for months, as opposed to only hours for alcohol.

Solvents have become the "high" of choice for young Aboriginal people for two reasons: they are cheap and readily available.

Traditionally, First Nations people have placed group rights over individual freedoms. Decisions must be made that are for the good of the weak and for the good of the whole community. In a First Nations system, the young woman would most likely be placed in care and supported by her family and the community. The liberal arguments about loss of freedom and civil liberties would mean very little in light of her imprisonment within her own addiction.

But the young woman is not within her community. She is dislocated in the city of Winnipeg. First Nations governments have few resources and a plethora of problems that all need attention. People like this woman continue to fall between the cracks, and they and their children are the real victims.

Unfortunately in Saskatchewan, a high percentage of people suffering from FAS/FAE are Aboriginal. Our social and economic conditions have bred many socio-economic problems, but this must be among the worst.

The justice system must face reality and address this serious issue because jail does nothing to improve the lot of people with FAS/FAE. And it follows that health authorities at all levels must stress prevention because this condition has no cure. The damage is permanent, and there is no going back. Aboriginal leaders and health professionals need to lobby for programs that help women during their pregnancies, and they need to educate the public about this serious issue.

Sexual Orientation Not an Issue in Traditional Societies

Traditional First Nations societies were very close family groups. Because they depended on each other for their very survival, diversity within the group was tolerated and often seen as positive.

People were not merely dismissed or thrown away for being different. In our modern society that breeds isolation and fear of the unknown, it is easy to dismiss groups and individuals who are not part of the mainstream.

One of the most isolated groups within contemporary society is the gay and lesbian community. This group is the subject of fear and contempt. Homophobia exists within all sectors of society, particularly among the religious right, rednecks, and many average people on the street.

Traditional First Nations societies also contained gay and lesbian individuals, but they were held in esteem and well-regarded for their insights and for their role as healers. Some tribes referred to gays and lesbians as the "third gender," which was a much more inclusive way of viewing them. Today, the term "two spirits" is used.

Writing in 1724, Jesuit missionary Joseph Francois Lafitau condemned homosexuality in the Aboriginal world, but observed, "They believe they are honoured." He noted that the Indians of the Great Lakes, Louisiana, and Florida all treated homosexuality as a special condition: "They never marry, they participate in all religious ceremonies, and this profession of an extraordinary life causes them to be regarded as people of a higher order and above the common man."

The French explorer Jacques Marquette also became aware of the position held by Indian gays and lesbians: "They are summoned to the Councils and nothing can be decided without their advice. Through their profession of leading an extraordinary life, they pass for spirits - or persons of consequence."

Since traditional societies consisted of individuals who were closely related, gays and lesbians, because of their special status, were used as mediators between men and women. They were also summoned to the Councils for advice because they contained the points of view of both men and women.

In some of the creation stories, the Great Spiritual Being is seen as neither male nor female, but is a combination of both genders. For example, the Zuni creation story involves a conflict between agricultural people and hunters. The people are brought together by a mediating spirit that is both man and woman. This spirit is able to unite the two and create the unique Zuni society of hunters and farmers. The Kamia of the American Southwest believe that the bearer of plant seeds who transformed their culture was a man-woman spirit named Warharmi.

When Christian missionaries and other do-gooders saw the perceived horrors of Aboriginal societies, they sought to impose their beliefs on a people who had developed healthy, stable societies. The role of gays and lesbians as healers and visionaries came to an end. An important and meaningful part of First Nations society was attacked and marginalized. Besides the obvious negative effects of the imposed culture on gay and lesbian individuals, the whole community suffered the loss of a valuable resource.

Today, First Nations can't claim the moral high ground with this issue the way we try to do with so many other issues. We are now just as backward and homophobic as the rest of society. The missionaries did a good job. But our societies are still small. Our extended families are still the most important single unit of our society, and we can't turn our backs on those who love us.

Today, some of our most creative people come from our gay and lesbian community. Writers such as Beth Brant and Tomson Highway, and videographer Zachary Longboy, have distinguished themselves in their chosen fields.

On a personal level, my niece is a lesbian, and through her I have learned about our prejudices and fears. I now know that all families contain people of three genders, and we have to return to our roots as inclusive societies to benefit from everyone's perspective.

Native People with Disabilities Suffer Twice

Being Native and having a disability is a double whammy, according to Georgina Morin who is quadriplegic. She has spent most of her life in a wheelchair, and she has to live in the city because her northern community is simply not wheelchair-friendly.

Aboriginal people who suffer from disabilities tend to do so in loneliness and poverty. Aboriginal society is poor to begin with, and the disabled must wait their turn at the end of the line. As a result, they end up in care off of the reserve in southern cities.

Young people with disabilities suffer the most. I spoke to one young man who had been sent to the city and placed in foster care because his family couldn't cope with his disability, which was caused by polio. He grew up in the city, and so he didn't learn his language or know his relatives, and he was very unhappy. When he got older, he returned to his community only to discover that he didn't fit in. He didn't know the language. He was regarded as a city boy and was shunned. He lived alone in a small cabin at the edge of town. Lack of support forced him back to the city and into a special care home. A few years ago, his wheelchair was found by the river in Saskatoon. Later, his body was found. It was concluded that he had committed suicide.

I have talked to other people with disabilities who tell similar stories. After years away from the reserve, they find it very hard to go back again.

The First Nations Network on Disabilities is self-help group of First Nations people from across Saskatchewan working to improve the circumstances of people with disabilities. They recently completed a survey, and the results are revealing.

First, it is no surprise that inadequate housing leads the list of problem areas. First Nations housing has fallen behind for able-bodied people, never mind for people with disabilities. Money for ramps, wider doors, and other basic modifications is not available and must be taken from the reserve's overall housing budget. Housing alone is the single largest reason that the disabled leave the reserve for the city.

The survey also concluded that the three largest causes of disabilities are diabetes, heart disease, and arthritis. These are lifestyle-related and result from our people's hard lives in poverty with poor housing. Disabilities caused from accidents and violence are actually the minority.

Now people with disabilities are organizing and helping each other. For a couple of hours each day, Georgina Morin goes down to the Saskatoon Friendship Centre where she does volunteer work with people with disabilities. She keeps in touch with them by phone and checks up to see that they are alright.

Many people with disabilities are returning to school to complete high school, take special technical courses, and in some cases, attend university. Recently, I attended the graduation exercises for the First Nations University of Canada. Dennis Sapp, a member of my reserve who has spent much of his life in a wheelchair, received his Bachelor's Degree in Indian Studies.

Another dream is to establish a home for Native people with disabilities run by Aboriginal people. It would have special programs and cultural practices. Even something as simple as bannock is a welcome treat. Dennis told me, "When we burn sweet grass, they (the staff) think we're smoking dope."

Dennis and his friend Louis Munroe sat on a committee of the Sherbrooke Community Centre and worked to develop a home for Aboriginal people with head injuries. They hope some day to repeat this with the development of a home for Native people with disabilities.

Aboriginal people with disabilities are often overlooked by our people. Now they are becoming empowered through education and increased communication.

As one young woman told me, "We're not stupid, and don't treat us like we are."

Youth in Crisis

Summer is supposed to be a happy time. It's a time for relaxing and taking a holiday. A time when people hit the pow wow or rodeo circuits and kick back. Instead, the summer of 2001 will be remembered as a summer of tragedy in Saskatchewan.

The Summer Games are an opportunity to showcase First Nations youth through competitions and cultural events. The 2001 Saskatchewan Indian Summer Games were overshadowed and diminished by recent tragedies across the province.

First, four young people were killed in a car accident north of Prince Albert. Three were from the Montreal Lake First Nation and one was from Black Lake. She left behind a 17-month-old daughter. Two of the Montreal Lake victims were brothers, and their father was in the car following them. They were returning from a funeral at Montreal Lake.

Next, the First Nations at File Hills have been shaken by four senseless murders. First Nations communities are close through kinship and friendship. They say, "Everyone knows everyone," and it's true.

Finally, to add to the tragic events, Aboriginal people in Regina and Saskatoon recently paused to reflect on the ongoing problems of young women and men on the streets in the sex trade. In Saskatoon, 30 names of young people – mostly women – who had died recently were read out. The list was haunting in its description of "overdose," "murder," or "unknown."

From the above-mentioned tragedies, we must conclude that today's youth are in crisis. Alcohol, drugs, and unhealthy lifestyles have taken their toll on our young people. We are one of the fastest-growing groups in North America, and the effects of this population explosion are being felt more and more.

Of our population of over 100,000, half are under the age of 18. Two-thirds are under 35. There have been over 20,000 First Nations people born since I started writing this column. This rapid growth puts serious stress on our communities. For example, half the regional budget for Indian Affairs is for education, and school construction in First Nations communities is at an all-time high. Our leaders and others like to point out the importance of the elders in providing stability and leadership for our young people, but with so many young people, the demographics indicate that the number of elders is very low.

Another issue facing many youth is the lack of opportunities in their lives. A young Aboriginal man has a better chance of going to jail than of graduating from high school. Unemployment is low to nonexistent in many communities;

all the best jobs in the band offices are held by the older generation, and they cling to them because they are some of the few existing jobs in the community.

Job opportunities for young people today are largely located out of the community, and that means getting an education, learning a trade, and competing in the job market. Many of our youth are ill-equipped to face these challenges, and the results are becoming negative.

The Chiefs at File Hills pointed out that drug and alcohol addictions were a large part of their problem, but in reality, addictions are a symptom of the larger issue of lack of opportunity and alienation.

Substance abuse is the end result of disenfranchisement, and it's a growing problem among the young. In the past, alcohol was a serious problem, and it took a serious toll. Today, most communities have AA groups and healing programs that have benefited the older generation. Today, many older people don't drink alcohol, and so their lives have been enriched.

But young people today face issues that many older people can't understand. We have a generation gap as serious as any other society. Simply telling the kids to "just say no!" is as useless as it was on the bumper stickers.

People turn to drugs and alcohol for a variety of reasons, and peer pressure is only one reason. In many cases, our young people are depressed and "self-medicating"; substance abuse is an escape-route.

I have spoken to some of the older people, and they told me that they were lucky that they only used alcohol. If there had been drugs around, they would probably be dead today.

Today's youth are looking at a crowded landscape with competition for education dollars, competition for jobs with good training programs, and peer pressure to use drugs and alcohol. Half the population isn't even on reserves; we now live in the cities with a whole other series of issues. Alienation and loneliness in the cities plagues our people. When I was young, we were considered poor, but we didn't know any better. Today, the good life is shoved in our face at every opportunity, and young people are aware of the disparity.

As First Nations people, we are at a serious point in our history. There is pressure on our leaders to provide opportunities for young people, but the reserve economy can only support a limited number of jobs. Education is the key, and steps must be taken to turn out quality graduates who can succeed.

Most importantly, we must take ownership of our problems and address them ourselves. Otherwise, our youth will continue to be alienated, and we will continue to face more tragedy and death in the years ahead.

Felix Musqua and My Uncle Adam:
Two Men Who Worked for Their Families and Communities

When both my Uncle and a good friend died close to the same time, I was struck by how similar they were even though they came from different generations.

When my friend Felix Musqua died of cancer, he was only 52. My uncle Adam Cuthand also died of cancer. He was 80 and had lived a full and rich life.

Felix and I served together as Vice-Chiefs for the FSIN. He was one of my closest advisors and supporters. He was steadfast in his beliefs and loyalties. He was not a fair-weather friend, a trait that is all-too-common among politicians.

Felix came by his beliefs from his father, Roy Musqua, who was the Chief of the Keeseekoose First Nation for 25 years and a Senator for the Federation of Saskatchewan Indians. His father schooled him in the treaties and the promises that were made to our people. He was considered an authority on the treaties and on their spirit and intent.

Even though the leadership changed from Sol Sanderson to Roland Crowe, Felix remained on staff as a consultant and treaty advisor to the Chiefs. Felix was considered above personality politics. To many people, including myself, he was the conscience of the FSIN.

My uncle Adam was also a product of his father and his grandfather. My grandfather taught him the meaning of service to one's people, and though none of our family has been a Chief, we were always there as headmen or advisors. My grandfather was an advisor and confidant to Chief Blackman, who was the lifetime Chief of Little Pine for many years. His father, Misatimwas, was the War Chief to Chief Little Pine. He was wounded at the Battle at Cutknife Hill and served three years in Stoney Mountain Penitentiary for protecting his people.

Uncle Adam carried on this legacy and served in the army as a sergeant during the war. He worked on the radar project that was in operation before the end of the war. My grandfather taught his children Cree syllabics, and Uncle Adam used to write letters to the family explaining what radar was. It was top secret, but he made my grandfather an "expert" on radar.

Following the war, Uncle Adam went to Saskatoon Teachers College and then taught at Ministikwan, Anerly, Pelican Lake, Montreal Lake, and Muskoday. Later, he went to Emmanuel College and became a minister in the Anglican Church.

When he joined the army, he lost his status as a Treaty Indian, and under the arcane laws of the day, he was considered a Métis. In 1968, after living in Manitoba for some years, he was elected to the leadership of the Manitoba Métis

Federation. Following his term in office, he coordinated the Métis land claims research for the Federation.

In later years, he was the student advisor to Native students at the University of Manitoba. Adam was always helping others, and as the student counsellor, he found a job that suited him perfectly. Nobody will ever know the number of students he helped or the money he gave them to help them out.

One of the virtues that Indian people admire and honour is generosity. Both Adam and Felix were generous with their lives and their money. It was only at my uncle's wake that one of the council told us that he had given $1,000.00 to the Little Pine School Library. It was typical of him to make a donation quietly, not expecting any special recognition.

In 1986, when the federal legislation to reinstate Indian membership or Bill C-31 came into effect, my uncle was returned to Little Pine membership. And when the Treaty Land Entitlement Agreement was signed, he was selected to be a member of the Band's Board of Trustees.

My uncle and my aunt Beatrice had three children and adopted two. They also helped out many more. Felix and his wife Earline raised four children and adopted four more.

While Felix and Uncle Adam were from different generations, they carried with them the principles and ideals of their ancestors. And they both left the world a better place.

Chapter 8

It's Justice for Some and Revenge for Others

Lock Them Up, Throw Away the Key

R eports from Statistics Canada and various think-tanks continue to point out that our people are over-represented in Saskatchewan's prison system. This sad fact comes as no surprise to the province's Aboriginal people, who have been aware of the problem for years.

In Saskatchewan, 76% of inmates in provincial jails are Aboriginal, the highest percentage in Canada. Manitoba was the second closest with 59%. These shameful statistics are proof of institutional racism at its worst.

We have a long history of this country's institutions maintaining a practice of racism. Over the years, government policies and practices have criminalized our people more than any other group in society.

For example, following the North West Rebellion, our people were incarcerated in large numbers. The government was determined to set an example and to show who was boss. So many men were put in jail that a new wing had to be added to Stoney Mountain Penitentiary. This was the first in a long line of jail construction specifically for the Aboriginal population. It was also one of the first examples of the government going after the victim while ignoring the root of the problem.

For years, we had special legislation for us that restricted us to reserves, forbade the consumption of alcohol, and allowed the government to remove children from their families.

And I'm not talking ancient history here: the government still removes children from their families and places them in different cultures, the prohibition on alcohol was only removed in the 1960s, and the last boarding schools were closed down only a few years ago.

Saskatchewan leads the nation in incarceration with 161 out of 100,000 people sent to jail, compared to Manitoba, which came second, with 127 out of 100,000 people sent to jail. Locking people up has become an industry in this province, and our people are the raw material.

Today, our people end up in jail for a variety of reasons. For example, if a person is unable to pay a fine, they will go to jail. Our people are poor, and so jail is often the only option. And poverty plays a role in the courtroom where the accused must defend him or herself. Our people usually can't hire top criminal lawyers or any lawyer at all. Our people will often plead guilty just to get things over with.

Compare this with some of the high-profile criminal cases where white people have fought in court, appealed, and remained out of jail even though they have been convicted. Look at all the fuss over Martha Stewart's five-month jail term at "camp cupcake" and then her subsequent house arrest.

The main reason our people end up in jail is due to alcohol and drugs. Whether it's a current problem or one from the mother, substance abuse is our greatest enemy. Many in prison are there because of fetal alcohol syndrome (FAS). Many persons with FAS are unable to understand the consequences of their actions and fail to learn from past mistakes. This is a serious affliction, but jail is not the place for sick people. The same holds true for people with problems with substance abuse. Drug addiction has been criminalized and not treated as the health problem that it is.

More effort must be put into rehabilitation and into addiction prevention programs. Instead, our society prefers to warehouse its problems and leave them for the next generation to worry about.

Our misery provides the economy with a thriving industry. In Saskatchewan, there are 831 prison employees in federal institutions, 1,036 in provincial institutions, and 193 in young offender custodial facilities. This is a staggering total of 2,060 jobs. If Indian people were properly represented in the jails, then only about half would be required. The cost to maintain the system is a constant drain on financial resources.

In Saskatchewan alone, the federal system costs about $60 million annually, the provincial system costs over $44 million annually, and the young offender system costs in excess of $12 million annually.

Former FSIN chief Roland Crowe, himself a former correctional worker, used to point out that in this province Indian people are the basis of a large and growing industry. However, it's an industry where we don't belong. Our people are the raw material, but when it comes to working in the system, we are significantly under-represented. Only 12% of federal employees, 15% of provincial employees, and 12% of the young offender system employees are Aboriginal. This is in stark contrast to the outrageous majority of Aboriginal people in the inmate population.

Also, most of the Aboriginal employees are front-line employees with only a slim minority in management positions. These are predominately white-run institutions locking up our people.

Contrast this sorry situation with the Women's Healing Lodge located on the Nikaneet Reserve outside Maple Creek. The majority of the staff is Aboriginal, elders are on staff full time, and the inmates are treated like human beings. The emphasis is on healing, not on revenge, which seems to be the driving force behind the mainstream institutions. The Women's Healing Lodge is working while the other institutions are miserable failures. In fact, the existence of the Women's Healing Lodge has increased the percentage of Aboriginal employees working in the correctional system.

Regardless of race, most inmates arrive at the jail's receiving room as hapless losers. There are few if any criminal masterminds in our jails. The biggest threat they represent is most often to themselves. The road to incarceration is littered with addictions, violence, and unhappiness.

It is a road that our people travel down regularly.

Saskatchewan has dug itself into a deep hole where it has concentrated on building and staffing jails. In the process, it has built up an industry based on our suffering. Turning the system around will mean reducing jail populations and laying off prison staff. This means making some hard decisions and standing up to union pressure.

What are the alternatives? Simply locking up more and more of our people isn't the answer. I know of very few people who have actually benefited from their prison experience. More than likely, they were released as more hardened criminals and were addicted to one or some of the drugs floating around the institution. Or they were infected with AIDS. Jails just make problems worse.

In Saskatchewan, we have a prison system reminiscent of the southern United States'; it is a system built to satisfy people's racism, fear, and ignorance. It lulls the public into a false sense of security that something's being done, even though jails create more problems than they solve. Someday, we'll look back on the antiquated prison system the same way we look back at boarding schools, slavery, and the death penalty – as institutions that simply didn't work.

Last year, 3,850 men and women were sent to jail in this province. Three quarters of them were Aboriginal. The system isn't working for us; it's only creating more problems. It's time for some serious change, and simply tinkering with the existing system isn't good enough.

Some More History

The Aboriginal Justice Inquiry is conducting hearings across the province, and many of the complaints and shortcomings of the police, penal system, and courts are being hashed and rehashed.

However, to truly examine the sorry state of Aboriginal justice in this country, one must take the long view of history and look at the laws, institutions, and failures of past Indian policy.

In the late 1960s, when I was in the social work phase of my life, I worked for the John Howard Society in Calgary. I visited the jails and supervised men on parole. At that time, the jails were just starting to feel the impact of the growing Aboriginal population. There were no special programs for our people, and they just did their time and went back to the reserve.

I noticed that the majority of the Indian inmates came from the Blackfoot Reserve east of Calgary. The Stony and Sarcee Reserves were much closer to the city, but they had few inmates in jail. I asked an Aboriginal leader why this was the case, and he told me that the Blackfoot Reserve had felt the impact of colonialism far greater than the other two. First, they had lost about half their reserve land in a forced land surrender around the turn of the century. Second, they had two boarding schools on the reserve. People sent their kids off to school in the fall and only saw them at Christmas and over the summer. This led to family dysfunction and guilt among the parents. It led to a high rate of alcoholism and related problems, which then led to the high rate of inmates from the Blackfoot Reserve in the provincial jail.

This story is typical of many reserves in Canada. Colonialism, with its paternalism and racism, has devastated many communities and families.

The next historical tragedy to land on us was the "big scoop" of the 1960s and '70s. Provincial social agencies thought that they should place Indian kids in white foster homes or have them placed out for adoption for their own good. Foster care and adoption led to more problems than they solved. Parents who needed help would have their children picked up by social services and dispersed throughout the country. If the parents were having problems, the despair of losing their children only made everything worse.

The social agencies actually wrote off a generation of parents as useless and beyond help. Their answer to the social problems created by colonialism was to impose more colonialism. The children, who were the products of this twisted system, lacked both a cultural and family base. They developed problems of their own, and many searched for their roots. They ended up stuck between two worlds and never really fit in or belonged to either. They created a new wave of inmates for the federal and provincial corrections facilities.

One of Canadian society's problems is that it generally sees all Aboriginal people as the same. If you are an Indian in Saskatchewan, you must be addicted, dangerous, and planning your next crime.

The reality is that Aboriginal people fill many valuable roles in the professions, government, and as employees for a wide variety of companies. It is the minority who has been damaged to the point that its members are dangerous to society and end up in trouble with the law.

The same holds true for First Nations and Aboriginal communities. Without naming names, some First Nations have a very low rate of men and women in jail, but have high employment and education levels. In other communities, it is practically a right of passage to go to jail, and the employment and education levels are very low.

The difference is found in leadership, self-government, and a strong cultural base. Communities that hold a Sundance and respect the elders tend to have less crime. Other institutions, such as a community school and strong, responsible, and accountable Band Councils, are able to address problems before they grow into major problems. Communities that organize a wide variety of sports programs have also driven down the crime rate.

But the real fight is in prevention. Steps must be taken to eliminate the root causes of crime and violence in Aboriginal society. History has shown that imposing rules and institutions on our people has not worked. Like so many solutions, change can only come from within a community itself.

Let God Sort It Out

*In the mid-1990s the Reform Party was calling for the return of the death
penalty. It would naturally have the hardest impact on the poor and dispossessed.*

Moves by the Reform Party to call for a national referendum on capital
punishment were mean-spirited and vengeful. They capitalized on the mood of a
nation reeling from the revelations of the Bernardo rape and murder trial.

This, coupled with the rhetoric to get tough on "welfare mothers" by
Ontario's Premier Harris, and the work-for-welfare schemes proposed by
Saskatchewan's Tories, capitalizes on a mean-spirited and angry mood in the
land. The silent targets of such policies are the country's underclasses. Blacks
in Ontario and Indians in the West are two obvious groups occupying the
bottom end of the economic food chain.

The United States practices capital punishment with no positive results.
In fact, they have the highest murder rate of any industrialized country in the
world. There are a disproportionate number of blacks and Hispanics who are
killed by state-sanctioned methods.

In Canada, the death penalty was abolished in 1976, but no executions had
been carried out for a number of years previous. There are disturbing examples
in our history, though. Following the North West Rebellion of 1885, the largest
public hanging in Canadian history was conducted at North Battleford. Eight
"rebels" were hanged together. They were all Indians who had participated in
the rebellion, and the public hanging was a message to all Indians that they
were truly defeated. The event was an example of vengeance and abuse of power
at its worst.

Are we heading back to where the law is used to get even with certain groups
of people?

The law, of course, does not discriminate. The abuse comes in the application of the law. There may be more white people than Indians arrested
and charged, but the jails contain mostly Aboriginal people. How come?
Many times, Aboriginal people will plead guilty to get it over with. They are often not
represented by legal counsel because they can't afford it, or they simply don't
know how the system operates.

In the 1980s, the Devine government killed the court worker program.
This proved to be a costly and stupid move because it denied support to Aboriginal people in the court system, and as a result, the jail population began
to swell. The cost to the taxpayer turned out to be far greater than the court
worker program ever was.

During the past decade, we have seen the jail population grow and the
subsequent construction of new and better jails. The real problems of poverty

and social breakdown have not been addressed. Instead, we seem to be headed down the same road as the Americans, by warehousing our problems and locking up more and more people.

A huge jail population becomes a subculture that serves as a graduate school for criminals working against meaningful rehabilitation. Very few inmates actually die in jail, and sooner or later, they're released.

The Reform Party capitalized on our revulsion of the evidence being presented at the Bernardo Trial. They wanted a referendum on capital punishment. They wanted a knee-jerk reaction that would take us back to the 1950s. They wanted the middle classes to condemn the poor, people of colour, and those who can't defend themselves.

The Donald Marshall case is an example of the "fairness" of the justice system. Marshall is a Micmac Indian who spent 11 years in prison for a murder he didn't commit. I wonder how many other Donald Marshalls are out there and how many would be executed in the new and mean-spirited Canada.

No Easy Answers to Mercy Killing

The Supreme Court upheld the decision of the lower courts to sentence Robert Latimer to life in prison with no parole for ten years for the "mercy killing" of his severely handicapped daughter Tracy. Latimer's sentence was condemned by a wide spectrum of the public, and the Supreme Court decision caused a groundswell of support for Latimer. I consider this support misplaced and caught up in the emotion of the moment. The Supreme Court was right to uphold the principle of the sanctity of life, no matter how exceptional the case appeared.

Latimer is the guy next door. He is a decent, church-going family man, and it is easy for him to obtain public sympathy. He should, however, answer to the law as it exists.

The rights of the disabled must be protected. Individuals unable to speak for themselves must be given a voice.

As First Nations people, we know what it is like not to have a voice. Our children have been abused for generations in boarding schools, foster homes, and other social institutions. We know the pain of not being heard and respected.

This case has also shown us that there are no easy answers to some of the complex legal and moral issues. Social policy must be carefully thought out and applied consistently.

I agree that Robert Latimer doesn't belong in jail, but many other inmates don't belong there either. Jail only serves as a post-graduate school for criminals. I'm not suggesting that Latimer will come out of prison a hardened criminal, but many young people have had their lives ruined in jail.

In Saskatchewan, we have a two-tier justice system with jail sentences for the poor and Aboriginal, and house arrest for the "white-collar" criminals (emphasis on the "white"). In sentencing a white-collar criminal, the judge will usually point out that the offender isn't a risk to society and doesn't belong in jail.

I agree that some people don't belong in jail, but I wish this decision were made much more often. Instead, the jail population in Saskatchewan has steadily grown, and the incarceration rate for Aboriginal people looks like something more from a banana republic than a country the United Nations has rated the best in the world. The provincial jail population could probably be cut in half with no threat to the public.

Another issue arising from Latimer's case is the problem with mandatory sentencing. Latimer was charged with murder, and the automatic sentence if one is convicted of murder is life in prison. The only room the law has is to determine the amount of time that must be served before parole can be granted. In this case, it was a ten-year minimum.

When capital punishment was abolished in Canada, the government made a compromise to the opposition for the imposition of long mandatory sentences. This places judges in a sentencing straightjacket. The Supreme Court and all the other courts have no choice but to interpret the law as it is written.

The situation is even more draconian in the United Sates with mandatory sentences for a variety of drug and property offences. The courts are really held hostage to law-and-order politicians. These right-wing politicians prey on the fear and ignorance of the public, and so the prisons are bulging with prisoners serving long-term sentences for relatively minor crimes.

The question now is: should the law be changed to allow for the oxy-moronic term "mercy killing"? When is a life not worth living, and who should decide? Who qualifies for a mercy killing, and when does it become a slippery slope that can't be stopped or controlled?

Today, passive euthanasia is practiced by withholding treatment for ter-minal cases. Family members agree that a loved one should not be resuscitated in the case of a severe heart attack or stroke. But to die with dignity is different than the act of taking a life.

This debate will not go away, but it is healthy for a society to examine its collective ethics and what it will accept or condemn.

The debate brings us back to the point of there being no simple answers. Politicians will have to search their consciences and make unpopular decisions that may more ethical and best for their society. It is not a time for glib ten-second clips and photo-ops. It is a time for leaders to lead and not get swept up in the emotions of the times.

Making Juries Fair

I once saw a cartoon that showed a cowboy sitting in the courtroom looking across at a jury that was all Indians. This was supposed to be a joke, but I knew that our people faced the opposite scenario all the time.

And so apparently does Justice Ronald Barclay. He ruled recently that defence lawyers have the right to question perspective jurors about their racial views. His decision was made at the trial of Dwayne Allen Fleury, a Métis who stood accused of murdering his brother.

His history-making ruling follows a decision of the Supreme Court that said when widespread racial bias is shown, it's reasonable to permit lawyers to question potential jurors about their views.

In his decision, Judge Barclay referred to racism as defined by the Saskatchewan Human Rights commission: "Racism is a combination of stereotyping, prejudice and discrimination that makes some races believe they are superior to other races."

If this definition clarifies what racism is, racism indeed exists across Saskatchewan. For years, our people have had their fate decided by jurors who harbour racial bias, but until now, we have had no weapon to counteract the situation. Now, armed with the Supreme Court decision, our people have the potential for a fair trial by jury.

The theory was that we had the right to be judged by a jury of our peers. Most often, Aboriginal people charged with crimes face juries of individuals who are foreign and hostile to them. For example, persons accused of a serious crime in the Athabasca area have to be sent down for trial in Prince Albert, where their fate would be decided by people who are not from their area or culture and who don't speak their language. This was not what would be considered a jury of the person's peers.

It has been said that justice must not only be done, but it must also be *seen* to be done. A jury that is foreign or openly hostile to the accused is not a jury that shows that justice is being done.

It's also time that Saskatchewan people woke up to the reality that racism is deeply ingrained in their province's history and social fabric. This conclusion has been reached by a learned judge and not by some Aboriginal politician or activist. This statement can't be ignored or dismissed; it comes straight from the province's courts.

In Saskatchewan, Aboriginal men and women are the majority population in the province's jails. There are a variety of reasons for this situation, including socio-economic status, unemployment, lack of opportunity, and racism.

Racism exists within the entire justice system. It permeates the police, the courts, the jail system, and the parole system. To point to the attitude of juries alone would be too simplistic.

If there were any doubts about the extent of racism in this province, the trial of Dwayne Fleury tells the story. Fleury's lawyer asked jury members if they could set their prejudices aside to make an "honest verdict according to the evidence." To the surprise of the lawyer and the Court, a total of five of the 26 people who were selected freely admitted that they could not ignore their prejudice when considering the evidence.

I should point out that the admission from the five jurors is to their credit. It takes courage to admit to one's shortcomings, and hopefully this experience will cause them to do some soul-searching.

This is a shocking revelation, and it indicates that over the years, people affected by racism must have infiltrated countless juries. How many of our people have gone to jail because jury members were unable to perform their duty with fairness free from racism and prejudice?

Thanks now to Judge Barclay's courageous decision, we can look forward to an improved and fairer jury system in Saskatchewan.

What to Do with Young Offenders: A Serious and Complicated Issue

Serena Nicotine was a young offender who suffered from fetal alcohol syndrome.
She killed a community care worker in her foster home and will probably spend the
rest of her tragic life behind bars.

Tragic events in North Battleford have once again brought out calls for a
crackdown on young offenders. Two young offenders have been charged with
the brutal slaying of a North Battleford community worker stabbed to death in
her home.

This tragic act has led to a firestorm of protest from the public with political and community leaders calling for tough action from the justice system.
These ghoulish exploiters of human misery seem to surface every time a spectacular or tragic crime occurs. They either call for the return of the death penalty
or the abolishment of the Young Offenders Act.

I find these reactions disturbing in their vociferousness and racial over-
tones. Minorities and the poor will bear the brunt of the proposed changes.

The overall population of Saskatchewan has not grown, but our incarceration rate has continued to increase. Simply locking people up is not the
answer; if it were, then the United States would be the most law-abiding
country on earth since they lock up the highest percentage of their citizens of
any developed country.

Opponents to prison reform maintain that "bringing back the noose" and
repealing the Young Offenders Act will make the country a safer place. The
opposite is more likely, though. Young people going to jail are entering an
institute of higher learning and coming out as more sophisticated criminals.
Inmates belong to their own subculture, which only serves to further alienate
and isolate them from society.

In the United States, one third of Black men are either in jail, awaiting
trial, or on parole. The situation facing Indian men in Canada is similar.

Every so often, appeals are made to create curfews and loitering bylaws,
and to toughen up treatment of young offenders. These appeals also contain
the undertone that it's Indian kids who are loitering, staying out late, and
breaking the law. This is further strengthened because about 70% of young
offenders are Aboriginal. In the process, a group of people are penalized and
discriminated against because of their race and age.

What isn't mentioned is how many non-Indians break the law who have
parents who can afford lawyers and get acquittals or reduced sentences. Indian kids tend to come from poor families and can only afford to plead guilty
and throw themselves to the mercy of the courts. And there is an element of
racism within the justice system that compounds the issue.

A cartoon in *The New Yorker* once showed a lawyer and his client discussing a case in jail. The lawyer asks his client, "How much justice can you afford?"

Most young Indian people live in a world of poverty, alienation, and rapid social change. In the past generation, a migration to the cities has created a society where half our people now live off the reserve and most are concentrated in the province's inner cities.

Also, years of alcohol abuse are now being felt as a new generation of children are being diagnosed with fetal alcohol syndrome (FAS). Children who are born with this condition are unable to realize the consequences of their actions. They lack responsibility and sometimes show no remorse. It's hard to generalize about the disease, however, because the damage varies according to the amount of alcohol the mother may have consumed, and according to when in her pregnancy it was consumed.

This is a serious problem, but young people in jail are not properly diagnosed. Accurate statistics don't exist, either. Many people in jail are there because they suffer from permanent brain damage. FAS is a time bomb that has created far more "criminals" than the public realizes.

Crime bashing makes good short-term politics, and all the political parties in the province have tried it. Ultimately, though, the issue will have to be addressed rationally.

The justice system must look to alternatives to the jails. Jails only create a subculture that breeds more crime. Instead of calling for longer sentences, we must come to the conclusion that the justice system isn't working and start looking for civilized alternatives.

Give Olsen His Day in Court

When Clifford Olsen made his bid for early release, the public recoiled in horror. As it turned out, the hearing revealed him to be a weak individual with limited intelligence, not the monster that the public perceived. In his case, though, justice had to be seen to be done.

The opportunity for Clifford Olsen to apply for early release under the "faint hope" clause of the Criminal Code is an example of equal representation under the law no matter how terrible the crime. It is also an example of the worst-case scenario with one of Canada's infamous criminals receiving access to justice.

The key here is *access* to justice. Laws in this country exist for all Canadians, and we cannot allow the justice system to pick and choose people we would rather exclude, no matter how distasteful an individual case.

This may not be a popular position, particularly with the law-and-order right-wingers circling the case like so many buzzards preparing for a feeding frenzy. There are even calls from the public for the return of the death penalty, the lash, the cane, and so on.

These hysterics bother me because I know who will suffer the most. In the United States, the vast majority of death sentences have been carried out on Blacks, Hispanics, and poor whites. The dispossessed people of society are the targets of the public's demand for revenge.

The United States is one of the few remaining countries in the developed world to conduct state-sponsored murder. More civilized nations have long since abandoned this practice. Our experience in Canada has shown us that Donald Marshall, Guy Paul Morin, and David Milgaard could have been executed if we had and exercised capital punishment.

I fear our people will be the target of this country's demand for revenge if it ever returns to the practice of capital punishment. We see the disparity in our jails and fear that this will be the same if capital punishment returns.

And it is a fear rooted in the past reality. Following the North West Rebellion in the Battlefords and the Batoche areas, so many Indian and Métis "rebels" were rounded up that a new wing had to be added to the Stony Mountain Penitentiary.

Many of our great leaders died in prison of consumption and trauma. Those who survived returned to their communities sick and beaten, and many died prematurely. Only a few were able to overcome the pain of their experience.

Much has been made of the hanging of Louis Riel, but an even greater shame has been downplayed by history. Canada's largest public hanging occurred right here in Saskatchewan when eight Indian "rebels" were hung together at Fort Battleford. Their grave was unmarked and is situated behind Fort Battleford near the riverbank. Today, a monument has been placed there, and offerings are regularly left at the gravesite.

Students at the Battlefords Industrial School and members from Thunderchild and Moosomin reserves were brought in and forced to watch the hangings. The message was clear: "this is what we're capable of, so don't step out of line."

The French took up the cause of Louis Riel, but nobody took up the cause of the Indian "rebels." The rebellion and its aftermath were to set the stage for Indian-white relations for years to come. This is why I fear loose talk about the need to return to capital punishment and harsher treatment for criminals. It means that Indian people will suffer more.

The Reform Party, which seems to want the Department of Justice renamed the Department of Revenge, found a gold mine of hatred in the Clifford Olsen case. He represents society's worst nightmare, and Reform knows it.

At a time when crime rates are actually dropping in this country, the Reform Party sees law and order as an issue. We as First Nations people are assuming control over our lives and taking ownership of our healing process and justice. The Reform Party would send us back decades.

Olsen will get his day before the review board and will be refused. He will spend the rest of his life behind bars. His only recourse will be to continue to be a pain in the butt. Olsen has always been an enigma because at his original trial for the brutal murder of eight teenagers, he made a plea-bargain and a trial was never held. The media and the public could only imagine what kind of monster he must be.

I would suggest that Olsen have his hearings but nobody show up. He craves publicity and politicians, and the media are giving him what he wants. A justice system can't be built around one person. It must represent society.

Canada's Throwaway People

According to a study done by the Mennonite Central Committee, Saskatchewan's justice and corrections systems are in a state of crisis greater than any other provincial jurisdiction in the country.

According to the report, Canada (especially Saskatchewan) has a system of crime control that is "expensive, inefficient, and ineffective." Responding to the report, University of Saskatchewan law professor Tim Quigley stated that the one of the major reasons for the problem was the "over-jailing of Aboriginal people" in Saskatchewan.

For years we have lived with the knowledge that far too many of our people are in jail compared to the rest of the population. About 75% of inmates in provincial jails are Aboriginal, while 61% of inmates in federal institutions are Aboriginal. The number of Aboriginals in the provincial women's institution is much higher.

The problem is systemic. In other words, it is ingrained within the system that justice does not serve our people.

Because of the impoverishment of our people, they may not be able to raise the money, so they stay in jail. And our poverty comes into play again in court because we often can't afford the legal council that would prove our innocence or reduce our sentences. When an accused stands before a judge, he or she may be unemployed and therefore have a lesser chance of being granted bail. A century ago, individuals would be sent to a debtors' prison if they couldn't pay their bills. This sounds ridiculous today, but if you look at the sorry economic condition of people in jail, justice is still something that you have to be able to afford.

Does simply sending people to jail solve the crime problem? Apparently it doesn't, because crime continues in spite of stuffing the jails. In the United States, crime is on the increase even though Americans are the most jailed people in the industrialized world. Jails are really crime factories. Young people who are sent to jail learn quickly and become better car thieves and break-in artists. Jail also alienates individuals and creates a subclass that becomes a culture unto itself.

But for most people, crime and jail are not long-term careers. Most look forward to getting off the merry-go-round and finding some form of normal life. I recently spoke to a street worker from Winnipeg who told me that most of the young people he knows in gangs want nothing more than a job. That's not the image one gets from the media or politicians who vow to get tough on crime.

Also, most criminals come equipped with a drug or alcohol problem that is at the root of their criminal activity. Governments need to confront this rather than simply jail people in some hope that it will solve the problem. Addictions should be looked at as health and social issues rather than as crimes.

Most criminals are usually burnt out and tired of jail by the time they turn 35 and 40. But what becomes of them? They have few saleable skills, no work record, and little education. Jail has done nothing to provide them with an alternative. Some of the individuals I know who have misspent their youth are little more that stay-at-home drunks and welfare recipients. This seems to be a sorry end for someone, but it is our reality. We are not welcome in this country, and we can feel it. Government policies over the years have been to place Indians on the shelf in some hope that we'll just go away.

From the reserve system that warehoused us while the country was being developed, to the welfare system that kept us out of the job market, and to the jail system that has locked up our young men and women, we have been treated as a group with no place in this society. We are the country's throwaway people.

I had a friend who was an excellent artist and writer. The only problem was that the only time he could function was when he was in jail. He would send me his paintings and poems, and I would marvel at his talent and insight. But he had a drug and alcohol problem that consumed him. He died too young, a victim of his lifestyle.

One day I spoke a mutual friend who told me that "he was too smart to be an Indian." I thought about it and discovered what he meant. In this society, very little is expected of Indian people, and if we have the insight and intelligence to see that, then we can't exist. His life was an endless frustration of diminished expectations. He was too smart for his own good.

Revolutions are not created by oppression or hardship, no matter what the political scientists think. Revolutions are created by diminished expectations. We have generations of Aboriginal people who have lived lives far below their potential, and now our challenge is to build a society with no throwaway people.

A First Nations Justice System?

The recent revelation from the Royal Commission on Aboriginal Peoples that First Nations have the right to their own justice system is long overdue and simply states the obvious.

The existing justice system hasn't worked, and its sorry legacy has been lost generations of Indian men and women. A few years ago, our people jumped from boarding school to jail as simply as white people go from high school to a post-secondary institution. Even today we have more young people in jail than in all post-secondary education combined in Saskatchewan.

The Province has largely been responsible for the continuation of this sorry situation. Bigger and better jails are built; sentencing circles are appealed; and the Crown even resists something as fundamental as a jury of one's peers. The justice system has failed and become an enormous waste of money.

It's no wonder the First Nations are tired of tinkering with the system and they want to develop their own justice programs that work for the benefit of the community. Western justice systems are based on the principle of vengeance and punishment. Traditional First Nations justice is based on healing both the offender and the community. The reason for this is obvious when you look at the fact that First Nations communities were formed from family groups which stayed together for protection and for the common good. When one member of a community broke the law and was a threat to the rest of the community, steps were taken to deal with that person. It was necessary that the community find out what was wrong with both the offender and his or her community.

Today, our communities have grown considerably, but by and large, they remain a collection of the original families. The spirit of closeness remains. People must belong to the society in which they live. It sounds simple, but if you are shoved aside and see no opportunity, the descent into frustration and drug and alcohol abuse are inevitable.

The time has come to seize the opportunity to establish our own justice system. This is one of the basic reasons for the drive for self-government. When people have lost control over their lives, the result is an increase in social problems and conflict with the law. The first tentative steps are being taken in Saskatchewan with the development of First Nations Police services. The Police services will be far more than simply Indian police officers stuffed into RCMP uniforms. The policing services will be under the leadership of a community policing board, which will be the important link between the community and the police. When the community sees the police as an institution that is responsive to its needs, reporting to the community, and situated within the community, then change will come.

The idea of taking unilateral action is not new; it goes back to our relationship with Canada through the treaties. The treaties did not give us self-government, but they affirmed our right to govern ourselves. Why else would our Chiefs be recognized as the legitimate voice of the Indian Nations, and why else would their mark on the Treaty give Canada the right to assume control of the land?

The RCMP has always played a significant role in the First Nations community, especially in Saskatchewan. The force was originally placed here to protect the First Nations from settlers and whiskey traders. The treaties signed by our ancestors called for both sides to keep the peace and to obey the laws of the land.

This was the ideal, but the reality was an abuse of power by the government, and often the RCMP was used to enforce the Indian Act with its political and religious discrimination. The RCMP was viewed as an occupying army rather than a police force. But the tradition continued, and the chiefs insisted that the RCMP be present at Treaty Day and other significant events to illustrate the importance of the treaties. This tradition continues.

The treaties turned over vast tracts of land and opened Western Canada for settlement. The treaty promises to the First Nations were largely forgotten in the feeding frenzy over the newly acquired land. In fact, the treaties granted certain rights related to land, and to social and economic issues, but the really important issues remained silent.

Our language, culture, religion, and right to govern ourselves were never part of the treaties. They were silent and retained for future generations. Lawyers will say that if an item isn't dealt with in an agreement, then it is not a part of the agreement.

This fact becomes even clearer when one examines the recent land settlements in the Arctic, the Yukon, and British Columbia. The settlements go way beyond land, and include watered-down self-government, provincial jurisdiction, and any other points that may be construed as recognition of traditional rights.

Section 35 of the Charter of Rights and Freedoms recognizes treaty and Aboriginal rights, and that alone is enough to recognize self-government. It's clear that the governments want to submerge the First Nations even further.

One of the important items of the treaties was a commitment from the leaders of the day that they and generations to come would abide by the laws of the land and keep the peace. This promise is remembered each Treaty Day when the RCMP attends in their traditional red serge uniforms.

The numbered treaties on the Prairies represent the best arrangement the First Nations ever received, not for what we gained but for what we kept. Our culture, religion, and self-government are the sources of our strength. The job now is to implement the spirit and intent of these treaties.

First Nations justice is an area where the promises made by both sides must be kept for the good of all.

Sentencing Circles Stress Healing, Not Revenge

The appeal court decision to overturn the sentence imposed on Ivan Morin places the autonomy of sentencing circles in doubt. Morin had originally gone before a sentencing circle, where he received an 18-month prison sentence followed by 18 months of probation and alcohol rehabilitation, for his role in a botched robbery where he physically assaulted a female gas station attendant.

The circle consisted of members of the Métis community, the victim and her family, the Crown Prosecutor, and members of the City Police. The members of the Métis community and the victims, including both the young woman who was assaulted and the gas station owner, were satisfied that justice was served. The City Police and the Crown, however, wanted revenge.

Over the past 20 years, Ivan had cut quite a swath across Saskatoon and was well-known to the police. He has been described as a career criminal, but that implies some plan or organized approach. In fact, most of his offences were committed while under the influence of drugs, alcohol, or a combination of the two. That was his problem, and he had to address it. In the words of Nora Richie, a Métis elder and former court worker participating in the circle, "The system failed Ivan."

Because Ivan lost his mother at an early age and his father was in long-term care in Saskatoon, he was placed in a series of foster homes where he encountered physical and sexual abuse. He was just one more rootless Métis kid lost in the system. He got into trouble with the law and was sent to juvenile institutions. He did provincial time and later was sent to the penitentiary where he did his "graduate work."

His story is one that is all too common in Indian country. Our social services and corrections create more problems than they prevent, and the Department of Justice often looks more like the Department of Revenge.

Canada's system of British jurisprudence has been used for the past century, but it has not served our people well. The current justice system is seen as "outside justice." White lawyers argue in front of a white judge, and the accused are sentenced and taken into custody by white authorities. Placing Indian people in these roles will not answer the problem. It will only co-opt our people into a system that continually fails us.

In the traditional court system, the victim and the damage done is often lost in the legal proceedings. The law is applied and the next case is brought in. The role of the sentencing circle is to have the guilty party face the victim and realize the damage of his or her actions. In a traditional sentencing circle, all the affected parties are present if they want to be. The guilty party must show remorse and make a commitment to make amends. Historically, this method of justice had been practised in various forms by the First Nations.

The case must be brought before the community affected to heal the wounds created by the perpetrator. This is because the individuals had an effect on the guilty party and so the community as a whole must be included in the healing process.

It may sound corny, but this is how traditional First Nations justice worked. The First Nations community members are now taking back control of their lives, and the sentencing circle is becoming an important part of Aboriginal justice.

The justice system must step aside to let traditional justice work. We must build a new system based on healing, not revenge.

The Wagner Inquest: A Metaphor for What Is Wrong
with the Justice System

The month-long inquest into the death of Lawrence Wagner was a failure that only served to illustrate the two solitudes existing in Saskatoon and across Saskatchewan.

Lawrence Wagner was a student at the Saskatchewan Indian Federated College who fought mental illness and drug addiction. His frozen body was found outside Saskatoon two years ago. No cause of death was determined, and so an inquest was called.

Three members of the six-member jury were Aboriginal, and the Aboriginal community packed the courtroom as they came out in support of the family. For a while, it appeared that they might find out what happened to Lawrence Wagner two years ago. However, it became clear that the police were more interested in protecting themselves than in digging for the truth and upholding justice.

It almost became a crime in itself to come forward with evidence linking the police to the questionable death. As far as the Saskatoon Police Department was concerned, Mr. Wagner was the author of his own misfortune, and the police's lawyer attacked every witness who presented evidence placing the police in a questionable light.

Two Aboriginal women came forward during the inquest and stated that they had seen two police officers place Mr. Wagner in a police car. The women were from his reserve and had recognized him. One of the witnesses even stated that she could identify one of the officers. The lawyer for the police attacked the women over the fact that they had taken so long to come forward. They both replied that they feared what the police would do to them. One of the women stated that she didn't want to end up like Darryl Knight. The women's fear of testifying is a telling and damning indictment of Native-police relations in Saskatoon.

Police violence isn't unknown among our people. In fact, it came as no surprise that police were dumping our people at the edge of town. It's been going on for years. The police even have a name for it. They refer to it as a "starlight tour."

Violence in the lockup isn't a deep mystery either: "They take a phone book, hold it against your ribs, and pound away," a friend of mine once told me.

Another witness, Dwaine Sutherland, went to the police and told them that he saw Wagner being placed in a police car. The investigating RCMP told him to take a polygraph (lie detector), but warned him that if he failed, he could receive a five-year jail sentence. Naturally, Sutherland refused because of his fear of a negative reading due to nervousness or some error in the machine that was beyond his control. However, none of the police interviewed or who gave evidence was subject to a polygraph test. This double standard brings into question the appropriateness of police investigating the police. It would be like the infamous Enron Corporation investigating itself.

Earlier this year, the inquest into the death of Rodney Naistus was inconclusive. Mr. Naistus was found frozen at the edge of the city under similar circumstances. The previous case of Darryl Knight reinforces this issue. Mr. Knight charged that the police had left him outside of the city to walk home. Fortunately, he was able to get inside the power station to call a cab. The temperature that night was colder than -20. Two police officers were charged, found guilty, and sentenced to jail.

The Federation of Saskatchewan Indian Nations accused the Saskatoon City Police of botching the investigation from the beginning. The scene where Wagner's body was discovered wasn't treated as a crime scene, and the police walked and drove all over the area, erasing any tracks or evidence. As far as they were concerned, it was the victim's own fault, and that was it. Furthermore, they lost Wagner's clothing and were unable to provide his socks, which would have indicated the wear as a result of walking six kilometers. No one reported the wear of the socks, and a civilian witness reported seeing a boot-mark on Wagner's back.

This whole string of events has left the Aboriginal community more cynical of the justice system and feeling more isolated. Race relations between the Saskatoon City Police and the Aboriginal community are at an all-time low and will remain that way for some time to come.

The process to determine the cause of death for Mr. Wagner has failed, and it's up to the police to reopen and solve the case. FSIN Senator Dave Ahenakew stated that this has been a destructive process because the truth was stopped from coming out.

One circumstance has improved, though: since the issue became public and the police have been scrutinized, no more bodies have been discovered at the edge of town.

Courts Push Social Change

Canadian courts are increasingly taking a leadership role in the absence of social and moral leadership from the federal and provincial governments. Years of deficit-cutting and a preoccupation with the bottom line have left a moral vacuum in all levels of government.

A recent court decision points out that the role of addressing these issues has now shifted to the courts.

In Saskatoon, Judge Mary Ellen Turpel-Lafond challenged the cruel treatment of young offenders at Kilburn Hall. She presented a 42-page ruling that released the accused and shifted the burden of guilt to the institution. For years, Kilburn Hall has been the entry point to a life of hardship and crime for many of our young people. Its results are at best dubious, and its tactics are like something out of the Spanish Inquisition. It and similar institutions have replaced the boarding schools as the primary method of institutionalizing our young people.

An elder once pointed out to me that the root of our problem is that we have lost control of our lives. He pointed out the way the boarding schools were run; the oppressiveness of the Indian Act; the draconian funding agreements; and how our young people are sent off to jails and youth detention with no input from the community. He saw what has continued to grow in spite of all the talk of self-government. No matter how we look at it, or how we analyze the social problems, it all boils down to the point that we have lost control of our lives.

The Supreme Court also recognized the problem when they pointed out the appalling numbers of Aboriginal people in Canada's jails. Calling it a "national disgrace," the Court urged judges to seek alternatives to incarceration. The Court also stated that "various inquiries in past years have concluded that the justice system is failing Aboriginals on a crushing scale."

I prefer to think that Canadian society as a whole has failed Aboriginals on "a crushing scale."

A young Indian man today has a better chance of going to jail than graduating from high school. That man is 25 times more likely to end up in jail than a non-Native man is. A Treaty Indian woman is 131 times more likely to go to jail than a non-Native woman. In Saskatchewan, Treaty Indians are ten percent of the population, but we make up 55 % of provincial jail admissions.

On every social indicator of health, wealth, and quality of life, we occupy the bottom rung.

One area where research needs to be done is in breaking down the statistics to determine the composition of the jail population. Some First Nations have low rates of people in jail while others have much higher rates. What are the differences between these communities? Was the boarding school impact greater on reserves than those that had day schools? Also, what about on-reserve versus off-reserve populations? Many First Nations are establishing wellness programs, but with the majority of our people living in the cities, new areas of concern are opening up.

The urban areas are now the battlegrounds for equality. One may not see it on the surface, but the high crime rate (including car theft, break-and-enters, robberies, vandalism, and other property crimes)is a sign of people taking action toward economic equality. When you are poor, and the good life is continually shoved in your face yet denied to you, crime becomes an alternative.

It isn't right, but it's the reality.

There is a crying need for urban wellness programs to address some of these issues, create jobs, and end the welfare cycle that places our young people in institutions. We need to create our own system of corrections that places offenders back into the community to be confronted with the pain and harm they caused. The issues of drugs and prostitution must be addressed realistically. These are crimes against our people, not real estate issues.

Most importantly, though, our people must take the lead. In the process, they can once again take control their lives.

Gang Activity New and Threatening

Aboriginal gang activity is on the upswing across Western Canada. It has its roots in various places, but to simply dismiss gang activity as racial and widespread is a mistake.

First of all, police will tell you that a small amount of people create a large amount of criminal activity, and crime creates equal opportunity when it comes to race. I once spoke to a police officer in Winnipeg who told me that in spite of the news reports and crime statistics, a small percentage of the Aboriginal community is actually involved in gang activity.

This also appears to be the case in Saskatoon and Regina. When you see a group of Aboriginal kids walking down the streets that's probably what it is, just a group. Indian people tend to be gregarious and often young people will hang out together for protection. This is not a gang.

Real gang activity is much more sinister. Gangs are a product of the prison system, the social welfare system, and other agencies that have been put in place to control the Aboriginal population. If you want to see the reasons for increasing gang activity, just look to the failure of the country's treatment of our people.

The boarding school system, the "big scoop" of the 1960s and '70s, and years of failed welfare policies have all contributed to the situation we have today. You can't just warehouse a people for generations and not expect to have some kind of backlash.

One of the greatest evils brought against us was the removal of the control over our lives. Indian agents, social workers, and bureaucrats always knew what was best for us, and the result was that our people lost control. When you look at the issues that face us as a people, the underlying factor is that we don't have control over our lives. It's only natural that our people have lost respect for the law, civil authority, and, worst of all, themselves.

And the government only made a bad situation worse. Today's gang activity began in Winnipeg and moved into the jails and penitentiaries. In their wisdom, corrections officials decided that the gangs should be broken up, and members were sent to facilities across the West. This only resulted in a recruiting bonanza for the gangs. Gang membership and activity blossomed as a result. It was a stupid move and one that we all will pay for.

Today, Aboriginal gangs are found in most western cities and on some First Nations. They have become a danger to Aboriginal people as well as to the general community. Gang violence is much more likely to impact on Aboriginal people than the general community. Therefore, as Aboriginal people, we see the urgency to limit gang activity.

Gang activity is, by and large, a male thing and again the reasons are found within our society. Aboriginal women have a greater chance of succeeding than Aboriginal men. The majority of graduates from university are women. Many more Aboriginal men have fallen through the cracks and face years of unemployment, drug addiction, and petty crime. This is a natural breeding place for gang activity. Gang power brings acceptance and a position that they don't have otherwise. In a gang, they have protection.

The federal government is also at fault for its treatment of off-reserve Indian people. The Department of Indian Affairs has washed its hands when it comes to Indian people who don't live on reserves. They have followed that practice for years, and the results of that neglect are what we see today.

The problems have been left for local authorities and police forces. This places a strain on the cities' resources, with the resulting incriminations toward the Aboriginal community. These incriminations come despite the fact that today we have many Aboriginal people who own property in the cities and are an important part of the tax base.

Recently, the Supreme Court ruled in the Corbiere case that off-reserve Indian people have the right to participate in elections on their First Nation. Legal opinion is that if the First Nation has a responsibility toward its off-reserve people, then it would follow that the federal government also has a responsibility. The Department of Indian Affairs has avoided dealing with this issue and continues to ignore the Supreme Court ruling.

Off-reserve Indians need recognition of their treaty rights. There should be off-reserve institutions and service centres to address some of the serious issues. Our tribal councils need the support to work with the people in the cities. If these steps aren't taken, the result will be that conditions will continue to deteriorate and symptoms such as gang activity will grow.

We must remember that crime, drug addiction, and gang activity are symptoms of poverty, loss of control, and unemployment, to name a few underlying factors. If we only react to the symptoms and ignore the root causes, we will continue to watch our youth turn to gangs for support and protection.

Leonard Pelletier: A Lifetime Behind Bars

Leonard Pelletier has spent over 30 years in jail for a crime even the United States government admits they can't solve.

Leonard Pelletier has been called the "Indian Nelson Mandela," or, as Amnesty International would agree, a political prisoner.

The story begins back on June 26, 1975, when the FBI was searching for stolen goods on the Pine Ridge Reservation. They pulled over a pickup truck and shots were fired. The incident quickly escalated into a full-scale firefight, with 30 or so Indian people going against 50 or so FBI agents. In the ensuing melee, one Indian activist and two FBI agents were killed.

The FBI wanted someone to pay. Two Indians were charged, but the jury acquitted them on the grounds of self-defense. The FBI then turned to Pelletier because he was identified as one of the leaders of the American Indian Movement (AIM). AIM had been a pain-in-the-butt for the American government. AIM participated in the standoff at Wounded Knee and other demonstrations. The movement was gathering support, and officials on both sides of the border were concerned.

After Pelletier was charged, he fled to Canada but was later extradited based on evidence that has since been proven to be fabricated. This issue has been presented to a series of federal governments, but Canada has yet to act. Part of the FBI evidence is an affidavit sworn by a woman alleging that she was Pelletier's girlfriend. As it turned out, this woman was mentally incompetent, never met Pelletier, and wasn't at the reservation on the day of the incident. Nevertheless, the FBI entered her statement as part of the extradition evidence, and it was accepted. The Canadian government dropped the ball in this case, but 25 years later, it still won't admit to it.

In the end, Pelletier was sentenced to two consecutive life terms, even though the FBI admitted they had no idea who pulled the trigger. Pelletier was found guilty of aiding and abetting; he was basically found guilty of being at the wrong place at the wrong time.

Pelletier now sits in prison at Leavenworth, Kansas. He is scheduled for release in 2040 at age 97. He lives in constant pain with a form of lockjaw that only allows him to open his mouth about half an inch. The prison doctor has performed two botched operations and a specialist from the Mayo Clinic has volunteered to help, but the prison won't allow it. There is no end to the pettiness and cruelty of this institution.

While in prison, Pelletier has not been idle, and he continues to work with his people. He sponsors an annual Christmas drive to collect toys for children on the Pine Ridge Reservation. He has established a scholarship and training program for Native American youth. He has sponsored children in El Salvador and Guatemala. He has served on the advisory board of the Rosenberg Fund for Children. He has also developed his skills as a talented artist and writer.

He is seen as a leader with a "firm commitment to humanitarian concerns." Pelletier is described as a model prisoner and no threat to society, and he has received a number of human rights awards.

For years, a loyal group of supporters has rallied around him, demanding his release. He has been visited by world leaders, such as delegates from the European Parliament, and Danielle Mitterrand, wife of the former French President. For a while, his case was also picked up as a propaganda project by the former Soviet Union. In the United States, this was the kiss of death during the Cold War. Pelletier was used as a pawn by both sides.

Mainstream political organizations shunned the Pelletier case. At the time, the political organizations were conservative and feared the tactics of AIM. Leaders worried that AIM would spread and be a threat to their policies and tactics.

It wasn't until last summer when the Assembly of First Nations and the National Congress of American Indians met in Vancouver and passed a resolution in support of Pelletier's release. On January 21st, top officials from the two organizations, including AFN Chief Phil Fontaine, met with Pelletier at Leavenworth. The two organizations have also approached both President Clinton and Attorney General Janet Reno, asking them to intervene and release Pelletier from prison.

Pelletier has been denied parole. A petition for clemency was presented to the Department of Justice, but it has gone unanswered for five and a half years. Pelletier's health continues to deteriorate.

Clearly, this is a case of political persecution. Governments on both sides of the border have sought out Indian leaders and militants for prosecution and persecution. The time has come to move on and leave the animosity of the past behind. A good way to start is by releasing Leonard Pelletier.

Leonard Pelletier is now 59 and has been in jail for 28 years. The American government continues its vendetta against Pelletier, refusing his application for parole even though he is no threat to the community, and even though the courts have ruled that the original trial was flawed.

Chapter 9

Indian Society: Led by Men,
Driven by Women

Education Is Liberating Indian Women

The other day I bumped into an old friend, and at first I didn't recognize her. She looked ten years younger, and she was self-confident and happy.

The last time I saw her, she was a single parent with limited skills, limited horizons, she drank too much, and she had bad luck with men.

So what happened?

"Well..." She said, "the first thing I did was kick that bum out of my life." The second thing she did was enroll in university and work on her Bachelor of Education degree. She was in her final year, and she planned to be teaching the following year.

This story illustrates what's happening out there in Indian country. Indian women are attending university in record numbers, and they are serious about their futures. Indian society has been male-dominated for years. For example, there are 72 Chiefs in Saskatchewan, but only three of them are women. However, while Indian politics is led by men, it is driven by women.

Women have traditionally been the leaders in fields such as education, health, and social conditions. When the fight was on for Indian control of education in the late 1970s, it was the women who ran the school committees and fought to control their children's education. Indian Affairs thought the school committees would serve as a group of ladies who would make lunches and little else. The women had other ideas, though, and they refused to settle for the crumbs; they instead went after the whole bakery. Today, there are 65 Indian-controlled schools in Saskatchewan, and the staff and school committees are mostly made up of women.

Two-thirds of Aboriginal students in university are women, and three quarters of university graduates are women. The group that fought the hardest is now reaping the benefits.

The federal government is obligated under the terms of the treaties to provide financial support to Indians who seek higher education. This support is by no means a gravy train; welfare, for example, can pay more. However, the money still opens avenues of opportunity that would otherwise not be available. Now a single mother doesn't have to settle for a dead-end existence on welfare. She can attend university and break out of the welfare trap. It is said that a human mind is an awful thing to waste, but all too often, single Indian mothers find themselves on the scrap heap.

The women attending university are mature, articulate, and committed to a better life. Many are former employees of the Federation of Saskatchewan Indian Nations, tribal councils, and Band offices. In these roles, they have developed good research and study habits.

This is the quiet revolution taking place in Indian country. The new professional class (including teachers, social workers, and lawyers) is mostly women.

Indian society wasn't always male-dominated. In the old days, there was a division of labour, and the women had their own societies that practiced healing of both the spirit and the body.

The sexism came from the boarding school system. The missionaries imported their Victorian attitudes and inflicted them on the students. The school policies were very clear: the girls would be trained as domestics who would make good wives, and the boys would be trained as farmers so they could operate a small farm on the reserve or work for a white farmer. The children were not even allowed to mingle with the opposite sex; the schools were built with a girls' side and a boys' side. The missionaries' hang-ups have now become a part of our contemporary culture.

Ironically, because of the large families and seasonal economies like trapping, the boys would have to leave school to work at home. They were often taken out of school at an early age. The girls, on the other hand, stayed in school longer and gained a more academic education. As a result, women continue to place a much greater emphasis on education than men.

The changes taking place in First Nations society are profound. The growth in awareness and the rising education levels of Indian women, coupled with migration to the cities, are creating a new Indian society that will be the future driving force of the Indian Nation.

Update: My friend taught school for a few years before returning to university and getting her Master's degree. She continues to teach.

Indian Women Bear Brunt of the Problems

A Regina woman was recently acquitted of killing her abusive husband. Her lawyer, Don Worme, argued that she was a victim of battered woman syndrome. At the same time, a young, pregnant Manitoba woman died in a police cell after being beaten by her husband. These stories are tragic and all-too-common in Indian country.

Many Indian women are forced to live in conditions of poverty and violence that would shock most Canadians.

Indian women bear the brunt of our social dysfunction. Often, they must deal with the suicides of their children, drug and alcohol abuse in the home, and physical and mental abuse from their partners.

I'm not painting a pretty picture, but it must be shown. Ovide Mercredi, the National Chief of the Assembly of First Nations, recently went public in declaring that more money must be made available to address our social problems. Demanding more money is an easy way for the politicians to go on the record and to show that they've expressed concern. Ovide is a political leader, and it's not good politics to criticize one's people.

While more money would be welcomed, it would only be a part of the solution. The answer lies in the hearts and minds of our people. Many of our leaders would prefer to ignore the social problems, hoping that they will simply go away. But we need a real change in attitude when it comes to family violence and other social issues.

People blame poverty, racism, and boarding schools for our situation. Someone once told me that alcohol was the problem. But there are plenty of examples of guys who have quit drinking yet continue to abuse their wives. Another theory is that since Indian men don't have much status or power, they take it out on their wives. Excuses are not good enough. A man makes the choice to abuse his partner. It's a conscious act.

It's easy to look around for excuses and reasons, but we ultimately have to look within ourselves for the solutions.

The healing process is underway in a number of communities and the decline of alcoholism is a good example. Alcoholics Anonymous groups function on most reserves without any funding. Public drunkenness is frowned upon, and people become ashamed of their behaviour when faced with peer pressure.

While money may have been spent for alcohol rehabilitation and other programs, the fact remains that shifting attitudes have forced the biggest change.

In the past several years, a number of men and wellness conferences have been held in both Canada and the United States; two held in Saskatoon have been well attended.

Many Indian men are starting to help each other and face the fact that they need help. This is what we must do to address spousal abuse. Peer pressure must be used to influence those who abuse their partners. Wives are not property, and if a woman is in danger, the home is not a castle. There is no humour in wife-beating jokes, either. We have to break down the old attitudes.

Self-government means that we are in charge of our destiny and that includes shedding all the baggage that we would rather forget about. And one of the first steps toward taking control must be the elimination of family violence. Otherwise, self-government will be meaningless.

Women Deserve More Recognition

The horrible and unbelievable story coming out of Port Coquitlam, British Columbia, is turning our attentions to the most vulnerable members of Canadian society.

A search for many of the 50 women who disappeared from Vancouver's downtown eastside since 1984 is being concentrated on a junk-strewn pig farm located up the valley at Port Coquitlam. Many of the women who went missing are Aboriginal.

This once again brings attention to the high cost Aboriginal women in particular pay when they fall into a life of drugs and sexual exploitation.

For the past 17 years, women have gone missing from Vancouver's downtown eastside. This area is notorious for being inhabited by prostitutes, heroin addicts, and other drug addicts. At first, the disappearances were viewed as another drug addict moving away or dying as a "Jane Doe." It took until August of 2001 and close to 50 missing women before the Vancouver City Police began to suspect that a serial killer might be preying on prostitutes.

This raises the question that is so often brought up: what if these had been women from another segment of society, such as middle-class women from North Vancouver or Point Grey? There would have been a general alarm and no expense would have been spared in finding the murderer. But the deaths of poor people, drug addicts, and Aboriginal women don't elicit the same visceral and urgent response.

Across British Columbia and Western Canada, Aboriginal communities are coming to grips with the fact that one of their friends or relations is dead and lost in B.C.'s Lower Mainland. For years they have been searching for their loved ones, and now the tragic reality is sinking in.

Aboriginal women who end up on the street generally don't do it by choice. In many cases, their home life was unbearable, or they suffered the effects of sexual abuse brought on by a dysfunctional society. Some have been ravaged by the pain and hurt of the welfare system, boarding schools, or years of grinding poverty. Often, moving to the street appears to be an escape from the pain in their lives. They see it as the only viable option.

But before we condemn what is happening on the West Coast, we should look in our own back yard. We have our own drug and prostitution problems in Saskatchewan, and Saskatoon had a serial killer who would be better known if he had preyed on white women. John Martin Crawford is serving a life term because he preyed on Aboriginal women. He killed four that we know of.

His victims must not be forgotten. They include Mary Jane Serloin from the Peigan First Nation in Southern Alberta, Shelly Napope from One Arrow, Calinda Waterhen from Waterhen, and Eva Taysup from Yellow Quill. Another woman, Janet Sylvestre, was killed at the same time, but no charges were ever laid for her death. Crawford preyed on Indian women because he was a loser, and because he felt they were cheap, expendable, and lower on the social order than him.

Today, the deaths of the four women haunt the Aboriginal community in Saskatoon and Regina. The streets are a dangerous place to be, and if it isn't white men abusing Indian women, then it is Indian men exploiting Indian women as pimps and drug dealers, or both. Indian women are exploited on both sides, and, in the end, escape is almost impossible. Some new groups and events are attempting to turn the situation around.

A self-help group has been formed across the country with a chapter in Saskatoon. The group is called Sexually Exploited Youth Speak Out (SEYSO). SEYSO is led by former street kids and including those who might still be working in the sex trade or who are at risk for entering the sex trade.

Sara Ninnie, a former street kid herself, heads up SEYSO. "The group meets each other on their own terms," she told me. "We meet once a week and be supportive of each other. We do peer-counselling and do positive things that they never do. For one day a week, they can forget what they're going through."

The group has received some funding from the National Aboriginal Healing Foundation and will be able to hire several full-time workers and a counselor.

This is one example of Aboriginal people helping each other to heal. We need more of these programs, and we need more young people like Sara who will work with their people to cure this horrible part of our history. Otherwise, we will have more death and violence, and more Aboriginal women will go missing or return home in coffins.

It has become an annual tradition in Saskatoon to hold a march in honour of the women who have gone missing or who have been killed in the sex trade. One of the ceremonies includes the reading of a list of names of killed or missing young women. The reading of the list is haunting and makes the missing women a reality. These are real people who had friends and family who loved them.

To the general public, street life and prostitution is a lifestyle that most people choose to ignore or can't understand. For us, it is a part of the sad reality of being Aboriginal in Canada. Those women who went missing are our relatives.

Their fate is the sad result of the legacy of racism, boarding schools, and poverty. Indian women can be beaten up and killed with very little public outcry. Somehow, they are not important.

This was made very clear a few years ago when the serial killer John Crawford killed three women in Saskatoon and one in Lethbridge, Alberta. The women were Aboriginal, and Crawford was tried and given a life sentence with little fanfare. At the same time, Paul Bernardo was being tried for the killing of two young women in Ontario. The Bernardo case grabbed national headlines but Crawford's trial received little press outside the province. Today, Bernardo's name is a household word but Crawford's is forgotten. It's a sad testament to the small value society places on Aboriginal women.

Young Indian women continue to suffer and die on the mean streets of Saskatchewan's cities. When you see a young woman on the streets, she represents only part of the picture. Behind her are the pimps and hangers-on who are eager to take the money she earns and use it for drugs. There is also a large group of johns who want younger and younger Indian girls. It's a vicious circle of supply and demand economics. The demand is for drugs and sex, and the supply is Indian girls.

The source of the problem lies mainly with men, both white and Aboriginal, who continue to perpetuate this soul-destroying lifestyle.

Over the course of my work as a journalist, I have done a number of stories related to prostitution and missing women. I have interviewed a number of former prostitutes, and I have been struck by the lifestyle of drugs and violence. Women have told me how they jumped from speeding cars, how they were taken out of town and beaten and raped, and how they lived in constant fear for their lives.

It's not the romanticized life that is portrayed in movies like *Pretty Woman*; it's a life of pain and suffering. One young woman told me that she was always cold and hungry, and the money she earned was mostly spent by other people. She, too, faced the constant threat of violence from the johns.

So what are the possible solutions to this social and personal tragedy?

First, it should be socially and criminally repugnant to try to procure sex from underage girls. I agree that the courts should seize vehicles, and impose heavy fines and jail sentences. Procuring or attempting to procure sex from a child is a serious offence, and it should be treated as such.

Second, pimps should be hunted down and charged with serious consequences for their actions. Sexually exploiting children and young women is a crime against humanity, and it should be treated as such. When I see Indian men involved in the sex trade as pimps, it disgusts me. I think back to our ancestors who were warriors and protectors of the women and children. They were known as the worthy men. Today, they are a large part of the problem. They are no longer warriors and men; they are leeches and weaklings.

The police and courts are addressing the first two issues and making it harder for people to profit from or participate in the sex trade. More should be done, but the law enforcement agencies are on the right track.

Third, I think that part of the solution lies in the legalization and regulation of the sex trade. Sex between consenting adults is not against the law, but communicating for the purposes of obtaining sex through a commercial transaction is against the law. However, having sex with a minor is child sexual abuse and must be treated seriously.

With legalization, the sex trade could be regulated and sexually transmitted diseases could be better controlled. Also, women wouldn't be treated as criminals, and they could rely on the police for protection. The key here is that the women would be adults over the age of 21. Sex trade workers under the age of 21 should be placed in custody and given opportunities for drug rehabilitation and counseling. Prostitutes should be treated as victims, not criminals. As it stands now, prostitutes operate outside the law, and so see the police as enemies, not friends.

Society needs to take a serious look at prostitution and what can be done to protect women and remove drug culture. Today, legislators and law enforcement agencies are treating prostitution as a crime, and the public is ignoring the problem.

Black Elk, an elder and spiritual leader, recognized the strength of women, saying, "When the women are defeated, then we as a nation are truly defeated."

We don't need any more days of mourning. We don't need parents and families looking for their children, or identifying their bodies in the morgue. We need a society that is safe for women and children, and we need to take back our streets and neighbourhoods.

Suffer Little Children

The sight of a pretty little Indian girl standing on a street corner prostituting herself is one of the saddest sights for me. It breaks my heart. As a father of a young daughter, I say, "There but for the grace of God....."

But this young girl, who is the object of my pain, is also the target of disgust, loathing, and lust. She ceases to be human. She is the cause for dropping real estate values, crime in the streets, traffic jams, and other social ills, real or imagined.

But her presence on that street corner is part of the story. The rest of the story most people haven't heard or don't want to hear because it would complicate their simplistic view.

Child prostitution is one of the worst crimes against children in any society. It is soul-destroying and a serious form of child abuse. A child prostitute is defined as a prostitute younger than 19, and it is estimated that 80% of the province's children in the sex trade are Aboriginal. This is a serious situation, and it reflects our status within society.

A notice on the Internet was brought to my attention recently. It stated that one didn't have to go to Thailand for "little brown girls," but instead they could be found in Saskatoon. This bone-chilling remark makes it clear that our province must not become a haven for sex tourists, but instead we must take serious steps to charge the johns, seize their vehicles, level serious fines, and send them to jail.

Right now, the majority of customers are white males who see our people as cheap and subhuman. Somehow, our young girls are less than important and can be abused with impunity.

The presence of any young girl on the street didn't happen overnight. Her story is likely one of family violence, sexual abuse, racial hatred, self-loathing and a life on the street that is better than her home life. She probably has a history of youth detention, drug abuse, and foster care. Men are the clients and the pimps who exploit her to feed their egos and their drug addictions.

And this is not unique to Saskatchewan or Canada. Racial minorities occupying society's bottom rungs make up a disproportionate number of people in the sex trade. In the United States, it's the Afro-Americans; in New Zealand, it's the Maoris; in Australia, it's the Aboriginal people, and so on. The reasons for this are many and varied, but they go back to lack of opportunity, social and economic conditions, racism, and colonialism. Demonizing and dehumanizing these people makes it easier to view them as a problem that should be eliminated, rather than as people who need help.

Many young people end up on the streets because of a poor home environment with violence, overcrowding, and a history of sexual abuse. They end up on the streets in search of a new family and a measure of control over their lives. What they find is much different. They are preyed upon by pimps and are subject to violence and even death at the hands of the johns. And drug addiction and prostitution go hand-in-hand.

Over the years, I have interviewed a number of prostitutes and street people for my documentaries. I have been told that the drug addiction became the only way they had to cover up the pain and guilt they felt. The average sex trade worker is not the "happy hooker," but a person in deep pain whose best friend is a needle. One commonality with the women was the deep anger they had for society, their families, and themselves. After they got off the street, they still had to deal with the pain and anger which hung around for years.

AIDS and other sexually transmitted diseases are a constant threat for people in the sex trade, and diseases such as hepatitis C are transmitted by intravenous drug use. Most drug addicts end up with hepatitis C through the sharing of needles.

I have also interviewed a number of drug addicts in my work, and I've been struck by the serious damage addictions cause. After an addict quits drugs, his or her life can be a constant struggle for years. Some have to take a shot of methadone every day to combat their heroin addiction, and this may go on for years.

Support services, such as outreach vans and street workers, provide controversial needle exchanges and condoms. For the good of society, we must fight AIDS, hepatitis C, and other diseases. Prostitution does not have to carry a death sentence.

There is a crying need for safe houses where men and women can come to seek help and counselling. They need a place where they can make some choices with proper information.

Over the years, I have known a number of former prostitutes and drug addicts. They all told me that the decision for them to change their lives came from someone who believed in them and gave them unconditional love and understanding. All their lives they had been told that they were no good and they believed it. Calling them down or harassing them is exactly the wrong thing to do; this only strengthens their resolve that they are worthless.

When your self esteem is at rock bottom, it's easy to become addicted to drugs and then turn to prostitution to feed that addiction. And it's not an easy habit to break; drug addicts face years of struggle and the constant fear of relapse. Their health is ruined with AIDS or Hep C. They must also change their lifestyle and move away from their old friends. The alternative is continued drug addiction or the move to something else, like alcohol.

I once asked a friend what happens to old drug addicts. He replied that the ones who don't die or end up in jail become old burnouts and stay-at-home drunks. Their lives are effectively ruined. Drug addiction is easy to get into, but it is hell to live with or overcome.

There is no easy solution or magic wand for prostitution and drug addiction. Moving the stroll to a different part of town or placing everyone in jail will not address the roots of the problem. Healthy living begins in the home, and it begins with love and caring. We were not put on this earth to suffer this way.

Alpha Lafond Worked for Her Family and Her Community

Back in 1972, when I first began working for the Federation of Saskatchewan Indians, I was in charge of the Federation's monthly newsmagazine *The Saskatchewan Indian*. It was an exciting time, the Federation was just beginning to grow, and we were involved in grassroots organizing and institutional development.

At the time, the Federation had taken over the community development program from Indian Affairs and had established Indian workers province-wide. The community development worker for Wichiken and Chitick Lake was an "older woman" (to me, anyway) named Alpha Lafond.

Alpha recently passed away after a lifetime of good works in support of her family, her community, and the First Nations of Saskatchewan.

My first impression of Alpha was that she was a tireless community development worker and a constant advocate for the First Nations she represented. This was back at a time when Indian women were supposed to play a supporting role and let the men do the "serious" work.

Alpha was born Alphonsine Venne. She attended Saint Michael's student residence and later married Albert Lafond, a veteran from the Second World War. My late Aunt Jean Goodwill was her maid of honour. Alpha was from the generation that witnessed the whole sweep of our history in her lifetime. She was a part of the five generations that went from the settlement on reserves to the present day. Her grandparents, George Greyeyes and Sarah Arcand, were among the first students at St. Michael's School at Duck Lake.

Alpha grew up in a world where our people lived independently, used horses for transportation, grew their own gardens, gathered berries, and hunted for food. People lived in log houses with no electricity or running water. It was a hard life, but in many ways it was also a good life. While child and infant mortality rates were high, and while the simplest tasks required a lot of work, our people were more independent and the language and culture were strong.

Alpha Lafond was a political pioneer. In 1958, she was the first Saskatchewan Indian woman to be a band councilor; in 1960, she was the first Saskatchewan woman to be a Chief; and in the 1980s, she was the first woman to be appointed a senator with the Federation of Saskatchewan Indian Nations. She was also appointed to the position of Chair of the Senate.

In the late 1970s, the FSIN and the Province of Saskatchewan established the Indian Justice of the Peace program. Alpha became one of the JPs and took on her new role with characteristic enthusiasm and commitment. It was a hard job, but once again, she was a pioneer.

Alpha's son George told me that she never stopped learning and growing. When she was in her late 50s, she took a university commerce course because it would help her in her work. Later, she would buy a computer, and she was on the internet and had e-mail.

While Alpha was well-regarded on the provincial stage, it was at the community level where she put a lot of her energy. She was a tireless worker for community projects, such as hockey and ball tournaments. She felt that by organizing community sports, she was helping the whole community, especially the young people. In the 1980s, Muskeg Lake hosted the Saskatchewan Indian Summer Games, and Alpha was one of the driving forces that made it happen.

Alpha remained a devout Catholic throughout her life. Each year, she would take the family to the pilgrimage at St. Laurent. George Lafond told me, "We would prepare for days, and sometimes we worried that our old car wouldn't get us there."

At her funeral, former FSIN Chief David Ahenakew spoke, praising Alpha's good works to her community and for the people of Saskatchewan. "She never let us down," he told the large crowd. Over the years, they had worked together, and the respect they had for each other was obvious.

Alpha was a rare and valuable leader for all of her people. In the end, mourners from across the province gathered for her funeral. She was loved by her community, but she was shared by the whole province.

Mrs. Pelly Was a Storyteller

Mrs. Pauline Pelly was from the Cote Reserve north of the town of Kamsack, and she was known across Saskatchewan for her work in education and for her political activism. But she was also known as a wonderful storyteller. One of Mrs. Pelly's favourite stories was of a frightening incident that actually happened to her.

It was the fall of the year. The snow had not yet come. The wind howled in the trees and rattled the windows of her house. It was the time of year when the life of summer slips away to be followed of by the long nights of winter. It was a time when the spirits walk the earth.

When she lived on the reserve, Mrs. Pelly and her family lived alone in the country. From time to time, she would drive into town. One night, she jumped into her car to head to town. Throughout this particular week, though, she had been experiencing a sense of foreboding that something bad was about to happen. She headed off into the night, deeply troubled.

She hadn't driven far when she heard the sound of someone breathing in the back seat. She felt the hair rise on the back of her neck. She felt shivers down her back. She glanced in the rear-view mirror and noticed something sitting in the back seat. She looked up again, and her blood ran cold: there was the outline of an evil spirit. It was a black shape of a person sitting in the back seat. In fact, it appeared to be the devil himself.

It was dark, so none of his features could be seen, but on the top of his head was the clear outline of two horns. At first, she couldn't speak. Her mouth was dry, and her mind was racing. She drove quietly in the darkness.

Finally, she summoned up her courage to ask, "Who are you? What do you want?"

There was no reply. The evil creature sat quietly in the back seat. There was no sound except for breathing, and the creature's breath was foul-smelling.

Now, she knew what was going to happen: the devil had come for her, and she was going to die. This was it. It was the end of her life. Again, she asked the devil what he wanted. Again, there was no reply. The creature just sat there in terrible silence. She knew what he wanted. He wanted her.

So she began to confess her sins. She went back as far as she could remember. She even made up a few that she didn't commit, just to prolong the inevitable. After she was finished, she glanced in the mirror. The devil sat still. He said nothing. She knew her end was near. The devil had heard her sins, and now she knew for sure that she was going to die.

Up ahead, she saw that she was coming up to an intersection with the main highway and there was a streetlight. She knew that the devil would take her before he was caught in the light. She was thinking rapidly now. What could she do? She decided that she would not go quietly. She hit the brakes and shouted to the devil that she was not ready to die. When she hit the brakes, the devil fell forward and dropped into the front seat.

There was a loud "yip!" She looked down, and came face-to-face with her tormentor. It was her dog! He had slipped into the car back at the house and was going to enjoy a trip to town.

She opened the door, grabbed the dog, and threw him out into the ditch. The poor dog sat there. He hadn't done anything wrong that he could figure. All he wanted was a ride in the car, and this crazy woman had confessed all her sins to him, yelled at him, and thrown him in the ditch. He sat there, miserable and shivering in the cold. But Mrs. Pelly had a good heart, and after the initial shock wore off, she took pity on her dog and let him back into the car.

From that day on, Mrs. Pelly always checked inside her car before she went anywhere, and her dog was always welcome, providing he didn't sneak in and scare her.

Anahareo: An Unsung Hero

Saskatchewan history is full of colourful characters, and one of the most celebrated is the naturalist Grey Owl. But few people are aware of the woman behind the mythical Grey Owl. Anahareo was Grey Owl's partner for ten stormy years, and she lived with him in northern Ontario, Riding Mountain National Park in Manitoba, and Waskesiu National Park in Saskatchewan.

Anahareo was also known as Gertrude Bernard, a Mohawk whose family originally came from Oka, Quebec. The name Anahareo was her Mohawk name, meaning "wild grapes." She was raised outside the reserve in the Ottawa Valley town of Mattawa. Her mother died when she was only four, and she was raised by her grandparents. When they were too old to care for her, she moved in with her aunt and uncle.

Anahareo planned to go to college in Toronto, but in 1925 she was working as a waitress in a tourist camp on Lake Temagami when she met a white man masquerading as an Indian called Grey Owl. His real name was Archie Belany, and he came from Hastings, England.

The fact that Grey Owl was not an Indian was never a secret as far as Indian people were concerned. He spoke Cree and Ojibwa with an accent, and he didn't look like an Indian. But if that's what he wanted to do, nobody seemed to complain.

Anyway, Archie and Gertrude became an item and set up housekeeping. Archie was a woodsman, hunter, trapper, and guide. Archie had been married before in England, and had lived with an Indian woman in northern Ontario with whom he had a son. But Anahareo was to become the great love of Archie's life.

In reality, Grey Owl was very flawed; he was a binge drinker, and he was abusive toward Anahareo. He was very insecure and had not had a successful permanent relationship. He, like Anahareo, had not been raised by his parents.

During the winter, Grey Owl and Anahareo went out on the trapline, but Anahareo became disgusted with the cruelty of trapping animals for their pelts. She had been raised in a town, so this kind of life was foreign to her. Once, Grey Owl killed a beaver, and as a result, two kits were orphaned. Anahareo kept them and named them Jelly Roll and Rawhide. They lived in the lake beside their cabin. It was really Anahareo who convinced Grey Owl to become a naturalist and conservationist. She was his inspiration and his passion.

Grey Owl's moods and drinking often got the better of Anahareo, and she would split and go prospecting in northern Quebec. Later, when they lived in Waskesiu, she would head north and work as a prospector on the Churchill River.

In 1931, Archie Belaney started to work for the Parks Branch, first at Riding Mountain in Manitoba and later at Waskesiu National Park. It was at Ajawaan Lake in Saskatchewan where Grey Owl and Anahareo found both happiness and fame. By now, Grey Owl was busy writing his books, and Anahareo had given birth to their daughter, Dawn.

In spite of this, Grey Owl would head into Prince Albert and go on a drinking binge. His health was not good, his heart was weak, but he became a common sight on a drunk in P.A. Ironically, here was a white man reinforcing the stereotype of a drunken Indian.

After awhile, Anahareo sent Dawn to live with friends in Prince Albert so she could get an education. Then she left Archie and went north prospecting. Grey Owl's fame continued to increase.

In 1936 and '37, he travelled over to England on a speaking tour where he played the role and became a famous Indian naturalist. He continued to drink, and his handlers were always trying to keep him under control. During all this time, he was suffering from tuberculosis. He died in 1938.

Anahareo became a forgotten person. The racism and sexism of the times would not allow people to recognise her as the driving force behind the development of Grey Owl the naturalist. She was just one more Indian woman who would not receive fair treatment.

She was the little Mohawk girl who left her homeland and travelled far to the West at a time when Indian people seldom left their reserves. She was a remarkable person.

Chapter 10

"It's the Economy..."

Starting Out

The high level of unemployment and poverty in our communities underlines the urgent need to create employment through business development.

At the turn of this century, there were only about 10,000 Indian people in Saskatchewan. In 1918, the Spanish flu pandemic would reduce the population even further. At that time, Saskatchewan was starting to fill up with settlers, and Indian people were seen as an anachronism with no future.

What a change. In the year 2000, Saskatchewan Indians were the province's fastest growing group with a population of over 100,000. Much of Saskatchewan's future success will be determined by how well we perform. It's sobering when you stop to consider it.

Currently, we are just beginning to enter the province's workforce and economy. For much of the twentieth century, we remained on the sidelines, either through legislation or government policy. Now in a few short years, we must move from being the consumers of government services to being creators of wealth.

The results will be disastrous if we fail. If we continue with high rates of unemployment, we will be a serious drain on the province's financial resources. But if we are able to create jobs and enter the workforce, we will be an asset rather than a liability.

Saskatchewan and Canada face two choices: either we create First Nations employment, or we become a chronically depressed region like Appalachia.

Are All Communities Viable?

There are issues in Indian country that need to be seriously discussed, but because of our history and the sensitivity of internal criticism, some issues remain silent. One issue speaks to the very existence of some of our communities. I'm talking about the economic viability of many of the First Nations across Canada.

A few years ago, I was shooting a video production in northern Manitoba. Each morning, we left our motel, and traveled two and a half hours on gravel road just to reach our location. It was a community of over 2,000 people, and it had no economic base other than government services and welfare. At one time, it had been an important trading and trapping area, but the world had passed it by, and so they were reduced to a welfare community. I wondered what effect this had on their people, and what the future would hold for them.

As Indian people, we are close to our roots, and our communities are rich in tradition and history. The only problem is that you can't *eat* history and tradition.

In every province, there are many communities that are not viable from an economic perspective, and the result is a people who are left behind, wallowing in the welfare trap. Communities that once had an historic reason to exist are now out of the mainstream, and, like many prairie towns, they are no longer able to sustain their populations.

This is not an issue that our leaders would like to address. It is political suicide to state that some communities need to move if they expect to survive. In First Nations politics, each First Nation is independent, and criticism of leaders and other issues is muted. The chiefs would consider it heresy and gang up on the hapless politician. His or her political career would be in tatters.

But the issue won't go away, and many of our people have already voted with their feet. Over half the Registered and Treaty Indians in Saskatchewan now live off the reserve. The educational and job opportunities are away from the typical reserve, and so it's only natural that our people move to the city.

Now when our people leave the reserve, it isn't like a scene from the 1930s, with the Joads saying a tearful farewell before they hit the road never to return. We may move away, but it's generally a reasonable commute to return, and it's easy to maintain contact. Like a bunch of homing pigeons, we return home on a regular basis. Saskatchewan has an outward migration, but less than 10% of the Aboriginal population has left the province.

Our First Nation, no matter where it is, remains our home. It's where our family roots are, where we bury our dead, and where we go to recharge our batteries. No matter how isolated or depressing it may appear, it is still home.

But the potential of First Nations hasn't been fully explored. For years, it was government policy to warehouse our people on reserves, treating the communities more like concentration camps than homelands. We have lived in poverty while resources and industries have been developed around us. Today, planes full of mine workers are flown into northern uranium mines while the local people watch. Only recently have our people found work in the forest industry, and it's only because of growing First Nations ownership in the forestry sector.

Also, the past few decades have seen the collapse of the trapping economy, and the soaring of the Aboriginal population. These factors have made it impossible for our people to continue with the old ways of living off the land. So today we are left with large rural communities with a limited economic base and a rapidly growing population. It is a situation that must be discussed internally by our people. Otherwise, the government experts and social scientists will move in and make the decisions for us.

In the past, relocation projects have ended in failure and resulted in years of dysfunction. For example, the government brought the people in from the community of Portage La Loche to the town of La Loche and created a welfare community. It wasn't until the local Dene First Nation took charge and set up their own community of the Clearwater First Nation that things improved.

The James Smith First Nation was an amalgam of several First Nations, and they are now in the process of unwinding the mess that government created. Sandy Bay is an artificial community designed to accommodate those displaced by the Island Falls Dam.

Forced solutions don't work. The answers must come from within, and the time has come to ask some tough questions. What is the future of some of our more isolated and economically-deprived communities? We owe it to future generations to deal with this issue before it gets dealt with for us.

First Nations: Part of the Future of the Rural Economy

A few years ago, The Action Committee on the Rural Economy (ACRE) issued a report that made recommendations on the future of the rural economy. The report recognized that the First Nations are and will be major players. ACRE was a committee set up by the provincial government with the mandate to examine the future of the rural economy in Saskatchewan.

First Nations are expanding land bases because of Treaty Land Entitlement and land claims. To date, by far the majority of the land selected has been both cultivated and uncultivated farmland. Much of this land has been selected with agricultural potential because First Nations recognize the importance and potential of the farm economy.

Also, while First Nations represent about 10% of the total provincial population, we are a young population that will play an important role in the province's future workforce.

Aboriginal participation was received overall on the Action Committee, as well as in all the subcommittees. We therefore had meaningful input which was reflected in the report's recommendations. The recommendations focused on job opportunities, partnerships, and access to resources. The committee also recommended that specific opportunities in Aboriginal tourism be identified.

While there are specific recommendations for Aboriginal people, it is clear that the remaining recommendations are designed to benefit all rural residents. Indeed, the purpose of the exercise was to develop recommendations that would benefit all rural residents.

Given Saskatchewan's reliance on the Aboriginal work force, it was disturbing to hear the results of the FSIN's study on Aboriginal education. The FSIN reported that the education system was failing Aboriginal young people. The study showed that 78% of Aboriginal youth have less than a complete high school education and 17% have not advanced beyond grade eight. Only three percent of Aboriginal people have a university degree.

The low education levels for Aboriginal youth are especially felt in the paycheque. The average personal income for Aboriginal youth is 75% less than their non-Aboriginal counterparts. The average annual income for a First Nations youth is $4,800.00 compared to $8,400.00 for non-Aboriginal youth.

Fifty-eight percent of Aboriginal youth reported income from social assistance compared to nine percent for non-Aboriginal youth.

More than ever, Aboriginal people are an important part of the future of rural Saskatchewan. In recent years, we have vastly increased our land base through Treaty Land Entitlement or land claim settlements. Governments would be wise to place more resources into First Nations and Métis communities for the benefit of the entire province.

An Indian Bank: Unheard of a Few Years Ago

As First Nations develop and enter the world of business and commerce, it is necessary to develop an institutional base of support. In Saskatchewan, the institutional base for education was established in the late 1970s with the establishment of the Federated College, the Technical Institute, and the Cultural College. As a result, First Nations education has flourished in this province. Economic development, coupled with the growth of self-government, has led to the formation of Canada's first Aboriginal bank.

The genesis for this new institution comes from the Saskatchewan Indian Equity Foundation (SIEF), founded in 1982 as the country's first Aboriginal capital corporation. Both the federal and provincial governments contributed capital and established an equity pool for loans to First Nations businesses. In time, SIEF was successful, and the capital grew to more than $7 million. In the next 12 years, SIEF issued loans totalling more than $30 million.

Incredibly, the loan loss ratio for SIEF has been less than 1%. No chartered bank or lending institution in Canada can point to that kind of record, particularly when one considers the tough economic times of the past decade.

In 1993, the board of directors for SIEF realized that they had reached the point where SIEF had to expand into something more than a lending institution.

SIEF met with financial institutions seeking a partnership for the development of a full-service chartered bank. The reaction from the banking community was mixed, with no small amount on scepticism. In the end, submissions were received from two institutions, and the Toronto Dominion Bank was selected.

SIEF and TD Bank began negotiations, and eventually a corporate structure and a business plan were worked out. An application for incorporation was submitted to the Office of the Superintendent of Financial Institutions, the body that incorporates financial institutions in this country. The application was accepted, and all the substantial issues were addressed.

Aboriginal leaders in business were sought out. The institution is a national institution, so its board will have to be representative of the national character of Aboriginal people. "Aboriginal" includes First Nations, Métis, and Inuit.

The First Nations Bank of Canada received financing from both the TD Bank and SEIF. The share structure will include common shares and both Class A and Class B shares. The common shares will be ownership shares and held by Aboriginal people only. Class B shares will be held by the TD Bank, and the Class A shares will be preferred shares available to all investors. The plan calls for all profits to be reinvested in the bank over a ten-year period, allowing the bank to become fully Aboriginal-controlled.

The TD bank will be providing $8 million investment, training, and access to their banking technology. SIEF put up $2 million, and contributes its knowledge of the First Nations marketplace.

The first branch has been opened in downtown Saskatoon, and the bank will offer a full range of deposit, credit, and financial services. The customer base will be open to any person or institution. First Nations Bank customers will be able to access their accounts at any TD branch and through their banking machines.

All new business will be actively pursued. The key to the success of the bank will be that it is open to all customers.

At first, the bank will be a schedule 2 bank with 80% ownership held by one group. The plan is for it to eventually become a schedule 1 bank with no single owner holding more than 10% ownership.

Land claims settlements and business developments are rapidly placing Aboriginal people in positions of financial power and influence. The next century will see even more rapid developments in the Aboriginal world. The First Nations bank is positioning itself to become the national financial institution that will grow and benefit from these changes.

Today, the First Nations Bank is now turning a profit and experiencing steady growth. Its mortgage portfolio is $83.5 million, deposits are $15.7 million, and it has total assets of $115 million. The bank now has four branches, located in Walpole Island, Ontario; Chisasibi, Quebec; Winnipeg and Saskatoon.

We Need More Rich Indians

When Michael Wilson was the Minister of Finance back in the Mulroney era, he made the comment that Canada needed more millionaires. The press and the opposition poured scorn on his remark. It was considered an elitist statement, but Wilson had a point. Wealth creation is just as important as job creation, and wealth creation has now replaced job creation as the motivation for economic development in Indian country.

Past and present government policies have been to focus on job creation programs. This may have made the government look good and decrease the welfare roles, but the programs left little lasting impression on First Nations communities.

Jobs can come and go at the whim of government programs, but business development can create jobs, cash flow, and wealth. Business requires infrastructure, sub-contractors, support services, and employees. As someone once said, "Money's like blood. It's got to circulate."

Construction jobs end when the work is completed, often in a few months. Administrative jobs create some work, but their effects on the community are felt only by those directly involved.

Economic development in Indian communities has always been difficult for governments. On the one hand, economic activity is necessary, but on the other hand, local businesses complain if the Indian activity is too successful. The old arguments of unfair competition have been used to thwart First Nations' economic development.

In the early days of this century, Indian farmers were very successful and regularly went to the local towns to sell their produce. Non-Indian farmers complained to their local Members of Parliament, and the Indian Act was amended to include a clause that Indian farmers could only sell their produce after receiving a permit from the Indian Agent. Also, the pass system required that all Indian persons obtain a pass from the Indian Agent if they left the reserve. This politicised economic development, and Indian farmers fell behind their off-reserve counterparts.

One area where Indian business people remained successful was with the raising and training of horses. Indian ranchers were the main source of horses for many settlers during the early days of settlement. Horses were so valuable to a farming operation that the government seldom interfered with this trade.

But the Indian economic activity mostly consisted of trapping, commercial fishing, and limited farming. Indian economics fell far behind the rest of Canada's, and the reserve economies fell into a state of dependency. In recent years, there has been a resurgence and growth in independence and business activity.

The English River First Nation purchased Tron Power, a construction and janitorial company with contracts in Northern Saskatchewan and Saskatoon. The Band had previously entered into a joint venture with the company, and the two had worked together for the past two years. This style of business development follows a pattern in Aboriginal business development. The community enters into a joint venture and obtains the management expertise. In return, the Band provides a workforce, some capitalisation, and access to contracts. This reduces the risk and increases the resources.

Kitsaki Developments, a company wholly owned by the Lac La Ronge Indian Band, has joint ventures with other companies and First Nations. NRT Trucking, for example, is a major contract hauler for the northern mines. NRT is jointly owned by Kitsaki, Trimac Transport, and several other northern communities and First Nations.

The newly formed First Nations Bank is an example of a joint venture between First Nations institutions and the Toronto Dominion Bank. This new bank will play a vital role in providing the financial infrastructure so badly needed to build an economy.

First Nations business development has been spearheaded by First Nations development corporations, but now individual entrepreneurs are coming into their own. This move is being supported by First Nations leaders, who are anxious to see jobs and business activity in their communities. First Nations development corporations also support individual enterprise since the development corporation is usually an umbrella that supports a variety of business activities.

The role of First Nations governments is increasingly seen as a support to business rather than as a participating party. Aboriginal business is now seen as one of the important building blocks to a secure future and as the financial basis of our communities.

Left Out in the Cold ... Again

The Gull Island Dam on the Labrador's Churchill River will cost $4 billion dollars, take ten years to build, and it will flood 85 square miles of Innu land. It will be the first in a series of dams on the Churchill River that will devastate Innu land. By 2003, the construction had not begun.

A few years ago, the media reported the cordial meeting between Quebec Premier Lucian Bouchard and Newfoundland Premier Brian Tobin as they signed an historic agreement to further dam the Churchill River in Labrador. The media also reported the demonstration by a group of Innu people from nearby reserves.

The land in question is in Labrador and Quebec and has been home to the Innu people for generations. The land, which contains traplines, graveyards, and cabins, will be flooded and its traditional use destroyed. This land is apparently inconsequential in light of the avarice of Quebec and Newfoundland. This is a clear illustration of our place in this country. We often end up on the sidelines watching others develop our resources and ruin our land.

Hydro dams have been one of the biggest destroyers of First Nations land. Northern Manitoba has seen the destruction of the fishing industry in the Nelson and Churchill River systems. Nothing was spared in the rush to dam the rivers to create hydropower for export. The five First Nations affected received a compensation package, but their land was destroyed, and Manitoba is now reaping huge profits from the sale of hydro to the States.

A few years ago, the people of the Peigan First Nation in Alberta tried to stop the construction of a dam on the Old Man River that flowed through their reserve. The dam has been built, and some of the traditional land of the Peigan First Nation is now under water.

In Saskatchewan, we have also had our problems. A proposed dam on the Churchill mercifully hasn't been built, although every so often there are rumblings that keep the idea alive. The Gardner Dam on the South Saskatchewan flooded the historic rock "Mistassini" that was shaped like a sleeping buffalo. This rock was an archaeological site that was a spiritual home to the Plains Indian people. Now it's gone forever.

And pollution has ruined First Nations land and communities. The Akwesasne Reserve in Ontario is upriver from a hydro dam and downwind from several industrial plants that have seriously polluted the area's plants and ruined its habitat.

The English-Wabigoon River System in Northwestern Ontario was polluted with mercury in the 1960s from a pulp mill in Dryden. The people in the First Nations communities downstream have now experienced the effects of mercury poisoning from their traditional fish diet.

And on and on it goes. Our people have been shoved aside in the past, and when you would think it would be time for change, the Newfoundland and Quebec governments perpetuate the old pattern of exclusion.

History in Indian country has a way of sticking around. Past injustices are coming back to haunt the country and the government. For example, the understanding of our elders is that the treaties call for the shared use of the land, but no mention of minerals was ever made. Any lawyer will tell you that if something is not mentioned in a transaction, it is not a part of that transaction. If you agree to buy a guy's house, you don't get his car as well.

In 1930, the natural resources in the Prairie Provinces were transferred from the federal government to the provinces. The First Nations were not consulted, even though under the treaties we had shared jurisdiction of the land. Since the mineral wealth was never mentioned in the treaties, it should have remained with us. The FSIN has raised the issue of resource revenue sharing, but so far, the provincial government has ignored it. The ignoring of problems in Indian country only results in bigger problems in the future. This has been proven time and time again.

Now we have hydro and resource projects all across the country that are ruining our traditional land and providing no financial return. We are a people that live in poverty, but we have the greatest potential of all Canadians.

The Innu were correct to demonstrate against the destruction of their land; they have been treated as a people that have no role and nothing to contribute. We can no longer afford to be shoved aside and marginalized. The time has come in this country for governments to recognise our role, our potential, and our rights.

Sharing Renewable Resources

A few years ago, the First Nations and the Province were busy negotiating co-management agreements on natural resources. These negotiations held the potential to solve the long-standing issue of Indian hunting rights.

Instead, the process has stalled. There has been a public rebellion, and the First Nations remain on the outside. The culprit, it would appear, is the federal government.

The Montreal Lake First Nation was negotiating a resources co-management agreement with the Province of Saskatchewan, and the federal government got in the middle, making negotiations take on a political tone just before the 2000 provincial election.

Under the Natural Resources Transfer Agreement, the provincial governments hold the rights to the natural resources. The federal government has not had any jurisdiction since 1930.

When the federal government got involved, the provincial government backed out, and the negotiations on other co-management agreements came to a halt. At the time, there were 22 First Nations involved in the negotiations, either by themselves or in traditional groupings.

The Montreal Lake process upset the local redneck element, and meetings were held. Racial epithets flew, petitions were circulated, and misinformation was rampant. In this case, truth was the first casualty.

Co-management agreements are in place in a number of areas, and First Nations, the Province, and local municipalities are cooperating and working things out. Of course, this goes unnoticed because there is no conflict or public outcry.

The keys to the process are cooperation and communication, and co-management is an idea whose time has come. In the past, the First Nations hunters and game wardens were always coming into conflict. There were a number of long and expensive court cases, most of which were won if the issue was treaty rights.

While others may dismiss treaty rights as unimportant, treaty rights form the basis of the relationship in the view of the First Nations. The treaties clearly state that the First Nations will be able to pursue their traditional lifestyle and be able to hunt, trap, fish, and gather unmolested.

For many years, this was the case, but with increasing settlement and a growing provincial population, more and more pressure has been put on the wildlife. It has been apparent for some years now that if there is to be proper wildlife management, the First Nations must be brought into the picture. Indian hunters were exercising their rights hunting on their traditional lands, and they saw nothing wrong in what they were doing.

Co-management brings the groups together; the jurisdictions of the First Nations and the Province are recognized, as are Indian hunting rights. In return, the two parties agree to work together to manage the resources in their best interests. As it turns out, it works. It works when the politicians and outsiders leave things alone, and both sides work in the best interests of the environment.

Bringing Back an Elk Herd

A few years ago, I was in Prince Albert when I ran into an old friend. Norman Henderson from the Montreal Lake Cree Nation was in town meeting with a group of wildlife officials, and he was all excited about what they were planning.

They were going to pick up a herd of about 200 elk from Elk Island National Park east of Edmonton, and then introduce them to the Montreal Lake area.

The plan sounded like a military operation. Relocating 200 elk is not something you do overnight. It requires planning and cooperation. The elk are shipped in trucks like cattle, and all indications are that they don't seem to mind it.

The Elk Island National Park is like an elk factory. About 300 to 325 elk must be culled or moved out of the park every year to prevent stress on the ecosystem. This was good news for the people of the Montreal Lake Cree Nation. The plan seemed to be a win-win deal for all the participants.

The restoration of the elk herd in the Montreal Lake area is a significant step toward the renewal of hunting rights and the cooperation of the Montreal Lake Cree Nation with the federal and provincial governments.

For years now, our elders have been cautioning us to use proper hunting methods and to maintain a healthy balance with nature. I recall one elder telling me that if we didn't use our hunting rights responsibly, we would have no wildlife to hunt, and so our hunting rights would be meaningless. Messages like these have been heeded, and dangerous practices such as night hunting are now outlawed.

The elk in the Montreal Lake area left some 25 years ago. The reasons are varied, but it was partly over hunting and partly due to loss of habitat from indiscriminate logging practices. However, the habitat has improved considerably over the years. Logging and forest fires are sometimes portrayed as disastrous to the ecology, but the opposite is sometimes true. Anyone who has gone berry-picking in a burned-over or logged area will agree about the profusion of plant growth that follows when an area is opened up. This new growth means good feeding if you're a large herbivore like a deer, moose, or elk.

The introduction of the elk herd is a project that includes advantages for a number of government agencies. The benefit to the Montreal Lake Cree Nation is obvious: they are having an important part of their culture brought back. In recognition of this, and to help the herd get established, Chief Henry Naytowhow has stated that the Cree Nation will prohibit hunting the elk for four years.

Saskatchewan has been able to work on a wildlife cooperation project that includes a study into the movements of the herd and how they interact with other herds in the area. Some of the animals are fitted with special collars and tags that will be used to track their movements through satellite and radio signals.

The return of the elk herd is also an important part of the cultural life of the Montreal Lake Cree Nation and neighbouring bands. Elk meat was once an important part of the reserve diet. Many First Nations people have a greatly reduced quality of diet, and traditional foods are needed to recreate a healthy lifestyle.

Children now grow up in reserve communities and lack the important education their grandparents received on the trapline. When these important links are broken, the health of the community suffers. The language begins to disappear in the young, one generation appears to have little to offer the next, welfare becomes a source of income, and social ills begin to develop. This has been the story in numerous northern communities as the trapping economy and lifestyle disappear. Today, many trappers go to the trapline out of habit and peace of mind rather than for economic gain.

Whether it is the return of the buffalo to southern First Nations, the annual migration of the caribou in the far north, or the return of the elk herd to the Montreal Lake Cree Nation, we are people of this land, and we need to be reminded of our roots.

The Need to Share Resource Revenue

The recent appeal by northern First Nations communities to share in resource revenue from northern mines is not a new request, nor is it likely to go away in the future. First Nations take the position that they must receive resource revenue since the mineral resources were not negotiated away when the treaties were signed.

Any lawyer will tell you that if something is silent in an agreement, then it is retained. In other words, if you sell your car and only your car, the new owner can't claim your garage as part of the deal.

This is the case for Saskatchewan's natural resources. Our elders have told us over the years that the treaties were agreements to "share" the land with the newcomers for settlement, but to share the land for farming only; the oral record of the treaties that our people remember is that the treaty negotiators wanted the land to the "depth of a plough," for farming only.

When the Indian leaders asked about the renewable natural resources, the treaty negotiators agreed that the First Nations would have the right to hunt, fish, trap, and gather "in perpetuity." In some cases, land was set aside to exercise these rights.

At one time, there was a string of little reserves down the eastern shore of Last Mountain Lake. These parcels of land were set aside so that the First Nations would have a place to camp when they came to the lake to fish. Last Mountain was also set aside as a hunting reserve for the Treaty Four First Nations. When travel was restricted and the land was no longer used, the reserve was liquidated. In Alberta, several Treaty Seven First Nations have timber reserves in the mountains where they can go to hunt or gather timber.

The oral record from our elders says that during the treaty negotiations, one of the Chiefs asked about the resources that lay beneath the earth. The Chiefs wanted to know what would happen when the land was settled and minerals were discovered. This was not a question that came out of the blue; it was an informed question. The First Nations that negotiated Treaty Four in 1874 had been in touch with the First Nations who negotiated Treaty Three. These First Nations were located in the Thunder Bay, Fort Francis, and Kenora areas. These First Nations had in turn been in touch with the First Nations along the north shore of Lake Superior. These First Nations had signed the Robinson-Huron Treaty, and they had received compensation for the minerals that had been extracted prior to the treaty.

It was common for important information to be transferred over long distances through the use of messengers and through meetings between Chiefs and leaders. Indian people were better informed than the treaty negotiators realized. This move created the precedent that the minerals were the property of the original inhabitants. When the chief asked about the minerals, he was told the minerals would be discussed at a later date. That later date never came, but it has been raised since by the First Nations.

The fly in the ointment appears to be the Natural Resources Transfer Agreement, which was signed between the provinces and the federal government in 1930. Under this agreement, the natural resources in the three Prairie Provinces were transferred to the provincial governments. This was done over the heads of the First Nations. In fact, I doubt that resource revenue was even considered for First Nations at that time, such is the racist nature of our history. The provinces latched on to the resources and profited handsomely as a result.

The First Nations languished in poverty, and to this day, funds transferred to First Nations are considered a social obligation instead of a legitimate cost based on treaty. The First Nations have asked successive provincial governments to open negotiations on resource revenue sharing, but they have been put off every time.

The Province is in no hurry to open this Pandora's Box and share resource revenue with the First Nations. Saskatchewan has built a healthy economy on resources such as potash, oil, and uranium. But they have not shared this revenue with the First Nations that hold a legitimate claim.

Is Gambling a Sure Thing?

I've said it before, and I'll say it again: whenever white people don't want something, they turn it over to the Indians. In the past, we've received old army bases, obsolete boarding schools, and swamp land. And it's no fluke that Canada's only desert is located on an Indian reserve.

The recent decision to turn gambling over to the First Nations is another case in point. In 1993, the Province and the FSIN announced with much fanfare that they had reached an agreement on gaming.

The Province originally allowed four casinos under First Nations management in addition to the one already proposed for Regina under a previous agreement with the FSIN. The Regina agreement remains in effect. A casino under First Nations jurisdiction is also being built on the White Cap First Nation south of Saskatoon, and another has been approved for Swift Current.

Gaming is a political hot potato that the provincial government has been trying to ignore and avoid. Gambling was seen as a good revenue-raiser, but the public has been reluctant to the point that Saskatoon voters rejected a proposed downtown casino.

The Province was feeling the pressure and wanted out. Gambling was bad karma, and an election was coming. The Province had the happy choice to pull out, yet still take the largest slice of the gambling pie. There are still some 3,500 video lottery terminals out there, and the Province controls them all.

So now the public perceives the First Nations as having cornered the gambling industry. We can count on at least 2,000 jobs and some profit. I don't want to complain, because as we prairie people say, it beats a kick in the pants with a frozen boot.

Is gambling all it's cracked up to be, though? Is it the key to our future prosperity? Some simple math shows the other side to this equation.

There are 120,000 Treaty Indians who are members of First Nations in Saskatchewan. Half are under 18, and they have presumably not entered the job market. That leaves about 60,000 adults. If 75% are employable, then that leaves 45,000 people who are in the job market. Our employment rate for these 45,000 people stands at around 25%. That leaves about 33,750 First Nations people who need jobs in Saskatchewan. Add to that the fact that about 2,000 to 2,500 young people are entering the job market annually, and you can see the magnitude of the problem and the small effect that casinos will have on our people.

The future of economic development lies in more pedestrian pursuits. The Treaty Land Entitlement Agreement will provide far more jobs in the agriculture sector alone. Resource development, in areas such as oil and gas, forestry, and mining, holds the potential to provide far more direct and indirect jobs. The tourist industry is another area that should be a natural for our people. The key to our development is not in the creation of new economic sectors, but in our entering into what already exists.

In the late nineteenth century, Indian people settled on their reserves and turned to farming. They were so successful that local farmers complained that the Indians were able to go to the nearby towns and sell their produce at lower rates. The farmers complained to the government, and the result was that Indian farmers had to have a permit from the Indian Agent before they could sell their produce. The result was the end of the short-lived First Nations agriculture economy.

The results of this are with us to the present day. We have been excluded from the economy and are blamed for our own misfortune. We are now too large a population to ignore or to place on the sidelines. Our future lies in the mainstream economy. The gaming industry is only one step toward that goal.

Politics and Jobs: A Sorry Union

In the movie *Blazing Saddles*, when Mel Brooks realizes that his meal ticket (a local politician) could be defeated, he shouts, "We got to protect our rinky-dink jobs!" This is a familiar lament around election time in most band offices. Elections and the fate of band employees are hopelessly linked together.

The sad reality on most reserves is that the only well-paying jobs are tied to the political system through the provision of government services. Everyone, from the head administrator to the school bus driver, owes his or her job to funding that is controlled by the Band Council.

This is not unusual. All communities must contain a civil service and jobs that provide government services, but in Aboriginal communities, it is disproportionate in that it represents the total economy. It is the classic case of crumbs thrown to a colonized people. In other Saskatchewan communities, government jobs only represent a minority of the economy. Couple this with welfare dollars, and we truly have a false economy.

This situation creates a system of uncertainty because one's job is only secure until the next election. As a result, those who hold jobs become protective and insecure about their futures. People on welfare are unable to plan further ahead than their next cheque, so band meetings are preoccupied with issues that may seem trivial to some, but are of great importance to others. For example, with limited funds for housing and infrastructure, assigning new houses and making improvements to water and sewer hook-ups can become the focus of a band council's decision making.

Most First Nations are run by people in their 40s and 50s. This is because they were young and educated when the government began transferring programs to bands in the 1970s and '80s. Over the years, this generation has done well for itself and has become entrenched in the running of the community. Today, while 60% of our population is under the age of 29, and while they are educated like no generation before, they find jobs and opportunities closed to them back on the reserve.

The lack of housing also plays a role since older families must be given priority. Young people are faced with the grim prospect of waiting at home for the band administrator to die. Clearly, members of the next generation can't look to jobs in the band office as their salvation. We need to develop a real economy.

Currently, a few reserves have the ability to circulate money through retail and service outlets. In most cases, welfare and salary dollars leave the reserve and are spent in local towns, providing no benefit to the community.

Young people are starting to see the opportunities and are taking the plunge into the competitive world of business. Saskatchewan Indians lead the nation in the creation of new businesses by two and a half times, and these are businesses created by young people in response to the insecure First Nations job market. New businesses cover a wide range of fields from northern development, urban businesses, and construction. Indian entrepreneurs are looking at mainstream opportunities.

Treaty Land Entitlement is also providing new opportunities as a new generation of farmers takes over a large land base with far more potential than exists on the crowded reserves. Treaty Land Entitlement holds the potential to position First Nations farmers and ranchers as major Saskatchewan producers.

But the key to our success lies in our ability to change our attitude toward our economy's potential, see beyond our borders, and, most importantly, support and encourage our young people.

Taxation Powers for First Nations

Taxation is not just the exclusive territory of the federal and provincial governments. It is also new territory for First Nations to raise revenue. The path to direct action began when the Whitebear First Nation went ahead and operated a casino on their land against the protests of the Province of Saskatchewan.

The resulting heavy-handed raid and subsequent trial strengthened the resolve of the First Nations to take direct action against a provincial government that was not prepared to negotiate in good faith. The Whitebear raid was a turning point in provincial-Indian relations.

First Nations are developing a whole range of businesses, and they are under the jurisdiction of First Nations self-government. "Jurisdiction" means the ability to license, regulate, and tax.

Cutbacks in federal government spending are causing shortfalls in band budgets, and so councils are looking for ways to raise revenue. This is a natural course of action for any government. All governments – federal, provincial and municipal – have the right to levy taxes and raise revenue, so why don't First Nations governments?

The problem is that the Province thinks that it has occupied the territory and that First Nations governments are their tax collectors. If a First Nation adds another sales tax on merchandise sold within their jurisdiction, the items will be over-taxed and sales will obviously be small or non-existent. The only option for First Nations is to replace the federal and provincial tax regime with their own.

The status of First Nations land is an issue with two sides. The federal and provincial governments regard Indian land as land that was given, as a form of largesse, for the use and benefit of Indians. The First Nations hold that under treaty, First Nations land is land that was kept as Indian land. They agreed to share the rest. Reserve land has never been a part of the province and never will be. The reserves were surveyed before the turn of the century, long before Saskatchewan even became a province.

Over the years, the Province has just assumed that it has jurisdiction over Indian reserves and has ignored any protest from the First Nations. Indian land and its resources are fully owned by the First Nations, and the jurisdiction of the First Nations must be respected. Also, if the First Nations are able to raise revenue from sales tax and other means, economic development will take a positive turn. Up until now, economic development has only been seen in terms of jobs. Now that economic development means taxation revenue, it takes on a whole new dimension: economic development is good for the whole community.

The issue is jurisdiction and the Province's reluctance to vacate the field. The Cowesses First Nation fired the first shot across the Province's bow, and the next move is to sit down and negotiate the orderly recognition of First Nation's jurisdiction.

The issue will not go away, and provincial government intransigence will only create a solid wall of resistance from more First Nations across the province.

Fur Bans Only Hurt Our People

Middle class, uninformed protest movements often do serious collateral damage to those who are least able to fight back. The European fur ban is an example where the traditional lifestyles of Aboriginal hunters and Newfoundland sealers have suffered because of naïve and close-minded do-gooders.

About 80,000 people have been affected by the European fur ban, and over half of Canada's trappers are Aboriginal. But our people fought back this time, and a pro-fur lobby was launched in Europe.

The European lobby was assisted by leaders and representatives from the Aboriginal organizations affected. Trade representatives admitted that the presence of the Aboriginal representatives made a difference.

As First Nations people, we have a long history of others acting on our behalf without a thorough knowledge of the issues. The anti-fur lobby is a good example of middle class North Americans and Europeans dumping on our people for trying to maintain a traditional way of life. These are people whose experience with wild animals consists of the stories told by Walt Disney and Beatrix Potter. They portray our people as either bloodthirsty killers of cute little wild animals or mindless dupes exploited by fur traders. In fact, they are just reinforcing long-held stereotypes of our people, and both descriptions are racist and demeaning.

These are obviously people who have never spent any time on the trapline or known trappers to appreciate their way of life. For over 200 years, our people have trapped commercially, and there has not been one case of any species harvested to the point of being endangered. In fact, the population of fur-bearing animals has been constant for years. This has been due to the large trapping areas and the traditional stewardship of the land.

The fur trade was of mutual benefit to both parties: the traders built an industry and opened up the North, and the trappers had a successful way of life with an improved economy. The myths of rip-off traders may be true, but these few guys were quickly put out of business. The traders depended on the First Nations for food, guides, and their incomes. They simply could not afford to create bad relations so far from their home base. Our people were not stupid.

Europeans who condemn our people do us a disservice and are destroying a healthy and self-sufficient way of life.

I once saw a news story on the fur ban where an environmentalist was asked, "What about the Aboriginal people and their way of life?" His reply was that it was up to the government to "provide programs for these people." This type of response is typical and places the onus on the victim. We know what the program will be: it will be the welfare program.

Many of these environmental activists take on causes with a religious zeal that would embarrass a televangelist. They are unable to reason or unable to see any side but their own. Their minds are like concrete: all mixed up and firmly set.

It is the height of hypocrisy and arrogance for the anti-fur movement to go after a people who have successfully managed and harvested fur resources for generations, especially when one examines the sorry plight of the European environment.

Eastern Europe is an environmental wasteland following the collapse of communism and the subsequent lifting of the iron curtain. The once-great forests of Germany are under attack from acid rain, and the Scandinavian reindeer herds are unfit for human consumption following the Chernobyl disaster. The list goes on and on, including the fact that fur-bearing animals in Europe have been nearly or completely wiped out.

This delay in the fur ban is welcome relief, but our leaders must continue to lobby and educate the Europeans so we can retain this valuable market and way of life.

New Leadership in Our Economic Growth

Positive change is occurring in Saskatchewan cities, if you follow recent events in Saskatoon.

In 2002, First Nations lawyer Leanne Bellegarde-Daniels was elected chair of the Saskatoon Board of Police Commissioners. Her appointment marked a number of firsts. She was the first person outside of city council and the police force to chair the commission, and she was also the first woman and Aboriginal person. She is also a board member of the Royal University Hospital Foundation and of the Board of Directors for the United Way. When I asked her why she was involved in the community, she replied that since Saskatoon was her home, she wanted to give something back.

Leanne's comment speaks volumes about the changing attitude Aboriginal people have toward their new lifestyle and social position. We now have second and third generation urban Indians who see a place for themselves in society that their parents couldn't see. Leanne is an independent lawyer who runs her own law firm in Saskatoon.

Traditionally, our people have migrated to the cities and remained on the fringes. The only community involvement for most would revolve around the school or minor sports – mainly activities involving their children.

Today's urban Aboriginal people are an important part of the social and economic fabric. For example, in Saskatoon CRESS Housing (an agency that provides housing for Status Indian people) spends about $285,000.00 annually on property taxes. Add this to the amount spent by Sask. Native Housing, the Yellow Quill First Nation, the Battlefords Tribal Council on downtown real estate, and individual Aboriginal homeowners, and you have a healthy chunk of change, likely approaching a million dollars. Since urban governments raise the bulk of their revenue through property taxes, Aboriginal people contribute their fair share.

It's no wonder then that our people see themselves as stakeholders in urban affairs and are participating on a number of levels.

In 2002, the Saskatoon Chamber of Commerce made history by swearing in its first Aboriginal president. Lester Lafond had been an active member of the Chamber for some years and had worked on a variety of committees. His appointment was seen by many as simply selecting the best person for the job.

Lester attended the University of Saskatchewan, and he has spent most of his working life in Saskatoon. He and his wife Shirley, along with their two sons and one daughter, have made Saskatoon their home.

The swearing-in ceremony was done in the Chamber's usual manner by a

Justice of the Peace, but was then followed by an honour song by two members of the Wanuskewin drum group. Reserve elders and Chief Gilbert Ledoux also attended. In his remarks, Chief Ledoux praised Lester for his work and for his position as a role model for the community.

Lester has been a pioneer and trailblazer in his work in the First Nations business community. For example, it was largely through his efforts that the Muskeg Lake Cree Nation was able to obtain the Sutherland urban commercial reserve in 1988 where they have since built three office buildings and the Creeway Gas Station. Two of the buildings are managed by Muskeg Lake and owned jointly with the Saskatoon Tribal Council. Another building has been built by Kocsis Transport, a successful Aboriginal business.

In addition, Lester was the FSIN representative on the Action Committee on the Rural Economy (ACRE) report commissioned by the provincial government. He is also the FSIN coordinator for the FSIN and the Province's First Nations Agriculture Strategy.

In his acceptance speech, Lester stated that while he was a First Nations businessperson, he was not a single-issue person. He pledged to work for all business development and to support all opportunities. Comparing society to a piece of twine where each strand makes the rope strong, he said, "By working together, we will all be stronger."

The appointment of Leanne Bellegarde-Daniels and Lester Lafond to leadership positions is a positive sign that race relations and an Aboriginal economy are improving at all levels. Our leadership and involvement is real, not token.

A friend of mine once told me that about 45% of society is on our side, the other 45% can be convinced, and the remaining 10% will never support us no matter what we do. With positive role models like Leanne and Lester, we are increasing the number of people who are on our side.

Chapter 11

The Life and Times of Abe Original

The Aboriginal Party Takes Shape

During elections I receive a lot of political propaganda in my mailbox. Some of it is interesting, but most of it is useless.

I was especially pleased to receive a kit from the Rhinoceros Party that included a barf bag to take to political events (thanks – I'm sure it will come in handy).

Another bunch of propaganda advertises a new party known as the Aboriginal Party. Apparently, it's named after its leader, Abe Original. The brochure listed the party executive as Luke Warm Water, Abel Duck Daisy Chain, and an elder, Joe Creemudgeon.

The aim of the party is to return Canada to traditional values – that is, values that existed prior to Columbus discovering America. It's a tall order, but they are serious, as I found out when I gave Mr. Original a call.

"We see ourselves as the only voice of reason in this election," he said. "Whenever white people get fed up and say, 'we should give the country back to the Indians,' we are going to give them that chance."

The Aboriginal Party's platform concentrates on many of the same issues that the other parties address, but the party has developed a uniquely Aboriginal approach.

For example, the deficit is a preoccupation with all parties. The solutions range from getting rid of it in three years, to five years, to never. The Natural Law Party plans to make the deficit magically disappear or to at least to saw it in half. The Aboriginal Party plans to attack the deficit in true Indian fashion: it plans to ignore it to death.

Employment will also be addressed in the Aboriginal fashion: "We should make a substantial attack on unemployment," Abe stated. "People who are story tellers, singers, artists, or dancers will be placed on government payroll and allowed to do their thing."

Aid to farmers will consist of buying their farms and giving the land to the Indians, who will turn it back to virgin prairie and raise buffalo.

The Reform Party has stated that it will reduce immigration considerably. The Aboriginal Party would like to go further and not only reduce immigration but also reverse it. The Aboriginal Party promises to reduce the immigrant population to zero within five years. An immigrant is defined as anyone whose ancestors didn't come across the land bridge from Asia 10,000 years ago.

There is a small amount of revenge built into the Aboriginal platform. All the economists, lawyers, bureaucrats, and politicians who got us into this mess will be taken to Wanuskewin where they will be stampeded over the buffalo jump. "It may seem a bit crude, but it will show that we mean business," Abe told me.

The Aboriginal Party is waging a serious campaign. Abe is seeking election at Cowichan Sweater on the west coast: Luke Warm Water is on the ballot in Lost-in-the-Barrens, Saskatchewan; Abel Duck is running in Saint Moustache, in Quebec; Daisy Chain is managing the national campaign; and Joe Creemudgeon is holding out for a Senate appointment.

I asked Abe if his platform wasn't a little bit outrageous. He said that while some of it was considered radical, he wasn't worried, asking, "Political promises are made to be broken, Aren't they?"

In Which the Belle of Batoche Turns Out to be a Bell

I hadn't heard from my old friend Abe Original for some time. I assumed he was laying low during the summer, but I was in for a surprise when he called me. He invited me over to his place because he wanted to introduce me to his new friend. That was all he would tell me, and my curiosity took over.

When I got over to Abe's apartment, I was greeted by Abe and his sidekick, Luke Warm Water. "Meet Marie Antoinette," Abe said. I looked around, but there was nobody else in the room, just an old bell sitting on the coffee table.

"That's Marie," Abe said, pointing to the bell.

"Is that what I think it is?" I asked. "Is that the missing bell of Batoche?"

It turned out that it was, and Abe's story of political intrigue and undercover work began to unfold.

"A few years ago, when the Métis National Council had a board meeting in Winnipeg, it was decided that they should liberate the bell from the Ontario Legion where it was on display as a trophy of war. They opened it up to tender, and Luke and I put in a bid. As it turned out, it was the winning bid."

"We thought the Belle of Batoche was a woman," Luke added.

"Yeah," Abe said, "we thought all we had to do was drive down and pick her up. It turned out to be more complicated than that, so we took Luke's pickup and headed east."

I looked out in the parking lot at Luke's beat-up red pickup truck, a.k.a. the "Rez Rocket." When the media reported that a red pickup with Saskatchewan license plates had been seen in the vicinity, I had had no idea it was them.

"So anyway," Abe continued, "we went into the Legion and had a few drinks, and chatted up the locals. Seems they were pretty proud of their booty and weren't about to give it up without a fight. I kept them talking while Luke cased the joint and figured out a way to steal the bell."

"Their ancestors who stole the bell were Orangemen and fervent anti-Catholics. They saw the Riel Rebellion as a war to keep the West Protestant and English. It's strange when you consider how things turned out. Nobody cares about your religion anymore, and the English are a minority in this province. It's strange to think that at one time, Canada was just as crazy as Northern Ireland."

"Anyway, after everyone went home, Luke and I went back and pried open the back door, slipped inside, and made off with the bell. We took a couple of medals for ransom as well. We figured we could threaten to destroy the medals if they caught us. It was our insurance policy."

"The poor old Rez Rocket barely made it home," Luke said.

"We hid the bell for several years, and this summer we wanted to present it to the Métis people at their annual gathering at Batoche," Abe continued. "But politics got in the way, and the whole thing became a media circus. The Province is desperate for friends and issues these days, so they jumped into the act."

"They even named highway number five 'Louis Riel Way,'" Luke added.

"They wanted us to give up the bell in return for amnesty," Abe said. "We didn't want amnesty. We're thieves and proud of it. It was a clean crime: they never found us, and we got away with the bell. Granting us amnesty was an insult. Besides, we were taking back something that was stolen in the first place."

"So what are you going to do with the bell?" I asked.

"We plan to give it back, but without the hoopla," Abe said. "Some night we plan to go out to the church at Batoche and place it back in the bell tower where it belongs. Meanwhile, we plan to polish it up and use it for a center-piece on this table."

I left them hard at work, cleaning the bell and discussing the return of totem poles to the West Coast, the Elgin marbles to Greece, and other loot stolen in the past by raiding colonial powers. They had discovered a new area of Indian economic development, and they were about to exploit it.

The New-Look Aboriginal Party

When a provincial election is in full swing, I like to look in on my old friend Abe Original. He and his motley group of friends contest various elections under the banner of the Aboriginal Party. Their results have been less-than-stellar, but they make up for it with enthusiasm and chutzpah.

When I got over to Abe's apartment, I found a small but dedicated group busily putting the finishing touches on its latest campaign plans.

At first, I didn't recognize the person who greeted me at the door. He was different; he had a plastic sheen to him. It was Abe, though!

"Com'on in," he told me. "Meet my new image consultant, Mini Moose. Mini's a professional campaign consultant from the United States, and her job is to remake me while we rebuild the party. This time, I'm going to get my office in the marble palace."

Mini had given Abe a whole new image. He wore contact lenses instead of his geeky glasses. He also had a hairdresser do his braids every morning. He wore stylish suits and flashy ties instead of his usual t-shirts and sweatpants. He even wore Gucci loafers in place of his moccasins. Overall, the results were striking. He looked more like a real estate agent than a politician, but if this was what the public wanted, then I figured they might be on to something.

Luke Warm Water was busy working on the party platform. He told me, "In the past, we haven't been able to attract the white people's votes. Only a flaky few vote for us. What we plan this year is to develop a platform that offers broad appeal and that reaches out to the average Saskatchewan resident. We'll forget them after we get elected, so we're no different than the other parties."

Abe came over and joined us. "Here's the first draft of our political platform," he said. "First, we promise full employment."

"We found a simple way to accomplish this," Luke said. "We plan to encourage women to give their jobs to men and stay at home."

"If women didn't work, then this country would have full employment," Abe stated. "Mini had some problems with this, but what the hell – she doesn't have to live here."

"We will also guarantee labour peace," Luke said. "Our plan is to repeal all the labour legislation, so when the next strike is threatened, we can tell them that we have no legislation, and they have no jurisdiction to strike. Let them try to figure that out!"

"And we have a solution for the problem of deteriorating highways," Luke said.

"It's so simple," Abe told me. "We plan to eliminate highways altogether. Do you know how much highways cost? It's so much easier to build an airstrip in each town and have everyone buy a plane. A half mile of airstrip is much cheaper than a hundred miles of road."

"And," Luke added, "few people know how to fly a plane, so we see a whole new growth industry training people to fly aircraft. It should create a whole bunch of new jobs. It's a win-win solution. We're amazed nobody thought of it before."

"We're stuck for what to do for the farmers," Luke said. "We will encourage all First Nations with Treaty Land Entitlement to purchase land to their full land quantum. That will help out some farmers."

Abe added, "Maybe we could buy their grain and feed it to the starving people of Africa and Asia."

"In the Manitoba campaign, there has been some controversy over the Tories presenting campaign ads that look like part of the evening news," Abe told me. "We plan to go one better. Our plan is to talk to Aboriginal reporters, such as Nelson Bird and Mervin Brass, and have them sneak our stories into the real news broadcasts. Mini's working on a whole series of bogus stories to feed those guys."

"I just hope that the reporters don't do something stupid like have scruples and ethics," Luke added.

A photographer was coming over to take pictures for buttons, posters, and billboards. Abe was going on about the furnishings for his new office in the marble palace, so I figured it was a good time to leave and let history take its course.

Planning an Indian Reality Show

When the dog days of summer are upon us, life is easy.

In the early days of reserve life, mid-summer was a time when people went berry-picking, visiting, and generally had a relaxing time.

It was the time following the Sundances and before the late summer when the men would go out to join the threshing crews or cut brush.

It was also the all-too-brief period when the children would be home from the boarding schools. Summer was an important time for the families because they would be reunited, and for two months, the parents could teach their children the important aspects of their culture and traditional religion.

Therefore, I thought it was a good time to look up my old friend Abe Original and see what he was up to this summer. I found him and his sidekick Luke Warm Water down by the lake fishing. They hadn't caught anything, but it looked like they were in no hurry to give up.

Abe's career had been less-than-spectacular since he became a television producer and consultant. "We had a bit of success with the cooking show," he told me, "but there are only so many First Nations dishes, like Kraft Dinner, Spam and boiled potatoes."

"We ran out of ways to bake bannock," Luke added.

"Besides, *Cooking with Luke Warm Water* was a dumb name for the show," Abe said. "I think it turned off the audience. The response was tepid at best. I told you *Original Cooking* was a better title, but *Noooo...!*"

"I think we have just the idea now," Abe told me. "The thing today is all about reality TV. They have those survivor shows where people go to some South Sea island or the Australian Outback."

"But that's not *reality*," Luke added. "How many people will actually end up in those situations?"

"That's right!" Abe stated. "Reality is more like what happens every day to real people."

Abe continued, "We have this idea for a survivor show where Indian people must survive in the cities, and the white people have to survive on a reserve. It goes like this: One episode would be to take a group of people from the reserve and drop them off on the corner of College and Yonge Street in Downtown Toronto. They would be left with nothing but a small amount of cash and their wits. They would have to survive on the streets, dodge the police and social workers, and try to stay out of trouble with the law. One by one, the participants would be scooped up by the authorities, and the last one to survive would be the winner."

"Now that's reality for our people," Luke added.

"The second scenario is even better," Abe said. "We take a group of white people and set them up on a reserve. They'll be provided with the tools to survive for one year, including a drafty old house, a Quebec heater, a bag of flour, a box of 22 shells, some snare wire, and a monthly welfare cheque of $100.00. They too will have to dodge the police and social workers, and try to survive and stay out of trouble. One by one, they will get sick, succumb to scurvy or rickets, or get thrown in jail on some minor charge because they don't have enough money to pay the fine. The last one left will be the winner, or 'survivor' is more like it."

Luke said, "We have some other great ideas, but I don't know if they will work. They may be too realistic for most people to understand. For example, we thought of putting a group of Indians on the streets of a small prairie city, and the last one to have the cops drive them to the outskirts would be the winner."

"Or we thought of putting a group of people on Baffin Island in January, and the survivor would be the individual who was the last to freeze to death," Abe said. "But we would have trouble getting people to volunteer, and I don't know what legal or insurance problems we would encounter."

"We have some other ideas that include prisons, universities, and trailer parks, but they need a little more work," Abe added.

I left Luke and Abe sitting on their lawn chairs by the lake, casting their lines for imaginary fish. I knew that they would continue to work on their ideas. While I doubt we'll see their survivor show any day soon, you never know...

In Which Abe and Luke Sit Out an Election

The federal election was drawing to a close and Aboriginal issues had been conspicuous in their absence. I decided to research this glaring failure by calling my old friend Abe Original.

You may remember that in the last election, Abe and his side-kick Luke Warm Water established the Aboriginal party and led a spirited national campaign. They finished somewhere near the back of the pack, but they were able to make their point, whatever that was. This year: nothing. The Aboriginal Party was nowhere to be seen.

I contacted Abe at his penthouse in Toronto. He informed me that he and Luke were busy selling new age philosophy to gullible yuppies.

"It's a seller's market," he told me. "We dress up as elders and lay our quaint, rustic view of life on these stressed-out but wealthy victims of modern life. We get rich, and they get a warm fuzzy feeling. Next month, we're taking our show on the road to California to make some serious bread."

"What about the Aboriginal Party and all your political ideals?" I asked.

Abe replied that they had been done in by the Elections Act. It demanded that to qualify as a national party, they had to have over 50 candidates and a deposit of $1,000.00 each. This spelled a temporary end for both the Aboriginal Party and their friends at the Rhinoceros Party. Besides, the idea of a national party failed to catch on with Indian people.

Abe had his own spin on the current election: "This year, Aboriginal issues have been ignored and not considered important," he told me. "The Royal Commission on Aboriginal People has been reduced to a $58 million doorstop, and self-government has amounted to nothing more than self-administration. Political parties are avoiding us like Bre-X stock."

"This is good because it gives us the opportunity to lay low, sneak up on them, and take them by surprise. It's an old Indian trick, and it has worked for years. They ignore us, we'll ignore them, and when they least expect it, we'll clobber them."

"So far, we've filled up the inner cities, educated record numbers of our people, and started thousands of new businesses. They keep looking at the people left on the reserves and assume that that's all we are. That's been the government strategy for years: warehouse our people on reserves, and when they act up, warehouse them in prison. They treat us like nothing more than a whole nation on the shelf. That's why Luke and I are sitting this one out. Next time, we'll have a national campaign ready to go."

I asked him what a new Aboriginal Party policy would contain.

"We plan to Indianize Canada," he replied, handing me their party platform.

The national debt would be eliminated by selling off part of the country in the same manner that the government used to sell Indian land as a way of raising revenue.

The calendar would be changed to have New Year's Day fall on June 21st, the longest day of the year and traditionally the start of a new Indian year. "Indian Summer" would become "White People's Summer," and it would take place in January so they can take their holidays down south. July and August would be designated as a national holiday, so everyone could follow the pow wow and rodeo trails.

The NHL playoffs would take place on a single weekend with one giant hockey tournament. Each game would consist of two fifteen-minute periods with stop time in the last five minutes.

No one would be allowed to get rich, but no one would be poor, either. Aid to farmers would consist of buying them out and turning the land back to grass for large herds of buffalo.

Abe had to leave. Someone needed a warm fuzzy fix, so he and Luke had to head out on a house call. But he had a point: sometimes it's best to be ignored and underestimated.

Both the Lease and the Jig Are Up

The other day, I received a call from my old friend Abe Original. He and his sidekick Luke Warm Water were in town, and they had something to show me. They came over to my office, and Abe very carefully laid out an ancient parchment document for me to look at.

"Luke and I just returned from a trip to Spain where we went to the archives at Castile. They have all the agreements that were made with the Indians of the Americas, including this document," Abe told me.

I looked at the document. It appeared to be a lease agreement signed by Christopher Columbus, and it was good for 500 years. It was signed by a Caribe Chief on behalf of all the First Nations of the Americas.

It was quite the lease. It saved Chris and his cronies harmless for any "diseases, atrocities, enslavement or genocide that may be perpetrated from time to time upon the said Indian nations." But the facts were clear: it was a lease that could only last for 500 years and then it expired.

"Do you know what this means?" Abe asked. "Their lease is up, and they will have to leave."

"It's right here in print," Luke said. "It also refers to appendix A, subsection 35 which provides the procedure to follow when 500 years are up."

"I have it right here," Abe said.

And sure enough, there it was: an addendum to the original agreement.

The document called for the peaceful return to Europe of all the settlers and the rehabilitation of the continent to its original condition; otherwise, they would have to pay a damage deposit.

Fences would have to come down, and cities would have to be abandoned to be dug up by archaeologists in the future. All power plants and nuclear facilities would have to be shut down and safely decommissioned.

"Any leasehold improvements are the responsibility of the Europeans, and they will have to leave what they can't carry," Abe stated, looking at the fine print.

"The lease actually expired in 1992, so they now owe us a few years rent," Luke mentioned. "There was supposed to be a 30-day period to renegotiate the lease, but that appears to have passed."

"So what do you suggest we do?" I asked. "It's not every day that you have to vacate two continents and a bunch of Caribbean islands."

Luke said, "We plan to take this document to the United Nations in New York and have all the countries in the world vote on it. Since the countries in North, South, and Central America are in a minority at the United Nations, they will be outvoted and forced to bow to world pressure."

"And if that doesn't work, we will take it to the world court at The Hague, located a little north of Saskatoon."

It was obvious that these two were on to something, and I hated to stick a pin in their balloon, but there was something about the document that just didn't sit right.

"If Christopher Columbus was working for Spain, how come the document isn't in Spanish or at least in Latin which was the language most often used in legal documents back then?" I asked.

"And on the back there is a symbol that indicates that the document is printed on recycled paper."

They were stuck for an answer.

"Maybe," I said, "somebody forged this document."

"You mean that nice guy at the airport sold us a bill of goods!" Abe shouted. "I should have known better than to listen to you," he said, threatening to wring Luke's neck.

"Wait a minute," Luke yelled, with panic in his voice. "We could redo this on real parchment in Latin and.....you know."

The last I saw they were heading off to the Office Depot looking for some parchment.

In Which a Carefully Planned Coup is a Non-Starter

A few years ago, I received a call from my old friend Abe Original. I hadn't heard from him since his last attempt to run for political office under the banner of the Aboriginal Party. Not to put too fine a point on it, but they failed miserably.

Abe and his friends lost their collective shirt, but now they were on the comeback trail. I met him and his sidekick Luke Warm Water at a pre-arranged secret location. Abe was clearly nervous, and he had a furtive, haunted air about him.

"After lots of thought, Luke and I believe that the time has come to save this country from itself," Luke confided in me. "Quebec is having an election, and its people will probably elect a separatist government. And the rest of the country is just liable to let them go."

"We must stop the English and French from carrying on with their centuries–old blood feud. We Indians are the only group that are united from coast to coast. The Cree Nation, for example, extends from Quebec to British Columbia.

"So here's our plan," Abe said, as he moved closer to me and looked around nervously. "We will take the country back in one fell swoop while everyone is asleep. We have carefully planned for this moment. Most of Canada's provincial legislatures and the federal government now have Aboriginal people in office. You don't think they got there by accident, do you? It's all part of my master plan."

"After everyone has gone home for the night, we will fly Judge Murray Sinclair from Winnipeg to Ottawa. He will meet with the federal Aboriginal caucus and swear in Ethel Blondin Andrew as the new Prime Minister."

Next, Senator Len Marchand will storm the Senate and seize control. We don't see any strategic value in the Senate, but Len wanted a piece of the action, so we're humouring him."

"The provincial legislatures will fall next," he said. "Keith Goulet will seize control of the Saskatchewan Legislature, and Don Cardinal will do the same in Alberta."

"Yvonne Dumont, the Lieutenant Governor of Manitoba, will issue a proclamation declaring himself the Premier."

"Where there are no Aboriginal members, we will send in war parties sealing off the legislatures and reclaiming them in the name of the local First Nation. All the lands passing through Indian lands will be blocked, and the Mohawks, of course, will block the seaway."

"Of course," said Luke.

"So, overnight the country will fall back into Indian hands, where it belongs. No more separatism, no more crazy ideas. It's all so simple," Abe said, sitting back, obviously proud of himself.

"I see only one problem with your plan," I replied. "What are you going to do with all the white people once we have the country? You're going to have to make some kind of treaty or agreement with them and settle them on their own land, such as reserves. And then they might disagree with the settlement, and you will have a whole lot of pesky land claims to deal with."

"And then they just might be unhappy with their lot, fall into unemployment and social dysfunction, and then all of our tax dollars will go to support them. It could be a real mess."

"And then we might have to take their children away to raise them in proper homes where they might have a better chance at life. It might even mean that we would have to take the children away permanently, placing them in boarding schools, because you know what can happen if the children aren't raised the proper way."

Abe thought about it carefully. "You mean we might save the country, but ruin everyone in it?" he asked.

"'fraid so," I replied. "The only solution is to try to learn how to get along."

"That's a crazy idea," Abe said, "but it just might work."

The Antiques Road Show Moves On

The other day, I received a visit from my old friends Abe Original and Luke Warm Water. These two characters' plans and schemes get stranger every time we visit.

This time, they had an old van loaded up with all kinds of odds and ends. At first, I thought they were on their way to the dump, but on closer inspection, I discovered they had landed a treasure-trove of Indian memorabilia. Abe was all excited about the recent sale of memorabilia from the Battle of the Little Big Horn.

"That guy got $60,000 for an old pistol that he said his great grandfather had at the Battle at the Little Big Horn," Abe told me. "We decided that we must have a lot of good stuff hidden away on the reserve. We got the whole reserve together for an 'antiques road show.' It's amazing what some people have saved over the years."

"Take this, for example," he said, holding up an ancient arrow. "This is one of the 27 arrows stuck into Custer's back. I got it from one of the Dakota reserves. This guy told me that his great-great-grandfather pulled it out of Custer's body while they were looting the battlefield. It's supposed to be the real thing."

"Here's a real prize!" Abe told me, holding up a wooden leg. "This is the actual wooden leg of Indian Commissioner Graham. He's the old so-and-so who sold off Indian land, sent our boys off to World War One, and held back on rations to the point of starvation. How we got a hold of it is a secret, but it includes some dark research and a little grave-robbing, so we will sell it with no questions asked."

"The elders told us that when the treaties were signed, they were told that no man with two legs would break the treaty, so they that's why they sent in Graham," Luke said.

"What on earth is this?" I said, pointing to a large pile of rope.

"This is the original rope that the Métis rebels strung across the Saskatchewan River to stop the Northcote," Luke replied.

"They didn't stop it, but they pulled off the smokestack," Luke added. "We got it from an old man at Batoche. It had been hidden in his barn because he thought they might get in trouble."

"But this was back in 1885! They should have got over it by now," Abe replied.

"You know how the government is: they never forget, and they never forgive," Luke replied.

"Check this out," Abe said, pulling out an old iron bunk bed. "This was taken from one of the boarding schools. It's a genuine-issue boarding school bunk bed. It's 28 inches wide and has springs like a hammock - a welcome addition for the serious collector."

"These things caused more backaches than I care to remember," Luke said. "They had no side rails, so if you fell off the top bunk, it really hurt," he added, obviously speaking from experience.

"Here's a neat little item," Abe said. "This is an original copy of a pass to leave the reserve. These things were used up until to the Second World War when they needed our boys to join the army. Obviously, you can't go to Europe if the Indian Agent won't let you leave the reserve. It should fetch a pretty penny."

"All this stuff should make us rich," Luke added. "Who ever thought that there would be so much money in old junk?"

"There is lots of other good stuff: the porridge maker from a boarding school, a can of Spork, and lots of old typewriters, carbon paper, and other stuff from the Indian Affairs bureaucracy," Abe said. "But now we have to go."

The last I saw of them, they had loaded up the van and were heading to parts unknown, dreaming of striking it rich.

Christmas on the Rez with Abe and Luke

'Twas the night before Christmas and all through the Rez,
Not a creature was stirring, so I sez...

"I think I'll go and visit Abe Original!"

Abe and his friend lived at the far end of the reserve, but it was a nice drive since the houses were all adorned in anticipation of winning the reserve trophy for the best-decorated house, barn, shed, or any combination of the above.

Abe and his friend Luke Warm Water were resting beside an open fire, which bothered me since Abe didn't have a fireplace.

"I bought a videotape of a fireplace and set it on the floor. It's great since you don't have to cut wood or tend the fire, and a video can't smoke up the house," Abe told me.

They both had an exhausted, worn-out look to them, and Luke looked the worst of the two.

"What happened to you guys?" I asked.

"It was horrible, absolutely horrible!" Luke said.

"We thought we could make a little extra cash by posing as Santa Claus at the reserve Christmas party," Abe told me. "They made me work as the Santa Claus, and Luke was my helpful little elf."

"The real Santa Claus was already busy, so they asked us," Luke added.

Apparently, today's children are a far cry from what they expected.

"What I couldn't get over was the gifts they wanted," Abe said. "I didn't know what a 'Pokemon' was until they asked me for one."

"And all the video games and CDs left me completely confused," Luke said, rubbing his head. "And what is this Furby thing?"

"What ever became of gifts like a new pair of skates, a sled, or a pair of mittens?" Abe asked. "This is going to be a difficult holiday season; it's already off to a bad start. The whole world is changing and Luke and I are just a couple of old Indians who've been left behind."

"We're just road kill on the information highway," Luke said. "Fish caught in the Internet."

I could tell that they were beginning to wallow in self-pity, so I suggested that they ask themselves what the coming millennium meant to them.

"It doesn't mean a thing," Abe told me. "The millennium is supposed to represent 2,000 years after Christ's birth, but historical records are all mixed up. Scholars feel that the millennium happened several years ago. Jesus is alleged to have been born during the reign of King Herod, but the historical record indicates that he died in 4 B.C. Something's fishy here."

"And whose millennium is it anyway?" Luke asked. "The Chinese will celebrate the year 4698 this year. It's 2544 for the Buddhists and 5102 for the Hindus."

"We've been here for about 10,000 years," Abe added. "I think it's quite ethnocentric and selfish for the Christians to impose their calendar on the world as if we all wanted to follow it."

"I think we should just celebrate the holiday season the way we always have," Luke said. "Let's go out on Christmas Day and visit everyone on the reserve, and then stuff ourselves with a big turkey dinner at your mom's."

"And a few days later, we can go to the round dance at the Band Hall and meet everyone all over again," Abe added. "That's what Christmas is all about for us: meeting family and friends."

"That's right," Luke added, "and on the reserve that includes almost everyone."

I got up to go, and Luke followed me out. I watched him as he walked down the road to his house. His outline was clear in the moonlight, and overhead the northern lights danced in the sky.

Chapter 12

Some Final Thoughts

Cell Phone Blues

Were you ever in a situation where a phone call broke out?

At a meeting I was at with some of the heavies in the Federation of Saskatchewan Indian Nations, everybody had a cellular telephone by their side for speedy communication. The meeting was making progress when "BEEP BEEP," a phone went off. Then, about three or four more went off. The meeting was interrupted and everyone was talking into their hands.

This left me wondering about the "advances" in communication technology and how many more advances in communication we can actually stand.

After the invention of the smoke signal, I can imagine that someone said, "What did we ever do before they invented smoke signals?"

We love technology. We embrace it. It doesn't matter if it's snowmobiles, computers, chainsaws, or cellular telephones. They are all just tools that are designed to make life easier and more fun. It's all part of the tradition of adopting technology to meet our changing needs. Knives, axes, and iron pots were the trade goods after contact with Europeans. Now it's colour televisions, pickup trucks, and the ubiquitous cellular telephone.

A band office might be miles from nowhere, but it always comes complete with computer terminals, a fax machine, and a telephone system with several lines. The band office is normally connected to all the councillors by the CB radio. And, of course, the Chief has the cellular telephone by his side. It is the Chief's symbol of authority, the modern-day talking stick. He is connected with the world. He can call the Prime Minister or order a pizza at will.

But the cellular telephone is quickly becoming a nuisance. It's like the high-tech bracelet they put on guys under house arrest. You can't escape; it's an electronic leash. If a guy turns it off, his wife will accuse him of committing some unfaithful act. If he leaves it on, he is bothered by calls about all sorts of trivial matters.

I've learned that if you call someone on their cellular telephone, they will answer, no matter what else is happening. The sound of a ringing telephone is one of the most compelling sounds in the civilized world. It's the modern day call of the wild. Total strangers will answer a ringing payphone even if they are just walking down the street.

And the love affair with cellular phones seems to be a male thing. I checked with the women chiefs (both of them), and they don't have cellular telephones. Other women don't bother with them. They consider them a nuisance and ostentatious.

I think that it's actually Freudian. There is something reassuring about holding on to this firm cylindrical object with its flexible aerial dangling off the end. It confirms that ones manhood is intact.

Cellular telephones have become a nuisance. They interrupt meetings and go off at the worst times, such as during the two-minute silence on Remembrance Day, at wakes or at funerals, in libraries, or even in the throes of passion.

And now I understand that they have developed the cellular fax machine. I pointed out to a friend that theoretically he could sit in a canoe in the middle of a lake and be sending and receiving faxes. He thought about it, and said, "I'll have to look into that."

White Consultants Go the Way of the Dodo

A few years ago, my Chief and Council invited me to sit in on some interviews they were conducting with banks. They were conducting the interviews, and the banks were presenting the proposals. A few years ago, these same people insisted we have a cosigner before we could get a loan.

My First Nation is one of 27 bands in Saskatchewan that recently signed a Treaty Land Entitlement deal. Over the next 12 years, we will receive $25.7 million to purchase 90,000 acres. The deal will eventually provide the bands with a total of $446 million and 1.6 million acres of the land. The banks are in a feeding frenzy. The settlement represents the only substantial new money to enter the moribund Saskatchewan economy.

It occurred to me that since the first fur trader wandered into this province, white people have been trying to figure out how to make a buck off of Indians. At first, it was iron pots, Hudson's Bay rum, and wool blankets.

But a few years ago, the pattern changed, and the sale of services entered the picture. The age of the white consultant was born.

At the time, any bright young lad who had recently left the Company of Young Canadians and had an Arts degree (or a part thereof) could work for a band or an Indian organization as a general consultant. The job usually consisted of writing letters, preparing proposals, and attending meetings with government officials.

Reserves became a dumping ground for social activists, anti-nukes, and other people trying to escape the twentieth century. Lawyers also began to troll for work in the Indian community. They saw it as an opportunity to increase their files.

A few years later, the scene started to change. Indian people began to get their own Arts degrees and quickly eclipsed the white consultants.

But the white consultants didn't give in easily. The dichotomy of being a community developer is that the community will eventually develop and not require your services any more. However, many of the consultants became impediments to change rather than agents for change. They refused to let go of their meal tickets in the face of their mounting obsolescence. Some of these guys are still out there: ageing hippies recycled as administrators and business consultants.

The same thing is happening to the lawyers, thanks largely to the work of the Native Law Centre at the University of Saskatchewan. Indian people have entered into the law profession in record numbers. Now we not only have Indian lawyers, but we also have Indian law firms and are rapidly becoming self-sufficient in legal services.

The latest gold rush for consultants appears to be the recently signed Treaty Land Entitlement agreement. However, appearances can be deceiving. The bands have the resources and their own people to do the organizing.

At a recent Chiefs' meeting, I was struck by the fact that the only non-Indians in the room were a couple of lawyers and Indian Affairs staff. Indian people will use consultants like any other group involved in land acquisition. Land specialists, agrologists, geologists, and legal specialists are some of the professional services required in the future. And these people will not be hired full time. They will be hired on a fee-for-service basis, a far cry from the social activists who saw Indian communities as societies that could be manipulated.

A few years ago, I met a group of chiefs from Northern Ontario. They were dressed in suits and well groomed; however, they were accompanied by a couple of scruffy white guys with shaggy beards and ponytails. "These are our consultants," they said. I wonder where those guys are now.

Nothing Exotic About Real "Indian Food"

The other day, I was going through my mail when I came upon an invitation to an event that looked promising. Among the items on the agenda was the major hook: Indian food would be served.

What, I wondered, is "Indian food"? Does that mean they will serve up a spread of curry and chutney? Somehow, I doubt it. Indian food, as it turns out, is stuff like wild rice, buffalo meat, bannock, and blueberries.

Now this is great food. But it's not necessarily everyday Indian food. Wild rice, for instance, is a recent import from Manitoba and Minnesota. It didn't exist in Saskatchewan 20 years ago. And as for buffalo, they are the latest product from Saskatchewan ranches. And a few years ago, it was illegal to kill a buffalo since they were all kept in national parks.

Bannock is also an import. The Scottish fur traders introduced it from their homeland. It was adopted by the Indian people as their staple, and now it belongs to us. Blueberries are fine in season, but they don't keep well. Dried chokecherries make more sense.

Now I've been an Indian all my life and I don't recall being raised on this exotic fare. Indian food is like looking for a New York steak in New York or a Denver Sandwich in Denver. It doesn't exist. It is the product of people from other places.

Events such as Folkfest, Folkarama, Folkfrenzy, or whatever, highlight this stereotype. We are left with the impression that each member of a national group heads home after work and chows down his or her national food. Italians eat nothing but pizza and pasta. Germans are into sauerkraut and schnitzel. The Chinese dote on chicken balls and sweet-and-sour spareribs, and Jews have a steady diet of chicken soup.

The reality is that people eat much more than foods from their homeland or the foods that are reinforced by stereotypical images. The idea that Indians rush home from work to a mess of wild rice and buffalo is ridiculous. We can't afford such extravagance. Wild rice, buffalo, and smoked salmon are not cheap.

Real Indian soul food is boiled potatoes, Kraft Dinner, baloney, neck bones, and Kentucky Fried Chicken. And the bannock is the real stuff – not the airy-fairy, fluffy stuff they hand out to the tourists, but the substantial stuff that must be cut with an axe and is the consistency of a hockey puck. A good piece of bannock should lie in your stomach like a lump of lead and keep you from being hungry for a day or so.

I was at the official opening of a reserve school once, and after the ribbon had been cut and all the speeches heard, the dignitaries, guests, and band members lined up at the buffet table for the obligatory feast.

The white people and city Indians tore into the moose meat, duck soup, and other good stuff. The band members, on the other hand, picked over the food with obvious boredom. Then one band member went over to the chief and asked, "Where's the chicken?" The chief apologized and said that they had forgotten to go to town for the Kentucky Fried Chicken. It seems that the Colonel was their preference for the special meal.

I'd like to see a buffet table set up with real Indian food the next time we have an important function. The reaction alone would be worth it.

Technology Double-Edged for Indians

I recently attended a Chiefs' conference. Normally, I avoid these boring events, but this time I was compelled to go by my band council. The meeting began in the usual fashion, and the speeches began. About an hour into the agenda, the cell phones began ringing, making it sound more like crickets on a warm summer day than a conference.

My bet is the chiefs left messages for their office staff to call by mid-morning to give them a polite excuse for leaving the meeting. Others sat and talked on their phones, further confusing those trying to listen to the speaker.

Cell phones became a fixture in Indian country shortly after their invention. They have been quickly adopted, replacing the smoke signal and accelerating the moccasin telegraph. In fact, Indians have adapted to high-tech faster than other groups. I recently received a letter from a municipal office that was typed on an old manual typewriter. Compare this with the average band office that has computers, faxes, and all kinds of other toys.

I have to admit, I'm a complete klutz when it comes to anything fancier than a pencil and paper. I come from the old school that thinks bits and bytes are some kind of snack food. When I did get a new computer, I sat staring at it blankly until a couple of band employees from my reserve dropped by and took pity on me. They plugged it in, loaded it up, and showed me what to do.

Today, it's women and computers that run most band offices. If you walk past the group of drones sitting around the front office looking important and in charge, you will find an office in back. This office invariably contains a woman bookkeeper and a computer. All the band accounts are processed here. She and her computer run the whole show. The guys in the front are mere window dressing. She holds the keys to the kingdom; she knows how to operate the computer.

Our people have a long history of adapting to change. The first outside changes came early in the fur trade. Iron tools like knives and axes were introduced. Firearms made hunting easier.

The economy changed with the introduction of the fur trade, and traditional gathering places became fur-trading forts. Later, after the treaties were signed, our people adapted as farmers. They were so successful that local farmers complained, and the government applied restrictions and controls that effectively killed the industry. Indian farmers who wished to sell their produce had to receive a permit from the Indian agent. This became a political tool, and certain farmers and even whole reserves were blacklisted.

Later, our people in the North would adapt cedar canoes from birch bark and then outboard motors followed. Later yet, the cedar canoes evolved into aluminum. Next came the power toboggan and now all terrain vehicles. All of these innovations served to enhance the traditional lifestyle, but along with them came goods that continue to cause problems.

The first fur traders brought "fire water," so named because it was potent enough to burn. Alcohol brought nothing but hurt and destruction to the Aboriginal world and remains a serious problem today.

Other products were less destructive than alcohol. The television, for example, sneaked into most Indian homes and became the centerpiece for entertainment. The stories from the elders had to take a back seat to the latest Hollywood sitcom. The television spoke only English, which is part of the reason that English became the dominant language of our homes. Today, educators are desperately trying to save our languages by teaching them in the classroom.

Technology is a double-edged sword. When our ancestors first met the fur traders and received a hunting knife and an iron pot, little did they know that a couple of centuries later we would be experiencing the best and the worst that newcomers had to offer.

Top Story: What's Hot and What's Not

In 1998, women fought and won the right to go topless in Canada. In light of more serious issues, this was trivial, but it got the media's attention.

Each summer, the media picks up an item and beats it to death. I think when the senior staff goes on holidays, the junior staff takes over and gets drunk with power. It's like the jester becoming king for a day.

In 1990, it was us. Indians were the hot topic, and anyone who went out and marched, blockaded, or occupied made the evening news. It was our 15 minutes of fame.

The issues are still out there, but we've now lost our cachet. Other more important issues have come along. Issues like pit bull dogs. At one time, the media was covering every dog attack in the country. You had the feeling that a vicious dog was waiting on every street corner. Then, they went away in the minds of the media. Of course, they're still out there, but now they're yesterday's news.

Pit bulls have been replaced by Elvis sightings, alien invasions, and, of course, the Royal family. This unfortunate lot of mediocre and licentious individuals never fails to keep the media amused.

In the summer of 1999, the media was fixated on bosoms. That's right: women's breasts. Topless women were discovered across the land, and the media had a field day.

Canadians ran around bare-naked for years, but the media treated it like something brand new, and that summer was dubbed the "Canadian summer of nudity."

We were treated to the unseemly spectacle of a topless woman riding in a Jeep down Albert Street in Regina. The woman wasn't unseemly; it was the camera crews that pursued her in their minivans, recording the whole event as a hot news item. The media behaved like so many horny bumpkins. Equally unseemly was the CBC placing the item as the lead story on the evening news so they could use the cute graphic "Top Story."

When I was just a tadpole back on the reserve, I remember that women breastfed their children as a matter of course. Whether in church, public, or private, it was regarded as natural act. It was a loving matter between a mother and her baby. I also remember restaurant operators in Southern Alberta refusing service to Indian families because (horrors!) they feared the mothers might breastfeed their babies in public.

So we bought the backward Victorian morality, and the women bottle-fed their babies. Not only was it expensive, but it also created a new bunch of health problems. Bottle-fed babies don't receive the nutrients and disease-fighting properties of breast milk. Our children's health has been sacrificed in the name of proper decorum.

Women's breasts are seen as evil, immoral, and liable to inflame men. Men are seen as weak individuals not in control of their passions. These views are hopelessly outdated and naive.

The problem is not with women going around baring their breasts. That's irrelevant. The problem is the attitude of men. Canadian men have distinguished themselves as a bunch of Peter Pans: boys who refuse to grow up.

One of the largest rallies ever on Parliament Hill was a demonstration a few years ago by women asserting their right to go topless. The crowd contained many rubber-necking males, some with video cameras. It was apparent that Canadian men had a long way to go.

It's also a strange dichotomy that at a time when scientists are urging us to stay out of the sun, more flesh is being exposed. Scientists have warned us for some years now that the ozone layer is thinning out to dangerous levels, and if we don't watch it, we will sizzle and wrinkle like so many strips of bacon on a griddle. This brings us to the real issue: going topless will be an academic argument if we can't go out in the sun.

Going unnoticed or under-reported are real issues, like child poverty, the decay of our inner cities, and race relations. Our natural habitat is under attack, and each day more species are endangered or go extinct. There are fewer than 300 Siberian tigers on the planet, but somehow topless women make the headlines.

This too shall pass, as they say. Next summer, look to some other trivial and irrelevant issue to consume the public's interest. Wasn't that Elvis bagging groceries at the supermarket?

Indians Get Stuck with White Man's Castoffs

While I was in Toronto on business, I decided to call up an old friend. "Meet me at the Buck," he said. In Toronto, the Indian bar is called the "Silver Dollar," but everyone knows it as "the Buck." Anyway, we got together and got up-to-speed on wives and kids and why draft beer is in cans (the latest oxymoron) when he sprang his thesis on me.

"You know that whenever anything is old, used up, or no more use to white people, they give it to Indians."

"Give me a for instance," I said.

"For instance, Spork," he said. "Back in the early '60s they brought tons of this stuff out to the reserves. We were raised on Spork. My mother was a Spork gourmet. She must have had 27 casserole recipes alone. Just the sight of a can of Spork turns me into a 12-year-old."

"Any other examples?" I asked.

"Lots," he said. "In the '70s the federal government had surplus army camps, such as the one at Rivers, Manitoba. They turned it into an Indian training centre. And when the government decided to close down all the old boarding schools, instead of blowing them up and erasing them from the face of the earth, they turned them over to the Indians."

"And then there's the Territorial Building in Regina. A few years ago, the Province transferred it over to Indian hands. It's over 100 years old and obsolete as hell," he said.

"It's even rumoured to have ghosts," I added.

"Do you know what the latest and greatest coup is?" he asked.

"Enlighten me," I replied.

"It's Treaty Land Entitlement," he said. "The first formula (called the '76 formula) would have given us Crown land, such as PFRA pastures and other useless acreage, but the new formula gives us money to buy land. As it turns out, though, it, too, is a wolf in cheap clothing."

"Right now, Saskatchewan farmers are fed-up. They are, on average, past their retirement age by a decade or more. Their credit and their patience have all run out. All they want to do is see their farm in their rear-view mirror as they head for the coast."

"And that's where we come in," he said. "Now that the white man has used up the land, put the Province hopelessly in debt, and grain is selling for two bits a truckload, they are willing to give the land back to the Indians."

"Look at the Inuit," he said. "They got most of the Arctic because nobody else wanted it. If the government was sincere, they would give us downtown Toronto and the Turner Valley Oilfield."

"What's next?" he asked rhetorically. "Are we going to inherit Air Canada? Inner-city neighbourhoods? The Montreal Expos? The national debt?"

"We'll just have to wait and see," I said. "Meanwhile. let's have another round."

If You Don't Know What to Call Us, Don't Try

The other day, a courier dropped a package off at my office. As he left, he said, "See you later, chief." That left me pondering why white people insist on calling Indians "chief," a title I neither deserve nor aspire to. We don't refer to white people as "Prime Minister," so why do white people call us "chief?"

When I was young, I was simply known as "a little Indian kid." There were lots of us, and we were singularly non-spectacular. I never questioned or doubted my heritage, but years later, when I joined the working world, I found out that Indians were known by a variety of names, some of which were downright disagreeable.

I always thought of us in terms of the various Indian nations, such as Cree, Blackfoot, Saulteaux, and so on. If you are an Indian, you recognize people from other tribes, and they are as different as the many nationalities of Europe. Europeans may all be white people, but they have many different languages, cultures, and religions. It is the same with Indians. Racism and misunderstanding lump us all together and treat us all alike.

Through the years, we have been called a variety of names. First, we were known as Indians because Columbus thought he had discovered India. As the tired old joke goes, "It's a good thing he wasn't looking for Turkey."

Another bit of folklore is that Columbus meant to say "Indeo," or "in the image of God." This is completely erroneous since it was reported that Columbus returned to Spain with two prisoners from the Caribe tribe. The objective of the exercise was to have them examined to determine if they were human or not. These were hardly the actions of a person who regarded the original inhabitants as being "in the image of God."

In the 1970s, bureaucrats lumped all of us together and called us "Natives." For a while, we became hyphenated Canadians, like the Italian-Canadians, Chinese-Canadians, Vietnamese-Canadians, and so on. This pejorative and colonial term held until 1982 when the term "Aboriginal" was used in the Charter of Rights and Freedoms.

"Aboriginal" never really caught on in Indian country. It sounded too much like "Aborigines," the racist catch-all phrase used to describe the first people of Australia. In Australia, the first people are called "Abos" or "Blacks," neither of which are very flattering names. And then there's the colour designation. The British press still refers to us as "Red Indians." If the press here were to try that, the Human Rights Commission would be on them like a cheap suit.

Colour is obsolete as a way of describing races and nationalities. Nobody today refers to the Chinese as "yellow" or the Italians as "olive-skinned." Even the term "Black" has fallen out of fashion in favour of Afro-Canadian or the double-hyphenated "Afro-Caribbean-Canadian." The only truly yellow people are on *The Simpsons*.

In fairness, we have to have a special name if we are to rise above the multicultural designation and take control of our birthright. The opportunity came with constitutional discussions, and we began to describe our place within the Canadian family.

The Constitution and Canada itself is based on the premise of two "founding" nations, the English and the French. This myth would have persisted if the original people hadn't stood up and pointed out that there were in fact other people – the First Nations people.

The term "First Nations" became the designation of choice and became our self-defining moniker. The other day, I was talking to a staff member from the colonial office who considers himself very hip and on the cutting edge of social change. He started to refer to us as "the First Nations." Well, I thought, "there goes the neighbourhood. Time to come up with something new."

The various tribes and First Nations have always described themselves in ethnocentric and self-adulating terms. The names, loosely interpreted, usually mean "the people," "our people," and so on. In the movie *Little Big Man*, Dustin Hoffman's character was adopted by a tribe that called themselves "the Human Beings," which prompted Chief Dan George to utter the famous line, "We Human Beings will never understand white people."

The term "Indian" is the common street term and is usually accompanied by a "suitable" adjective, such as "stupid," "lazy," "drunken," and "no good." Moving from the ridiculous to the sublime, the adjectives "stoic," "proud," and "wise old" may be used.

Somewhere in the middle sit the 90 per cent of Indian people who could be described as "honest," "hard-working," "self-supporting," "loving," and "decent." So there you are. We are as varied a bunch of Canadians as you are likely to find, and if you must call us something, don't call us late for supper.